Dr Gloria Mark is Chancellor's Prof[...]
University of California, Irvine. She [...]
researcher at Microsoft Research since 2012. She is a tw[...]
recipient of the Google Research Award and has received a
prestigious NSF CAREER award. She received her PhD from
Columbia University in psychology.

have declined to an astonishing 47 seconds. If you are interested in your well-being and how to gain agency in this digital age then you need to read this book.'

Susan David, bestselling author of *Emotional Agility*

'Interruptions are a fact of life. This has long been true, no fancy technology required, but today, we have bright, shiny technology, some deliberately designed to distract and thereby to interrupt. Gloria Mark's book is a thorough review of the impact these interruptions have on our lives and mental health. Some interruptions are welcomed, deliberately self-created. Most, however, are not. All interruptions impact the focus of attention, and attention is a critically limiting aspect of human cognition. Don't be distracted by my review – go read the book. It is an important and valuable contribution to living in this world of interruptions.'

Don Norman, author of *The Design of Everyday Things*

Attention
Span

Attention Span

Finding Focus for a Fulfilling Life

Gloria Mark

WILLIAM
COLLINS

William Collins
An imprint of HarperCollins*Publishers*
1 London Bridge Street
London SE1 9GF

WilliamCollinsBooks.com

HarperCollins*Publishers*
Macken House
39/40 Mayor Street Upper
Dublin 1
D01 C9W8
Ireland

First published in Great Britain in 2023 by William Collins

First published in the United States in 2023 by Hanover Square Press,
an imprint of HarperCollins*Publishers*
This William Collins paperback edition published in 2024

2

Printed and Bound in the UK using 100% Renewable Electricity at
CPI Group (UK) Ltd

This book contains FSC™ certified paper and other controlled sources
to ensure responsible forest management.

For more information visit: www.harpercollins.co.uk/green

To my mother, who focused on what is important.

TABLE OF CONTENTS

INTRODUCTION:

Breaking the Myths of Attention

*We think our civilization near its meridian, but we are yet only
at the cock-crowing and the morning star.*
                                                              —Ralph Waldo Emerson

Imagine opening your laptop at the beginning of the day. Right
away, you are faced with an onslaught of emails. You glance
over them, a number of them demanding some thought, and
you begin to answer them, realizing each takes quite a bit of
effort. You then switch to work on a project that you have to
finish today, take some phone calls, but then you receive a notification of another email from your supervisor. You jump to
that right away to communicate implicitly to her that you are
doing your job. But then your calendar notifies you of your next
Zoom meeting. It is only 10 a.m. but you are already starting to
feel fatigued. By three o'clock you can barely think about that
project coming due. You start to work on it and find that you
have trouble focusing and keep making mistakes.

Or perhaps your plan for the day is to work on your taxes.

But you first check Facebook and find yourself caught up in your friends' posts. A link to an interesting video brings you to YouTube, and then you notice recommendations on the sidebar and become immersed in watching other videos. You break away from YouTube and go back to your taxes but then remember you have to send emails about that remodeling job on your house. Once you are in your inbox you see other emails you should deal with. Three hours have gone by and you no longer have the energy nor the inclination to focus on those taxes.

We have developed unbreakable bonds with our computers and phones for much of our waking hours. When you hear a chime on your phone signaling an incoming text you cannot ignore it. The ubiquity of smartphones and internet accessibility has changed norms of both work and personal life with expectations for us to be available 24/7. It is not uncommon for people to report that they wake up in the middle of the night and check their phones for emails and text messages. I have heard this a lot during my research. Any individual who tries to disconnect pays a price for not keeping up with information and messages. Between our competitive world of work and our interconnected social web of relationships, no one can afford to be out of the loop.

A new type of behavior has emerged with the rise of computing where we dynamically switch our attention among different apps, screens and devices. As a research scientist, I have been fortunate in that I have been able to watch (and empirically track) this pattern of attention-switching, and with it, stress and exhaustion buildup, over the last twenty years as we became more reliant on our devices. Simply put, our use of personal technologies affects our ability to pay attention. What I have seen is that in the last two decades, human minds have collectively undergone a striking change in how they focus on information. But I have also seen how stress is associated with attention-switching—we need to take this seriously as the World

Health Organization identified stress as a health epidemic of the twenty-first century.[1] At the time of this writing, the world has been struggling through a pandemic, people are spending more time than ever on their devices, and stress has increased.

I am, by training, a psychologist, but I almost didn't become one. The microbiologist Louis Pasteur wrote that "chance favors the prepared mind," and it was by chance and with a mind open to opportunity that I entered this field. The truth is, I started out as an artist and never thought I would do anything else. I studied fine arts at the Cleveland Institute of Art, specializing in painting and drawing. I was deeply entrenched in abstract expressionism—so deeply, in fact, that years later when I read the notebooks that I kept while painting, I couldn't make sense of them. The writing was too abstract from my current perspective as a scientist.

After graduating, I received a fellowship from the British Arts Council and went to London to paint murals. But during that year, I experienced the reality of how difficult it was to make a living as an artist. I also learned that one recent talented art school graduate was now studying to be a dental hygienist to make a living (a fine profession, but not one that requires years of art training). I had also heard that another artist I knew was working as an elevator operator. While some people might be so dedicated to their art that they were willing to spend eight hours a day at a job that they didn't like to support their passion, I quickly realized that this life was not for me. Fortunately, I was also good at math, and I knew that it was a lot easier to make a living using those skills.

This is how I ended up at the University of Michigan pursuing a master's degree in statistics, which would pave the way for me to study psychology and computer usage. But at the time, I just needed to work, and so I applied for a research assistant position with Manfred Kochen, an information scientist. When I came into his office for the interview, Dr. Kochen asked me:

Can I code? (no); Do I know fuzzy set theory? (no); Do I know network theory? (no). I picked up my backpack and started to walk out of his office. Dr. Kochen then called after me, "Well, what can you do?" I turned around and told him that I could paint. He told me to come back and sit down.

Dr. Kochen told me that before getting his PhD at the Massachusetts Institute of Technology in math, he took classes at the Art Students League in New York. We then talked about art for two more hours. Finally, he said to me, "I have a grant to study the discovery process. Do you think you could work on that?" With the arrogance and naivete of youth, I told him most certainly I could. I knew how artists made discoveries. I just needed to find a way to describe it in scholarly terms. I dived into studying cognitive psychology, and that work eventually grew into a paper presented at a conference. I became immersed in the world of psychology and information science, ultimately getting my doctorate at Columbia.

Chance crossed my path again when, in my first job after graduation, I was hired at an information technology company to apply psychological ideas to study technology use. This company, Electronic Data Systems, had set up a laboratory affiliated with MIT. Known as EDS, it was experimenting with how computers could support business meetings and had set up a conference room with networked computers so that we could study how people collaborated. The company had the foresight to believe that they needed a psychologist to understand how people used computers during business meetings. Today, networked computers in a conference room are not something we would blink at, but back then, I remember feeling thrilled, thinking that I had stepped into the future. The idea that I could study technology use in a real work setting was exhilarating.

That job was the beginning of what would become a decades-long journey into studying technology use and overuse from a psychological perspective. This book is the result of my journey, capturing what I have learned about our deeper human and social natures, how we think, work and interact with one another, and how that is affected by the tools we use. Those "tools" have come such a long way from the EDS networked computers, to a point that digital devices are intertwined with our working, social and private spheres, so this book therefore is also about how our lives have changed in the digital age. Technology use is so commonplace and ubiquitous that it can no longer be disconnected from who we are. Human behavior and the design of computer technology mutually influence each other, and the changes are happening at lightning speed.

When I later entered academia, I created what I call "living laboratories" to study how people use technology. As a psychologist, I am trained to bring people into laboratories to study behavior, in order to control as many variables as possible, but I felt that to really understand how people use technology and how it affects them, I had to go where people are in their everyday lives. In this way I can get a fuller picture of their emotions, relationships, work pressures and conflicts, and of course their multitasking, distractions and stress, as they use their computers and phones. This is how I ended up sitting behind people in their actual offices, clicking a stopwatch every time they switched computer screens or picked up a phone (we were later able to upgrade our technology to track this digitally, much to my graduate students' relief). It was also how I found myself standing in a boardroom convincing a table full of executives to let me shut off their employees' email for a week and attach heart rate monitors to them. Or how we discovered that wearable cameras designed to periodically snap photos of faces, to measure in-person interaction while working, might occasionally mistake a toilet seat for a human face if the male participants forgot to turn off their camera before heading to the restroom. Science, especially outside of controlled laboratories, is never perfect.

In the thousands of hours that I have studied people in the course of their daily work, I have heard a common sentiment. People report that they are overworked and exhausted because they have to deal with too much information and too many messages. Getting to inbox zero is as hard and futile a task as Sisyphus's struggle—as soon as we get our emails down to even a manageable amount, a new avalanche arrives. People also say that it is just too hard to focus when they are on their computers and smartphones. We will see in this book that distractions are not just due to the notifications popping up across their screens or the chimes of their phones. Surprisingly, people are nearly as often distracted by something within themselves—a thought, a memory, an urge to look up information or a desire to connect with others. When you are immersed in the world's largest candy store, it is hard to resist sampling the wares.

We have come to spend much of our waking hours in what I call the digital world—an experiential environment that we access through our computers, smartphones and tablets. We do not need to be in a full virtual reality environment to be able to experience the deep immersion that we feel everyday just by using our devices. By spending so much time immersed, we have developed new habits, expectations and cultural practices which in turn have led many to ask: How can we take back control of our attention in this digital world?

Why is it that we may feel in control of our lives in the physical world but don't feel in control of our attention when in the digital world? This is just one paradox that we face with the rise in computing. Technology has been designed with the intent to augment our capabilities and to help us produce more information, but instead we feel distracted and exhausted. Managers send out messages and expect we will respond right away, yet they also expect us to be productive. One case that I will describe later in the book is of an employee's manager who continually delegated work to him via email and yet expected this employee to fulfill his other work obligations. When we cut off email in this company for one week, rather than phone or visit the employee in person to assign him work, the manager just stopped giving him tasks. It is far easier to delegate work electronically. There is also a paradox in the very design of the internet itself—a structure that makes it easy to find information and maps onto how our memory is organized as a network of associations. But the node and link structure of the internet also goads us into spending countless hours surfing the internet. We may have the illusion that we are doing more and that our human capacity has expanded when we shift our attention, or multitask, but actually we are doing less. Multitasking has repeatedly been shown to be associated with lower performance when objectively measured.

There are also other downsides to multitasking. There is a switch cost—the time lost because whenever you switch your attention, you need to reorient to the new task at hand. The cost would not be so high if you immediately picked up an interrupted project, but unfortunately our data show that we don't. Rather, we switch our attention to at least two other projects with over a twenty-five-minute lag before we return to that interrupted task. This is enough time and change in contexts to significantly disrupt our work.

Yet another cost of multitasking is that it is associated with negative emotions—anxiety, stress and burnout. Email, one of the main culprits for distraction, is especially associated with stress. In one study that I will describe, we discovered that when email was cut off for one week, people were able to focus significantly longer on their computers and switch their attention less frequently. Even better, we learned that without email, heart rate monitors showed measurably different variability in heart rate by the end of the week, demonstrating that people were also significantly less stressed.[2]

The science consistently shows that multitasking causes stress—our blood pressure rises, our heart rate increases—and this matches our own perceptions that we feel more stressed. Even our immune response against disease has been shown to weaken when we multitask. There is also a cost where we often still think about the last thing we did while we work on our current task—that gripping personal story you just read online might stick in your mind and interfere with your task at hand. But the highest cost is in using our precious and limited attentional capacity, or cognitive resources, especially when we have to keep track of multiple interrupted tasks. It is like having a tank that leaks and leaves less fuel available for actually doing our work.

The perception that it is hard to focus when using our personal devices is actually backed up by science. My own research, as well as those of others, has shown that over the last fifteen years, our attention spans have declined in duration when we use our devices. Our attention spans while on our computers and smartphones have become short—crazily short—as we now spend about forty-seven seconds on any screen on average. This is true for everyone: baby boomers, Gen X and millennials, as well as Gen Z.

The internet began being widely used less than thirty years ago. We often forget that our digital lives are still quite young—younger than the fall of the Berlin Wall, the formation of the European Union, and when HIV/AIDS was first identified. Almost 30 percent of the world's population are Gen Z, born after 1997, and having grown up with the internet and smartphones, they have not experienced what life was like before this revolution. Having straddled pre-internet and internet generations myself, I still marvel at our ability to get news updates, seek out medical advice, discover what places our friends are currently visiting, collaboratively work on documents with colleagues, and tweet our thoughts to the world—all within seconds. Yet we have become so dependent on the internet that we panic when our connection goes down even for a moment.

Our digital society and our attention

With advances in computing and our unbridled adoption of computers, smartphones and the internet, our everyday relationship with technology has undergone a rapid-fire shift, and this is particularly evident with changes in our attention behaviors. Most people now spend a significant portion of their waking lives on their digital devices (including when they wake up in the middle of the night). What is it about how we use our devices that impacts our ability to focus and makes us feel so drained?

Though written well before the rise of the internet, the Nobel-Prize-winning economist and cognitive psychologist Herb Simon captured the essential dilemma of our lives in the digital world when he wrote that "a wealth of information creates a poverty of attention and a need to allocate that attention efficiently."[3] Technological progress has paved the way for continual data creation and nearly unlimited access to information and people. Every day, across most of the world, we have the opportunity to dive into the vast pool of information that technology offers us. We can use computer applications and artificial intelligence to augment our ability to process information on the internet, yet ultimately the human mind acts as a bottleneck.

If we were superhuman, we would have an unlimited capacity to focus and absorb information, and unlimited memory to store it all. Perhaps in the not-so-distant future, humans will be able to have chips implanted in the prefrontal cortex that provide high processing capabilities and vast memory banks. But for now, that is a speculative dream, and the story of how digital media affects our attention and our moods is far more complicated than just the sheer amount of information at our disposal.

When we talk about our fast-paced tech culture, the question of attention deficit hyperactivity disorder often comes up. But the difficulty in sustaining attention on our computers and phones is a problem experienced by a much more expansive population than just those with ADHD. The best estimate I found of prevalence of ADHD among adults is 4.6 percent based on a 2021 review of forty studies conducted with over 107,000 individuals.[4] Among US children and adolescents ages two to seventeen, a 2016 survey of over 50,000 households revealed that 8.4 percent of this age group was diagnosed to have ADHD based on parental report.[5] Some research does suggest that people with ADHD may have more problematic phone usage than non-ADHD individuals. A survey of 432 people who self-reported both their ADHD and their phone use found a correlation between the two.[6] While the result is intriguing, it is important to emphasize that we still know too little about the relation between ADHD and the use of personal devices—more research is needed to see if there is any causal connection. But we shouldn't dismiss the issue of attention and devices as one that is only experienced by those with ADHD—in our current culture, everyone is affected.

Modern myths about our distraction

In the public conversations about our fast-changing culture, four modern myths have arisen about our relationship with computing technology. These narratives, though popular, are proven false by the science that I will describe in this book.

The first myth is that we should always strive to be focused when on our computers, and in that way, we can be productive. We should feel guilty if we can't focus. But it turns out that focusing for lengthy periods of time, especially without breaks, is not natural for most people. Just as rhythms abound in nature, our research shows that our attention also follows rhythms. People's focused attention naturally ebbs and flows. There are times during the day when we are at our peak focus, and other times not. Further, sustained focus is associated with stress. We can't meet the high mental challenge of being focused for long stretches throughout the day, just as we can't be challenged to lift weights nonstop all day, without performance starting to degrade when we run out of energy (or cognitive resources), which usually happens well before the end of a typical eight-hour workday.

The second myth is that flow is the ideal state we should strive for when we use our technologies. *Flow*, a term developed by the psychologist Mihaly Csikszentmihalyi, is that optimal state of attention where we are so caught up in an experience that we lose touch with the outside world and are unaware that time has passed. We feel joy, excitement, and are at our utmost creative peak. Most of us have experienced flow at some time. You might have experienced it if you play music, or when listening to a great symphony by Mozart or a rock song by Led Zeppelin. Or perhaps you've been in flow when you were playing soccer and all the players seemed to magically synchronize together. If you are a painter or ceramicist, you probably have been in flow while creating artwork—you felt limitless inspiration and you easily remained focused.

The ideal of flow is a fine ambition, except that flow is rare in our everyday lives, especially if you happen to be a knowledge worker, meaning that your job primarily deals with using digital information. While it is not uncommon for flow to occur if you are an artist, dancer, musician, woodworker or athlete, for most of us who now spend the majority of our time in front of a computer or phone screen in the day-to-day world, flow rarely happens. It's not the computer per se that hinders flow—it's more about the nature of one's job. You might easily experience flow if you compose music on your computer, or if you do complex coding, but not so if your job is scheduling meetings or writing reports. Flow does not occur while playing word games or watching Netflix—this engages our attention but is not a peak creative experience. Instead of flow, our attention in the digital world is usually short in duration and has a quality of being dynamic and shifting from screen to screen—what I call kinetic.

The third myth is that the distractions, interruptions and multitasking we experience while on our devices are due primarily to the notifications we receive and to our own lack of discipline. While much has been written about how algorithmically tailored notifications play a role in hijacking our attention, less is known about how our attention is subject to other pressures. We do not use technology in a vacuum. Our behaviors in the physical world are influenced by the culture we live in. Similarly, our behaviors in the digital world are also influenced by environmental, social and other technological forces. These influences also do not just occur in the Western world, but are universal.

Some of these influences might be unexpected. First off, humans think in terms of associations, and the internet has leveraged this well, with its network design so perfectly in tune with your thinking that not only can you easily find information, but you often don't stop seeking interesting nuggets once you find what you are looking for. Also, while you know that individual differences are what make humans unique, you may not realize how personality traits can affect our attention spans. For some, it is easy to self-regulate behavior and not check Instagram, while for others, practicing self-control is a great feat. You may also not be aware of how some personality traits can influence one's attention duration on the computer and phone, or how often one checks email. Another influence is the fact that we are social beings and are thus susceptible to social forces of others. We receive social rewards when we interact with others, we bow to peer pressure, we respond to power, and we want to maintain a net positive account of social capital with our colleagues and friends, which in turn drives us to keep checking email and social media. Also, while you are undoubtedly aware that we are immersed in a culture of media beyond just computers or smartphones, you may not realize that the habits you pick up from other media can carry over to influence your attention span on your computer. The four hours a day that the average American passively spends watching TV and films (average viewing hours rise with age), but also watching YouTube and music videos, has accustomed the viewer to experiencing continual fast scene changes, which in turn can reinforce screen habits on the computer.

The fourth myth that is widely shared is that the rote, mindless activity that we do on our computers and phones has no value. In this narrative, we are pressured to cut out mindless activity like playing silly puzzle games, browsing social media, or surfing the internet so that we can be productive instead. The short answer is that yes, we are wasting time when we get stuck in a rabbit hole of, say, social media, especially when we have important things to do and deadlines to meet.

This is an attention trap that I will cover in the book. But it's possible to take short breaks and do such rote activity intentionally and in moderation to relax. There is a reason why people are drawn to such rote activity—in short, we found empirically in our studies that it makes people happy. We are happiest when we use our attention for easy, engaging activity that is not challenging and stressful. Letting our minds wander while taking breaks with easy tasks, both online and in the physical world, helps us replenish our scarce cognitive resources, and with more resources, we are better able to focus and be productive. The Pulitzer-Prize-winning author Jean Stafford used rote activity such as gardening to help de-stress and rebuild cognitive resources for writing.[7] I will show how rote activity not only works in concert with focused attention, but also plays a role in helping us achieve well-being.

In this book, I will dive deep into the research that shows the reasons why these popular myths do not hold true. One reason that these myths arose is that the science of attention was not considered in describing how we use our personal technologies. Our attention on our computers is affected by so many things— the work we do, the amount of cognitive resources available, time of day, stress, quality of sleep, and a host of other factors. If we buy into the idea that distractions are primarily our own fault, then we ignore the fact that we are part of a larger socio-technical culture that exerts influences on our behavior.

Reframing our goal from productivity to well-being

In 2009 I experienced a wake-up call. In that year I received a diagnosis of Stage III colon cancer. I thought I was the healthiest person I knew. I jogged daily, ate healthily and kept my weight down. Suddenly I was being told that I had a 69 percent five-year survival rate. I was determined to be in that 69 percent group, and I am glad to report that I was. I have been cancer-free for fourteen years at the time of this writing and intend to stay that way. At the time of my diagnosis, the cause of the cancer was not known. A genetic screening showed no gene responsible for it, and no familial genetic link. But in the years prior I had been experiencing a tremendous amount of stress, and I do remember thinking that at some point I was going to pay the price for that stress. While I know that I cannot attribute my cancer diagnosis solely to my screen time or work life, it is known that stress weakens the immune system. Also, when one experiences a life-threatening event, it makes one realize that time is finite. My diagnosis was a wake-up call for me to think about how I was spending my time—quite a bit of that time was on my devices, and I was experiencing a lot of stress because of it. I also realized how, in our current digital age, feeling such intense time pressure and stress is widespread—I just needed to look around me and hear what my colleagues and study participants were say-ing. These experiences made me think even more deeply about the role that our digital devices play in affecting our well-being.

Despite that, digital devices have brought us so many benefits, and there has been so much progress in making our lives easier: enabling us to work from home, connect to loved ones, receive expert medical care, find information, and so much more. My health scare made me deeply aware that we need to rethink how we use our devices while maintaining our health and well-being.

We constantly hear that we now have the technical means to be ceaselessly productive in our digital age and that we need to optimize our time to pack in as much as possible. My own life experience and my research have led me to a different conclusion: we should instead think about how we can achieve our utmost well-being. We need to change the conversation from adjusting our lives to being maximally productive, to adjusting our lives to feeling balanced. Our goal when we use our devices should be to maintain a positive store of mental resources, so that we can ultimately experience a higher level of well-being. As a result, we'll be more productive.

Our modern digital era has caused a fundamental shift in how we think and work, and in how we focus our attention and achieve fulfillment. The technology we use on an everyday basis, our cultural and social environments, and our individual human nature together make it hard to focus. We now need a new paradigm for understanding how to keep ourselves happy, productive and fulfilled. The silver bullets that we have been promised to enhance our focus and be more productive are rather blanks, based on wrong assumptions about attention. Rather than consider attention as a binary state where we are either focused or not focused, we should realize that attention is far more nuanced. In the chapters ahead, I will show how each different type of attention—being focused, doing rote activity, and even feeling bored—has value and purpose when it comes to maintaining a positive balance of cognitive resources throughout the day. This means that focus is not the sole "optimal" state of attention, but actually works best when balanced with other types of attention that tax our resources less.

This book is divided into three parts. In the first part of the book, I begin by presenting some important science about attention. The study of attention is a vast field covered in thousands of research articles over more than a century, going back to William James, considered the father of psychology. Covering all the aspects of attention that relate to our experience in the digital world would comprise volumes. I have therefore restricted my coverage to just a few key concepts, such as the theory and role of our limited cognitive resources, that will help you understand your behavior when you use your devices. The rest of Part I covers research that I have done with colleagues showing how much people really do multitask and are interrupted, and how our attention spans have been declining with the rise of personal computing and smartphones. I will address the first myth by showing that rather than striving for nonstop focus, it is important to consider a balance of attentional states. I will also discuss the second myth and explain that finding your own attentional rhythm is more attainable than achieving flow. In Part II, I will take on the third myth, and review reasons for why we multitask and are distracted, taking a deep dive into the individual, social, environmental and technological influences on our attention, distractions, interruptions and multitasking in the digital world. I will also address the fourth myth, presenting research results that show how mindless activity actually has benefits and can help us replenish our resources. In Part III, I will discuss solutions: how we can develop agency to control our attention, based on research that shows how people can be their own successful agents of change, and how you can use your devices and follow your own rhythm of attention.

Over the years, many colleagues, students and peers have expressed to me how much they identify with my research results. You will likely realize that your perceptions about your attention have been verified scientifically. This book is intended to help you to consciously understand why you have such a hard time staying focused, why you get distracted easily and self-interrupt, and why your attention shifts so much when you use your devices. Real change starts with awareness, and developing agency to control our attention is about understanding why we behave as we do so that we can self-reflect and course-correct. If your goal is to achieve a healthy psychological balance, then you will keep your mental resources replenished and then as a byproduct will be more productive. As our digital world continues to accelerate, I am optimistic that we can also find balance within it.

Part I:

The Anatomy of Attention

CHAPTER ONE:

Your Limited Cognitive Resources

Most people are familiar enough with their computers, tablets and smartphones to know how to adjust settings. Chances are that you have a basic idea of how the internet works, and when your device loses its internet connection, you can troubleshoot the problem. While most have a good sense of how their devices work, fewer may know how our attention works when we use our devices. In order to understand why we switch our attention so rapidly on our devices, why we succumb to distractions, and why our days feel so draining, in this chapter we will open up the mind's black box and look at the deep psychological processes that explain our unique digital behaviors. Later in the book we will also take a holistic view of the underlying forces that can explain why we multitask and are so distracted. But first, we will start with the basics of attention, how it works, how much energy it actually takes to perform "simple" tasks, and how the digital tools that we almost constantly use are uniquely demanding of our limited attentional resources.

My changing relationship with technology

My journey in studying why our attention is drained so rapidly when using our devices started in 2000, when I began my life as an academic. Though the dot-com bubble had burst, that year ushered in a new decade of accelerating advances in digital technologies. Over the next ten years, five million new startups would be founded. In 2003 we would see the birth of a social media giant spark a wave of other social media giants that changed life not just for individuals but for society as a whole. In 2007 we would be introduced to a small pocket-sized computer that changed how, when and where we accessed information and people.

Not only was the year 2000 a pivotal point in the digital evolution, but it was also pivotal in my own relationship with technology. I had recently moved back to the US after working in a large research institute in Germany, where I had enjoyed an extremely well-balanced work life. There, I did not have to write grants, did not have to teach, did not have to sit on committees, and was able to focus on a single project. Now, starting work as an academic at the University of California Irvine, I was suddenly thrust into a different culture: I was working on multiple projects, writing grants to secure funding for more projects, teaching, mentoring students, serving on committees, and building a new network of people. I knew I should put the brakes on some projects, but how could I say no to so many exciting things?

I became glued to my computer screen as I tried to keep up. I noticed how my attention on the computer kept shifting among my different projects, and also to different applications and websites often not even related to my projects. Sometimes these shifts were driven by email or other notifications, but also sometimes by my own internal thoughts. I found it very hard to spend time finishing even a part of one project before I started to work on something else. My attention seemed to be shifting from screen to screen faster as the decade progressed.

A story that illustrates this changing relationship was how I spent my lunchtime. In Germany, a large, warm meal, *Mittagessen*, is eaten at lunchtime. When noon approached, a colleague would usually walk around the office and gather up colleagues to go to lunch. We all eagerly awaited this nice long break, which lasted for about an hour. We would walk to the cafeteria, have a hot meal, and spend the time in a lively discussion, catching up on gossip and new technology. Then, as a healthy add-on to the lunch break, my colleagues and I would take a *Runde*, walking around the research campus for twenty minutes. We all returned to work refreshed and thinking about new ideas. Once I came back to the US, my lunchtime practice changed dramatically. Right after teaching my first class, I would rush to the cafeteria to buy my take-out lunch. I would speed back to my office and then down the hallway, passing by the open doors of all my colleagues, peeking in, seeing each of them eating their sandwiches in front of their computer screens. I would then slide into my chair, turn on my computer and do the same. Lunchtime was no longer a break from work but rather a brief interlude to secure food before getting back to the screen.

As I started to discuss with colleagues and friends how I was both attached to my computer screen and yet having a hard time staying focused on what was on that screen, I was finding that others were reporting the same types of behavior. The more I talked to people, the more I discovered that this experience was quite widespread. People described switching their attention frequently, while spending more time on their devices than ever before. It was disturbing, but as a scientist, intriguing to me at the same time. What was happening? I began to think seriously about studying this phenomenon objectively.

I feel so lucky to have been in the right place, at the right time, in the right field, when many new technologies, so commonplace today, were first introduced. I remember the first time I used a cell phone. It was the mid-1980s. I was a student and was riding in a taxi through Central Park with a friend. Motorola had introduced its DynaTAC 8000X phone, which few owned as it cost about $10,000 in today's dollars. It also had only thirty minutes of talk time. My friend, who prided himself on being at the forefront of adopting technology, handed me his cell phone and said I could try it. The phone was huge by today's standards. It's hard to describe the exhilaration that I felt barreling through Central Park in a cab when I heard the call connect. I would feel that same exhilaration a few years later when I saw those networked computers at my first job in the EDS conference room, and later my first encounters with a graphical web browser, streaming video, physical immersive virtual reality spaces called CAVES, and online virtual environments, smaller versions of what now is called the metaverse. I was also fortunate to be in the right profession, working as a psychologist equipped with the training and methods to be able to observe and study how our attention and behavior were changing as these technologies came into our lives.

Your control over your attention

Psychology is a relatively young scientific field compared to chemistry, physics or medicine, which span centuries, and even millennia. The person who pioneered the study of attention is also known as the "father of psychology," William James. Born in 1842 in New York City into a wealthy and cosmopolitan family, his godfather was Ralph Waldo Emerson, and his younger brother, the novelist Henry James. When he was young, he was not sure of his path and bounced around trying different pursuits, first studying art, then chemistry, and then medicine, until finally settling on psychology. But there was no psychology department in the mid-1870s when he was hired as a professor at Harvard—the first psychology lab was opened in

1879 by Wilhelm Wundt at the University of Leipzig—and so James also bounced around academic departments, first on the physiology faculty, and then later in the philosophy and (newly formed) psychology departments. The exposure to these different fields that touched on different aspects of the body and mind generated his interest in understanding a very basic aspect of humans—their attention.

James was a prolific writer, eventually completing his great treatise *The Principles of Psychology* in 1890, which comes to nearly fourteen hundred pages. Remarkably, James was able to write over two thousand words per day. In fact, James cleverly used psychology to limit distractions and to use his time efficiently for writing. In what would be highly unusual today, he scheduled his office hours with students during his evening meal at his home so that he would not be disturbed while he worked during the day. Most students were indeed too timid to come to his house, and this limited the number who would visit. Any student who did come was then ushered into his dining room to meet with him as he continued eating.[1]

James was the first to define attention from a psychological perspective. His definition is not so different from how most of us think about attention today: *"Every one knows what attention is. It is the taking possession by the mind, in clear and vivid form, of one out of what seem several simultaneously possible objects or trains of thought. Focalization, concentration, of consciousness are of its essence."*[2]

But also importantly, James believed that our choice of what we pay attention to is consequential, as we construct our life experience this way: *"Millions of items of the outward order are present to my senses which never properly enter into my experience. Why? Because they have no interest for me. My experience is what I agree to attend to. Only those items which I notice shape my mind—without selective interest, experience is an utter chaos."*[3]

In other words, James believed that what we decide to pay

attention to becomes part of our lived experience. I might be walking in a beautiful garden and have my cell phone out. I am texting with a friend, and I'm trying to spell correctly and dodge autocorrect, which often guesses wrong. It is the texts that have entered into the record of my experience, and not the softness of the ground, the trill of the warbler or the scarlet of the azaleas. I have focused my attention on texting, and I could have been in Times Square.

To James, then, as we move through the world, we are confronted by a host of different kinds of stimuli, and we select what to focus on by our own volition. In other words, we can control where we pay attention. Oh, would that it were so easy as James envisioned.

Your attentional networks

You might imagine, then, from James's description that there is one central place in your brain where attention resides. But it turns out that attention is actually a system of different networks, located in different parts of the brain, that together make up the attentional system.[4] It is like the financial system in that there is no single entity that we can point to, but rather it is made up of different financial services, carried out by investment firms, banks, insurance companies and so on. In the attention system, our attentional networks perform diverse operations when we try to pay attention to something, like focusing on our screens or managing interruptions. First, there is *alerting*, which is used when we maintain vigilance during a task, like trying to concentrate on writing that report to meet a deadline. Next, there is *orienting*, used when we prioritize and select stimuli to focus on, such as when we find that email from our manager in our inbox that must be answered first, or when we choose to respond to that chime signaling an incoming text. Last, there is *executive control*, which manages interference of irrelevant stimuli like an offensive lineman does in football, so that we can maintain focus,[5] such as when we try to restrain ourselves from responding to distractions.

Another way to think about how these systems function in practice is to imagine you're a member of an orchestra. Alerting is used when you are counting the measures and watching the conductor so you don't miss your cue; orienting is making sure you're in the right place in the score, that you have the right key signature, the right dynamic, and you know who else you're supposed to be playing with; executive control is used to prevent distraction caused by a camera flash in the audience or by others you're performing with, even if you're caught up in a beautiful solo that someone else is playing.

When we try to focus attention and pursue our goals, we utilize a set of mental processes known as executive function, which you can think of as the governor of the mind. Executive function has the heroic task of managing different types of processes: prioritizing and switching tasks, decision-making, sustaining and allocating attention, using working memory, and also practicing self-regulation.[6]

The governor can work impeccably when tasks are easy, like when we're browsing Facebook. The trouble starts when our tasks, and the effort to manage them, gets hard. This happens when we try to deal with multiple tasks and when we're experiencing a lot of interruptions. A lot of things happen then: we need to allocate attention to our task at hand, but then suddenly we attend to the interruption, trying to keep track of the interrupted tasks in our minds, all while resisting new distractions. When we do all this under time pressure and for an extended period, the overtaxed governor of your mind struggles to keep you on your goals. That's when you start to see an impact on performance.

When we use our devices, we're in front of an interface that challenges us to keep our attention on our goals. It is not only the visual cues like browser tabs, social media icons, and notifications on your computer and phone that represent a gateway to information—it is also the *idea* that there is a vast reservoir of information at hand that you can access. You might not welcome the proximity of this excess information when you're trying to work on a single task, such as that overdue monthly report, and so you force yourself to resist the temptation to switch to any of these other information sources. But even if you succeed in not switching to another task or distraction, your executive function is still working constantly to inhibit that behavior.

Your limited pool of cognitive resources

Let's now consider why it is that you feel so drained at 3 p.m. and why you find yourself turning to social media for a break. A long-standing, well-accepted theory in psychology, with over fifty years of research behind it, is that the mind has a general pool of attentional, or cognitive, resources that we use in our everyday functioning.[7][8] These resources can be thought of as your attentional capacity, or rather, as the amount of attention you have available. A basic assumption is that these resources are required when you process information, and this pool of resources is limited. Your cognitive resources can drain, and that affects your performance in the short term, say when working on an hour-long effortful task and dealing with interruptions. But in the long run over the day, homeostatic variation (the time elapsed since you woke up) is also associated with declining performance.[9] The reason you feel drained and start making errors is likely that you have been using these limited resources like there's no tomorrow, and the demands on them exceed what you have available. So compared to earlier that morning, when it's 3 p.m. after managing email, texts and phone calls and being in meetings all day, and not taking time for meaningful breaks, you likely have fewer attentional resources available to maintain alertness, and for your executive function—your mind's governor—to help you avoid being distracted by social media.

The theory of limited cognitive resources can explain your performance when your workload is high.[10] This happens in your everyday life, like when you've been trying to keep focused, but then you're also being interrupted, switching tasks and trying to resist distractions on your computer and phone. We selectively allocate our attentional resources to different activities: reading, making phone calls, handling interruptions, or even to internal thoughts, just like how we allocate our financial resources to spend on different things. Imagine that you just went to an ATM, have cash in your pocket, and go to a farmers market that only takes cash. You spend your money on artisan bread, truffle cheese and grass-fed beef, but then your money nearly runs out. You have just a few pennies left, and the only thing you can buy are some wilted vegetables. If you want to buy something of good quality, you have to go back to the ATM and refill your wallet. Your attention works the same way. When your attentional resources are spent, you can't do very much, and you have to take a break and replenish. Performance suffers when the cognitive resources we need exceed those we have available.[11]

The cognitive load you experience from your activities, i.e., your mental effort, is believed to correspond with the demand on your cognitive resources.[12] Cognitive load has long been measured in the laboratory through performance: a person performs a task such as searching for a target letter (say, the letter H) among other distractor letters displayed on a screen. Over time, performance degrades, and the assumption is that cognitive resources have been expended. Another measure is pupil diameter, which has been shown to increase with cognitive load. Typically it is measured in laboratory studies while people do cognitive tasks such as mental arithmetic, sustained attention performance or decision-making.[13] Unfortunately it's just not possible to measure pupil dilation in the wild because pupil diameter varies with light in the environment, and there will never be perfectly consistent lighting at home or in real workplaces. Still another measure of cognitive load is facial thermography using a thermal imaging camera, since temperature changes in the face correspond to mental effort. But again, this method poses challenges for use in the wild as a person's head movement must be restricted in order for them to be monitored by a camera.

It turns out that there is a real physiological basis in the brain that underlies how cognitive resources are being used. Neuroscience studies show that when people focus their attention, a region of the brain becomes metabolically active, and carbon dioxide in the blood increases. In turn, the increase in carbon dioxide causes blood vessels to dilate to remove waste in that activated part of the brain.[14] But as people spend more time in sustained focus, their vigilance declines, and blood velocity decreases.[15][16] The change in attention and performance suggests that cognitive resources are not being replenished while the task continues. In order to replenish, an individual needs to stop the hard task and have time to build their resources back up. Thus, blood flow in the brain appears to be a metabolic index of how cognitive resources are used when people are focused. It provides neuroscientific evidence for the theory of cognitive resources and explains what happens when our brains are hard at work trying to maintain focus.

The emerging field of neuroergonomics tracks people's brain activity as they perform work to measure their cognitive load—in other words, their mental effort. Researchers have measured brain activity when people use sustained attention with techniques like positron emission tomography (PET) or functional magnetic resonance imaging (fMRI). The problem, though, is that people have to lie very still for PET and fMRI, and this severely restricts the kinds of activities they can do, making it hard for psychologists to study their attention behavior. But another technique has solved this problem: transcranial Doppler sonography uses sound waves to measure the velocity of blood flow in the middle cerebral arteries, which provide much of the blood flow to the brain. This technique is usually used to diagnose strokes or blockage of an artery, but it can also measure what happens when people are doing a task that requires focused attention. To measure blood flow while paying attention, people come to a laboratory and put on a headband with an embedded small transducer, which does not restrict body motion the way the PET or fMRI does. They then perform tasks, such as monitoring a screen for thirty minutes and making judgments about whether one line is longer than another. Still another promising approach for measuring cognitive load based on cerebral blood flow is functional near-infrared spectroscopy (fNIRS), which measures changes based on light reflection of oxygenated and deoxygenated hemoglobin. A study in a simulated office environment showed that it could detect workload differences in various reading tasks, even amid interruptions, though not in writing tasks.[17]

Brain–computer interfaces like transcranial Doppler sonography or fNIRS work well in restricted settings such as in airline cockpits or a simulated office environment in a laboratory. But outside of such a restricted environment, it is harder to measure our attention and the cognitive resources used with most of the tasks we do. What we typically do in our lives is not so controlled as it is in a laboratory, and there are so many things that can affect our performance. In everyday life, your mental performance depends not only on the amount of cognitive resources available but also on the type and difficulty of the task, and how many tasks you are attempting to perform at once. We might assume that an easy task such as passively watching a YouTube video may not use many resources. But a hard task like writing a report requires you to search for, read and summarize material, and make other complex decisions, and we can assume from lab studies that this uses a lot of cognitive resources. We also know from years of laboratory research that two different tasks can be performed simultaneously with no performance degradation if at least one of the tasks requires little or no effort, such as listening to instrumental music while reading text on your computer. Now consider that you are switching among more challenging multiple tasks, such as texting, updating your CV, searching on the internet, checking email and answering phone calls. We can assume that more cognitive resources are being expended to navigate between these different tasks compared to, say, just talking on the phone while walking, because we can walk automatically without much thought. And of course, with our attention to the phone call, our awareness of our surroundings decreases.

Cognitive resource theory also holds that different cognitive resources are used for different types of tasks. You would expend different resources when you do visual, auditory or spatial types of operations.[18][19] Examples of such distinct operations are when you read a news article, speak on the phone or play a video game that involves spatial skills. Tasks that require and compete for the same types of resources, like two auditory tasks that involve listening to an audio conference and a separate phone conversation, will have more interference, especially if you switch between them rapidly, and you'll have a lot of difficulty doing both without errors.

This is why when you try to focus and are continually interrupted and find yourself switching your attention among multiple tasks, over time you feel so exhausted. Your mind's executive function is in full gear doing the work needed to maintain performance. When you try to maintain this type of task-switching over time, performance inevitably degrades, and this is shown over and over again in laboratory studies. After a full day or even after a few hours of switching furiously among different tasks, without a substantial break you just don't have the capability that you had early in the day. You are knackered, as the British say.

Fortunately, cognitive resources can be flexibly allocated back and forth among tasks. If you are talking on the phone while driving and a car suddenly swerves in front of you, then your attention is suddenly fully reallocated to driving, and you abruptly stop speaking on the cell phone. If you are texting while your partner at the dining table is trying to converse with you, and if they raise their voice in an annoyed tone, then hopefully you will pause your texting and devote your attention to your partner.

While we know that switching back and forth between answering emails, handling interruptions and completing that quarterly report can use up your resources, other activities can replenish them. Some ways of replenishing resources are intuitive. If you have just returned to work from a relaxing weekend where you have caught up on your sleep, then you should have sufficient cognitive resources on Monday morning. A good night's sleep, with a reasonable amount of deep sleep and especially REM sleep (which benefits memory and the ability to sustain attention), can stockpile resources. When people psychologically detach from a stressful situation, they can also recover their cognitive resources.[20] Going on a vacation, especially to a peaceful environment, can allow the mind to reset. Even a mere twenty minutes of contact with nature can refresh your mind.[21] But what you may not realize is that playing a simple mindless game like Two Dots (an app where, like it sounds, you connect dots) can also allow your mind to take a break.

Cognitive resource use is an important long-standing theory that can help explain your attention performance. Throughout this book, I ask you to imagine a fuel gauge that indicates how much you have left in your tank of cognitive resources. When you subjectively feel spent and your performance starts to suffer, your gauge would read near empty. But if you feel refreshed at the start of the day, your gauge should register as full.

Sustained and kinetic attention

Our attention can change moment to moment, fluctuating between being alert and letting our mind wander. Psychologists have measured these moment-to-moment fluctuations by developing a clever technique called the gradual onset continuous performance task (gradCPT).[22] In this test, subjects are brought into a laboratory and are shown different photographs, say of either mountain or city scenes, that fade in and out and change every eight hundred milliseconds—which is just under one second.[23] Subjects are told to press a button when they view the city scene but not the mountain scene, and they do this for hundreds of images. This enables the researcher to discern moment by moment whether a subject is paying attention or distracted. Perhaps not surprisingly, the more the mind shifts between an attentive state and nonattentive mind-wandering state, the worse is the measured performance.[24]

Studies of sustained attention such as those using the gradCPT task are almost always done in the laboratory, measuring moment-to-moment fluctuations. But what happens with our attention when we are in our everyday environments, outside of the laboratory? In my own research, I have been interested in studying attention in the wild. Whereas we would expect, based on the gradCPT results, that people's attention would fluctuate between being focused and distracted moment to moment while on the same screen, it is also the case that people's attention shifts among different screens and apps, and I have found that sometimes these shifts are quite fast. Unlike laboratory studies that measure how people pay attention or not with relatively uniform stimuli like letters or images, in the real world, people are actually shifting their attention among quite different types of tasks with very different stimuli. People might attend to some things quickly in short bursts, while they might allot their attention to other things on a longer timescale. Also, unlike laboratory studies that typically use neutral symbols like letters or numbers, different activities in the wild can evoke different kinds of emotions: sadness on reading a news item, or amusement in reading a text from a friend.

But what also happens when people switch attention between different tasks is that they need to reconfigure their internal representation of one task to the internal representation of the next task, in what psychologist Stephen Monsell describes as "mental gear-changing."[25] These representations are known as schemas,[26] which you can think of as an internal script describing your pattern of behavior in a particular activity. We use these mental schemas to interpret the world and organize how we do things. When you write a report, you might invoke a schema of opening up a Word document and then starting to type. When you answer email, you have a different pattern of behavior: perhaps you click on your email client, scan your emails beginning with the most recent, select what to respond to, and delete or file others. Each time you switch tasks, your attention is redirected. This task-switching is like erasing your internal whiteboard and writing notes on it for the new task. When you are interrupted a lot, then you are reconfiguring your internal schemas at a fast rate—erasing that whiteboard, writing on it, erasing it again and so on. You can imagine how fast your cognitive resources decline.

As I was writing this chapter, I realized there was not a vocabulary to describe this type of attention-switching that we observe in the wild when people use their devices. Sometimes it seemed purposeful and other times chaotic. At times people might appear to have sustained focus, but then sometimes, inexplicably, they seem driven to switch their attention to something else: a different project, email, web surfing or social media. Their attention can be stimulus-driven by a chime or pop-up, but also it can be triggered by nothing that is discernible to the observer, and instead by something inside of them: a memory or an inner urge. I searched for some time for a word to describe this type of rapid attention-switching. It was certainly energetic. I began to look at terms used in physics. Suddenly the term *kinetic* jumped out at me and seemed to fit. The word *kinetic* means dynamic, in motion, marked by vigorous activity. Kinetic attention refers to a dynamic state of attention characterized by rapid shifts, such as between applications, social media and internet sites, or between the computer and phone. While in the real world it is hard to measure whether one is momentarily attentive or mind-wandering since we don't use controlled stimuli in a laboratory like in the gradCPT task, what we can observe are people's actions such as when they click on email, switch screens or surf the web. In and of itself, kinetic attention is neither good nor bad—it is simply a descriptor of real-world attention behavior. In many ways, it could be said that kinetic attention is an adaptive response to the wealth of information and distractions created by digital media, or an attempt to allocate attention more efficiently. But my research has also shown that we are, for the most part, not very good at utilizing it—our use of kinetic attention can result in widespread stress, fatigue, poor performance and even burnout. And again, a reason for this is that such rapid switching taps into and drains our cognitive resources. Next, we'll talk more in-depth about reasons why people have trouble in focusing their attention.

CHAPTER TWO:

The Battle for Your Attention

I often receive emails from people who describe their struggles in trying to control their attention and ask for advice. For example, I recently received the following: "Trying to articulate the difficulty with workplace distractions is like chasing a greased pig. I feel like every day my work is to deftly navigate complexities of this job with accuracy while being bombarded with emails, personal appearances by fellow coworkers, phone calls and texts. I leave work drained. Not physically, but mentally... I detest these devices that I think we are all slaves to."

This is a common refrain I hear. In this chapter we'll examine reasons we have so much trouble focusing our attention when we use our devices.

When attention is not under your control

When I'm driving a new route, even if I outsource the navigation to my GPS, I still have to pay attention to follow the directions. When we do tasks that might be unfamiliar or difficult, we engage in what's called controlled processing, which uses cognitive resources, sometimes quite a lot.

Not all attention, though, is under our willful control. Remember when you got your first cell phone? The first time you answered a call, you may have had to spend a bit of time searching for the right button to press or where to swipe the screen. But now, when you receive a call, you pick up your phone and press or swipe to answer it automatically. Similarly, after seeing an email notification on your screen so many times, you might automatically click when a new one appears. In these cases, our brain employs a type of cognitive processing that is automatic.

Automatic processing occurs with tasks that are very easy and well-learned and that we're familiar with. When you perform the same actions over and over again, like checking email or driving a familiar route, automatic processing develops. It does not deplete our attentional resources, which is why we can follow a straight route and talk at the same time, because we don't need to consciously think about the driving. But then if the light suddenly turns yellow, we flexibly allocate our attention to hit the brakes and stop talking. This type of automatic attention is called exogenous attention[1] and is usually driven by something external to us, by some kind of stimulus, like a traffic light.

Because automatic processing is fast, nearly effortless, and not generally under our control, we tend to respond quickly to notifications on our computers and phones—these are well-learned responses. Interestingly, the use of alcohol affects our ability to do controlled processing but has little effect on automatic processing.[2] So when under the influence, you would likely still grab your phone when an incoming text chimes, but you may have some trouble typing in a response.

In fact, it can be hard to *not* respond to a notification, in other words, to inhibit automatic attention. This is shown by a classic psychological test known as the Stroop Color and Word Test, which was invented by J. Ridley Stroop in 1935 to study cognitive interference when people are presented with two different stimuli.[3] Before the Stroop test was invented, as early as 1912, it was found that when subjects were trained in typing, and then the keys on the typewriter were switched, they had a hard time resisting typing as if the original keys remained.[4] Their well-learned habit interfered with the new task of typing with different keys. The Stroop task tests the same type of interference but with the well-learned habit of reading. In this test, one receives two sets of color names on paper or a screen. In one set, the font color matches the written word (i.e., the word *blue* is in blue font), but in the second set, the written color name and the font color are different (the word *blue* is now written in a yellow font). The task is to name the font color, and in the first set of words it's easy because the font colors and word names match. But in the second set of words there is an automatic tendency to read the word instead. It requires effort to inhibit the automatic response to say "blue" and instead say the correct answer, "yellow."

In order to perform the Stroop task accurately, one needs to actively maintain in one's mind the goal to "focus on the color" in order to block out the competing urge to read the word. Executive function works to inhibit competing responses in order to solve the task but is not always successful. In everyday use of our devices, we are continually challenged to inhibit automatic responses. Think, for example, of your computer interface as a dashboard. If you're trying to work on that overdue monthly report, when you see your browser tabs and icons, they represent gateways to activity that is way more fun and interesting. You need self-regulation to resist the temptation to automatically click on, say, a browser tab, and change screens. You will also likely have an automatic response to attend to an ad that flashes on your screen when you're on a website. As our actions become more automatic, it becomes harder to modify them and thus harder not to be distracted by stimuli like notifications. We'll see later in the book how trying to block automatic responses can get us stressed.

Some recent work on the neural basis of attention (the mechanisms in the brain that manage attention) suggests that if people have to continually employ cognitive control to resist behavior for a long period, then they end up making more impulsive choices over time. Most laboratory studies have tested self-control over short periods, say one hour. Whereas many people might be able to practice self-control in such a short time frame, it can be much harder to do so over an entire workday. In order to do a more realistic test of self-control, French researchers Bastien Blain, Guillaume Hollard and Mathias Pessiglione conducted experiments with participants over a six-hour period. People were brought to a controlled laboratory setting and performed difficult tasks like listening to a list of numbers and having to remember the ones that were presented three digits back. For example, when presented with a continual stream of numbers, e.g., 9, 7, 4, 2, 8, they would have to remember 4, then 2, then 8, and so on as more numbers were presented. As the experiment progressed, they were asked to periodically state their choice between waiting for a delayed reward of 100 euros or receiving an immediate reward of lesser value. Over the six-hour period, their resistance broke down and they made more impulsive choices, measured by choosing the immediate but less valuable monetary rewards rather than waiting for higher monetary rewards.[5] However, when doing easy tasks over six hours, the same impulsive behavior was not found. The experiment showed that over a period of time, when we exert cognitive control, trying to stay focused on hard tasks, we become more impulsive and gradually relinquish our ability to filter out distractions. Functional MRI data collected at the beginning, middle and end of the task showed that the increase in impulsivity was traced to a lowering in the activity in a region of the brain related to working memory and task-switching. The authors called it cognitive fatigue, and it shows that resisting distractions over time is yet another way to wear down our cognitive control. But also, while most laboratory studies test the ability to maintain cognitive control in experiments lasting one or even two hours, this study showed how our control can degrade the same way over a longer period, much like in a typical workday.

Keeping our attention on our goals

Recently I was talking with a friend and wishing I could have an unbroken extended period of time to work on this book without getting interrupted. My friend, who works at one of the tech giants, in turn was lamenting how each year a new source for interruptions is produced. As he explained, "We already have to navigate email, texts, phone calls and social media. If you don't let yourself get interrupted, you're out of the loop; as we keep inventing more interruption channels, we keep worsening our performance."

Indeed, it is too easy to find ourselves getting knocked off course from our goals. Our ability to perform a hard task like writing that report (or writing my book) involves maintaining that goal in your mind. Of course, tasks like writing a book have a long time line, and we can't possibly stop all interruptions during the process. When our attention is goal-driven, we are in control of and decide where to place our attention, and this protects us from distractions that are extraneous to our goals—this is what William James meant when he said that we use volition in choosing where to pay attention.[6]

So when we direct our attention to a goal in a top-down manner, this is called endogenous attention.[7] If my goal is to work on a book chapter, I would then allocate my attention to writing, reading, searching for information, or doing whatever I need to do to reach this goal. But when we simply react to stimuli in the environment automatically, like to phone calls or text notifications, then our attention is not goal-directed but rather stimulus-driven, in a bottom-up manner. This exogenous attention is the same type we experience when we're driven to brake by the sudden change of a traffic light to yellow.

In our everyday life, we are in constant negotiation between controlled and stimulus-driven attention. When we perform any action, we try to follow our internal goals (like writing that report) yet may succumb to external influences, like social media notifications, or even to our inner urges, like yearning to finish that crossword puzzle.[8] Attending to distractions is likely something we have evolved to do, to retain flexibility to respond to potential dangers in our environment. It remains important today. A person crossing the street and texting their friend can get clipped by a bicyclist if they're not monitoring the environment. But it turns out that people are not all that adept in monitoring the external environment when they use their devices: they can be so absorbed in texting while walking (and also driving) that they lose situational awareness and have a greater chance of getting injured.[9] It is ironic how, from an evolutionary standpoint, being able to monitor the environment as our ancestors did for predators while they hunted and gathered was beneficial for survival, and yet in today's digital world, our devices can capture our attention so completely that they even cause us to miss danger signals in the physical world.

So to act in accordance with our goals, we need to actively maintain them in our thoughts. When our attention is goal-directed, we can act purposefully. It is easy to imagine in the physical world the consequences of not keeping our goals in mind. Take the case of Andrew Devers, a twenty-five-year-old hiker, whose attention wandered while on a day hike in Washington State in 2021. He let his attention to the trail slip and found himself lost for eight days. Fortunately, he survived by eating berries and drinking creek water and was finally found with only minor injuries. But it was a terrifying experience for him. He described it this way: "I wasn't really thinking much about it. I just went with what I thought was the trail, and after like 45, 50 minutes of being in my own head, I just looked back and there was no trail anymore."[10] Similarly in the digital world, we often lose touch with our goals when we're using our devices and find ourselves off the trail. Without top-down control of our attention, we open ourselves up to stimuli that steer our attention for us. Our mind becomes like a pinball propelled from lever to lever by text chimes, social media notifications and targeted ads.

We all have the best intentions when we set goals like exercising every morning, but it's so easy to let these goals slip. As soon as, say, bad weather comes, we lose touch with the goal and instead spend thirty minutes on social media. What exactly happens in the brain when we try to keep our attention on our goals? A lot goes on behind the scenes, with a lion's share of the work done by our executive function.[11] First, we have to select the right goals, which can be the easy part. We might look at our to-do lists and see what our priorities are. Next, we must be able to hold a representation of the goal in our mind over time, which is much trickier as we have to guard against interference that might sabotage it. I can turn off external notifications, but it can be hard to control those inner urges. Fearing that I might be missing out on news and social media updates makes it a challenge. This is the role of our executive function, which can sometimes go into high gear to resist distractions. Last, we need to be agile to adjust our goals when necessary.[12] If you're not getting that critical information you need from your colleague, then you may need to change to a plan B goal. But here is the kicker. Trying to stick to our goals and resist distractions slowly depletes that precious gas tank of cognitive resources.[13] Once we're distracted and low on resources, it is harder to get back to maintaining our goals.

Attention traps

Now let's turn to some specific reasons why people have trouble managing their attention on their devices. Through observations, interviews and speaking with many people over the years about their use of their personal technologies, I found that there are several common behavioral patterns, what I call *attention traps*, where people report not being in control of their attention when they use their devices. You might relate to some of these patterns, which can help you reflect on your own behavior and potentially avoid them.

Framing errors

How do we get caught up in such patterns of behavior where we feel we have lost control of our attention? It starts with how we frame our choices of what actions to take. Framing refers to the particular perspective you give to the context in which your choice will be made. For example, say you have a pressing deadline coming up at work and your friend calls to invite you to take a weekend getaway at a nice resort. You could frame the choice of taking the weekend getaway in a positive way, as taking a break and relaxing to help you perform better during the week, or else you might frame the choice more negatively, as taking time away from working towards that deadline.

When you make a conscious decision to do something, you likely frame your choice, but you probably don't realize you are doing so. (At other times we react automatically to stimuli like clicking on a notification, and we don't have a chance to frame our choice.) Your situation, your emotional state and your mental energy all set the stage and will likely influence what you choose to do. If it is the start of the workday, and you don't feel pumped up with energy quite yet, then you might choose to take on something easy before starting hard work. If, however, it is four o'clock, and you are feeling emotionally drained after a day of meetings and work, your perspective might stem from what you could do to relieve exhaustion.

We can make framing errors, though, when we choose an activity, misjudging how worthwhile we feel it is. We might misinterpret or inflate the value of the chosen activity. For example, you might feel that working on the Sunday *New York Times* crossword will be a good break from work but then realize that it only served to make you frustrated.

We also can make framing errors when we wrongly assess how long we believe we will spend on a particular activity. People, nearly *all* people, are notoriously bad at estimating time. One study found that people err in estimating how much time they spend on a computer by 32 percent—heavy users underestimate their time, and light users overestimate their time.[14] You might decide that you want to take a short break from work, say ten minutes, to refresh yourself. You head to a blog, but the blog links to another interesting blog, and before you know it, an hour has passed and you have a meeting in five minutes that you haven't prepared for. We can easily fall victim to such attention traps. Later in the book, we'll talk about techniques that you can use to pull yourself out of these traps. For now, let's look at some specific patterns of behavior people report when they lack control of their attention.

The attention-wandering trap

I always smile when I call on a student in class who has been staring off into space and then fumbles to avoid admitting that he has no idea what I just asked him. Our attention naturally wanders between external stimuli and our internal thoughts. Mind-wandering in a strict sense is when people's attention is focused inward. It is so commonplace that people can spend between 25 and 50 percent of their thinking during waking hours just mind-wandering.[15]

When we use our devices, the visibility of browser tabs and

apps provides triggers that can lead the mind astray. In fact, we don't even need the visual cues of an interface to lead us off course—often just the mere exposure to our phones or computers can do this. Also, the internet facilitates our minds jumping from topic to topic, from outer content to inner thoughts, and back again. The flexibility of the internet's node and link structure reinforces this pattern of wandering attention. (We will go into this type of behavior in much more depth in Chapter 6.) In and of itself, such mind-wandering is not bad and can even be beneficial—it is an easy, non-taxing engagement of our attention and even replenishes cognitive resources. We can also discover and learn about new things. Sometimes putting a problem aside and letting your thoughts meander can open up new avenues for creative solutions.[16] But we can get caught up in attention-wandering on the internet to such an extent that we take away too much time from other things we want to get done.

There are so many digital activities where a key word or topic stimulates internal thoughts and starts a process of attention-wandering. For example, if you happen to read a Wikipedia article on the history of the suffragette movement, then you may start thinking about the #MeToo movement. You then go off and search for an article on #MeToo, and then other related topics capture your attention. When you end up in such internet meandering, you likely have made the second framing error of failing to predict the amount of time you would likely spend on Wikipedia when you made the choice to visit it— because you were so absorbed, you might not even have thought about time at all. People with good executive control are able to focus more on an external task and are better able to prevent mind-wandering[17]—and potentially incessant web surfing along with it. However, this ability to focus holds true when the external task is demanding. When the task is not very demanding, then executive control matters less, and just about everyone can be susceptible to attention-wandering. We are especially prone to this type of attention-wandering when we are low in cognitive resources. We succumb to doing what is easy, and we let ourselves be driven by external stimuli like clicking links on a web page.

However, one study found that meditation practices such as mindfulness techniques can be effective in controlling mind-wandering: people who had been through a mindfulness meditation course showed that they spent significantly more time on each task with less attention-shifting—in other words, they multitasked less.[18] These practices also teach people to gain an awareness of their present state, knowledge that is generally not available to them, and which we will learn about more in Chapter 13.

The rote attention trap

Another common behavioral pattern happens when people report not being able to readily stop doing easy and engaging activities on their devices. Playing simple online games like Candy Crush and browsing social media sites lightly engage our attention and can help us step back from stressful work and replenish our attentional resources. When you scan Twitter posts or do the same routine actions over and over again in a simple game—in either case you experience little or perhaps no challenge. You might see such rote activity as a good choice when you feel your cognitive resources are low.

But then the second type of framing error can occur. You might have wrongly estimated how much time you would spend taking a break—with such repetitive simple actions, one can easily lose track of time. The nature of the activity itself draws people to do such simple activities and keeps them engaged. Our research has shown that people receive emotional rewards and feel happiest when doing such rote activities (we will take a deeper dive into this in Chapter 10). The happiness itself becomes a reward and keeps you bound to the rote activity. This is why people spend so many hours watching TikTok (which we'll get into more thoroughly in Chapter 7).

These rote activities involve a type of stimulus–response behavior that includes immediate gratification, i.e., simple rewards such as laughter, earning points, achieving a new playing level or winning the game. The learning psychologist Edward Thorndike described this in 1911 as his law of effect, where responses that produce a positive effect in a situation are likely to be performed again.[19] Further, the greater the satisfaction, the stronger our connection to the behavior. One does not even need to receive a reward after every move in the game. This is called intermittent reinforcement, which is what the behaviorist psychologist B. F. Skinner studied, and it explains why people can be drawn to play a simple game over and over again even though they may only get a reward occasionally. Intermittent reinforcement strengthens the habit of engaging in the activity until it becomes ingrained.

Now, rewards in a simple game are easy to picture: one gets points, or advances a level. But rewards can also be generated from within us through our imagination, which triggers positive emotions. Scrolling through a real estate site can trigger your imagination of what it's like to live in a fabulous home. Retail therapy can reward us through imagination but can also bring intermittent rewards—sometimes we hit upon a great bargain browsing through shopping sites. Habits of turning to simple activities can form easily and go unnoticed, blinding us to time passing when doing them. We may not even realize we have these habits until we try to stop. As the English writer Samuel Johnson said, "The chains of habit are too weak to be felt until they are too strong to be broken."[20]

The social media trap

Quite a few people report that they feel their attention is trapped when they use social media. We are drawn to social media and texting because we are social beings and crave social support, social connectedness, and social capital, and want to satisfy our curiosity about others. Ideally, we can use social media to take breaks and connect to others, supporting our work and personal goals. When choosing to go on social media, framing errors occur easily. We can overestimate how much value we get from, say, Facebook, because in reality it is not designed for us to develop deep relationships. We can also underestimate how much time we might spend there because we may not realize how prone we are to social forces that lead us to participate and stay on the site. (We will talk about this more in Chapter 8.) In this type of behavioral pattern, we often prioritize short-term gains such as satisfying social curiosity over long-term gains of finishing our work.

Intermittent conditioning from social rewards can also function to keep people trapped on social media. Facebook likes are a great example of this: the number of likes on one's posts can increase one's sense of social worth. So you keep posting because you hope that one of your posts is bound at some point to hit a jackpot of likes. Every TikTok video may not be funny, but you know that eventually one will come up that is hilarious. Framing errors, the social forces that draw us to social media, and the social rewards we receive once there are a perfect storm for trapping our attention.

The identity trap

A behavioral pattern that I hear about more often from young people is that they spend a lot of time and attention on designing and maintaining their online personas. The philosopher Jean Baudrillard writes that we live in a world of simulation where people define themselves by the signs and symbols of society.[21] Such models determine how people understand themselves and relate to other people. But on the internet, what symbolizes the real becomes real. To some individuals, their persona on social media can be an expansion of their real identity, and for some can even become more important than their real-world persona. Having lots of followers on Twitter or TikTok can make one feel more important than anything experienced in the physical world. For some, careers are built on being an influencer where identity is paramount. Facebook likes help validate one's identity, and it can seem like a badge of honor to have one's tweet get retweeted. For young people in particular, online identities are important as that is how they present themselves to their social group and the world. But online identity is important to people of all ages, for example, in how they portray their work identity. Everyone wants to appear successful. We carefully construct our online personas because we want to display our real-world selves in the best possible light. Maintaining identity is a powerful basic human desire. Because online identity is so valuable, some individuals can spend a lot of time crafting and refining their posts and profiles. This can even take precedence over goal-directed attention to work or studies.

The sunk cost trap

We can get stuck in a behavioral pattern on our devices by making a sunk cost error: you have already devoted so much of your time and attention on a site or playing a game that you feel it would be a waste to pull your attention away. Sunk cost errors happen often in the physical world. For example, you have put an investment into a business of producing a new product hoping for a big gain, but it turns out no one is buying and you are losing money. You have already invested a lot of money and effort into it, and you would rather continue with the business, hoping it will pay off, than stop production with a certainty of loss. Gambling is another typical example of the sunk cost fallacy. If a person is playing a slot machine in Vegas and has already put $500 of quarters in, it's not easy to walk away. Just one more try and you might win it all back. Sunk costs can happen in relationships: after being together with a friend, spouse or partner for years, even if it's just not working out, to break up would seem like a waste of all that effort put into building the relationship. But if it's just not working, the rational choice is to end the relationship, call it a sunk cost, write it off as a loss and move on. But humans are not always so rational.

Similarly, we have trouble recognizing sunk costs in the digital world. You might choose to take a short break to read an article online, and you frame it as being worthwhile. After reading it for thirty minutes, you realize that it does not really have much value for you. Your time is lost, though, and can't be recovered. But you might feel that if you stop, all the time you put in so far would be a waste, so you press on, hoping the article might have a good ending. Games such as World of Warcraft have multiple levels, and players try to ascend to new ones by doing various activities like quests. The sunk cost trap is what the game company leverages to get people to continue playing the game. Companies design games knowing that people generally don't pull themselves out of sunk cost situations. If a person has already reached a high level, having already invested time, money and emotional energy into it, they don't want to stop. A recent study showed that the average amount of time in one stretch that people play video games is one hour and twenty-two minutes.[22] This is fine if you have an extra hour and a half a day to play games. But most people don't.

The activities described here are not necessarily detrimental, and can be positive in helping relieve stress and replenish resources. We'll return to that possibility later in the book. But when you feel that you are no longer in control of your actions, if you're unable to stop watching TikTok or spend too much time on Wikipedia or shopping sites, then they have become detrimental to you. Consider the framing errors you might make and see if you are susceptible to any of these attention traps discussed here. Later on in the book, we will discuss how you can develop agency when you use your devices, which can help you be more goal-directed, and thus better focused.

How we choose where to focus our attention

Since we now know how easy it is for our attention to be diverted, and since we have a limited capacity of attentional resources, we have to make choices as to how to willfully use our attention. Choosing where to focus is essentially a choice of how to allocate resources. It is like having money in your pocket and deciding what to buy at the farmers market. But how do we choose where to invest our attention?

Traditional models of attention propose that where we choose to focus our attention is governed by individual decisions based on our preferences, our priorities and the resources needed.[23] For example, we may choose to start our day with email; our priority might be that we need to finish that report by noon; and importantly, we would consider how much resource this task will require.

However, I argue that while individual factors of preferences, priorities and resource needs can sometimes explain our choices of where we direct our attention, they are not the full story. We are creatures embedded in a social, cultural and technical environment. We are subject to a number of influences on our attention and behavior beyond ourselves. In other words, to truly understand how we allocate our attention in this digital world, we need to understand the complex interplay between the social world we live in and the technology we interact with. How we choose where to focus involves our individual preferences and priorities but also is based on the broader social and technical world we are part of. Our minds, and our attention, are influenced by our external as well as our internal worlds.

Our social worlds can affect how we use our devices. As an example, let's look at the story of Google Glass. Introduced in

2014, it had a short-lived run as a personal product, and, worn like eyeglasses, was intended for people to be able to view content on a screen hands-free. But it also included a tiny camera mounted in the frame that could record what the wearer looked at as they moved around. Unless one was very close to the wearer, it was not apparent that the camera was operating, and people felt uncomfortable that they might be recorded. The wearer might have been intent on focusing their attention on the small eyeglass display, but they soon found out that in using this technology in a social environment, other people felt surveilled. The early version of Google Glass failed for social rather than technical reasons. Similarly, we use our devices as part of a larger social world, and as we will see later in the book, social influences affect what we do on our devices, particularly our ability to focus.

William James conceptualized attention as under an individual's volition.[24] We need to expand our thinking about attention in our twenty-first century digital world to consider that our attention while using our personal devices is also subject to influences by social but also environmental and technical undercurrents. We must take a *sociotechnical* approach, a wider view beyond just the individual, to understand the influences on our attention when we're on our devices. So, in such a complex world with all these influences, how can we fully control our attention, stick to our goals, and harness our tendency for kinetic, dynamic attention to work for us? Before we get to this question, we will first look at the research to understand people's actual attention behavior when they use their devices in the real world. From studying people in the wild, we'll see just how much they really do switch attention and are interrupted, and how focused attention follows a rhythm throughout the day. Science can be stranger than fiction, and the results might astonish you as much as they did me.

CHAPTER THREE:

Types of Attention

The great writer and poet Maya Angelou wrote her memoir *I Know Why the Caged Bird Sings*, and the rest of her work, in a hotel room. She rented it by the month and still spent the night at home, but would show up at 6:30 a.m., sprawl on the bed, and write until early afternoon. She never allowed the hotel staff to change the sheets for fear that they would throw away a slip of paper containing a precious thought. She removed the paintings from the walls, as they were unwelcome distractions. However, in addition to her tools of the trade like yellow pads, *Roget's Thesaurus*, a dictionary, a Bible and bottle of sherry, she also brought a few distractions of her own, like crossword puzzles and a deck of cards.

As she explained it, these distractions gave her "something to occupy my little mind. I think my grandmother taught me that. She didn't mean to, but she used to talk about her 'little mind.' So when I was young, from the time I was about 3 until 13, I decided that there was a Big Mind and a Little Mind. And the

Big Mind would allow you to consider deep thoughts, but the Little Mind would occupy you, so you could not be distracted. It would work crossword puzzles or play Solitaire, while the Big Mind would delve deep into the subjects I wanted to write about."[1] As Angelou described it, both the Big Mind and the Little Mind were integral to her writing process.

The Big Mind may have been the more powerful force of literary inspiration, but it needed the Little Mind to provide a respite. In my research, I've learned how Maya Angelou's idea is actually backed up by science. They are complementary ways of thinking, parts that comprise a whole.

The idea that we have different types of attention was first recognized by the philosopher John Locke over three centuries ago. In *An Essay Concerning Human Understanding*, Locke's description of attention was somewhat similar to Angelou's: registering thoughts and fixating on an idea, as well as what he called mind-wandering or reverie. Locke saw these distinctions as universal truths: "This difference of intention, and remission of the mind in thinking, with a great variety of degrees between earnest study, and very near minding nothing at all, everyone, I think, has experimented in himself."[2] Locke was likely the first to describe attention as more nuanced than just being focused or unfocused.

William James also referred to different types of attention. To him, full control of attention was opposite from "the confused, dazed, scatter-brained state which in French is called distraction, and Zerstreutheit in German."[3] James also referred to "stream of consciousness," in which a procession of thoughts and emotions passes in and out of our conscious awareness, like mind-wandering.

Our dynamic digital world is vastly different than the environments in which Locke and James lived and worked. The number and intensity of distractions in our digital age have amplified and our attention spans have declined and changed to such a degree that we truly need a new model for how to think about attention and focus. In this chapter I will present research that points to a new framework that features different types of attentional states, which we switch between and use for different purposes.

The language of attention

The language we use to describe attention reveals the different ways that we think about it. We might consider attention as something illuminating a subject and that we can control ("shining a spotlight," a "searchlight" or a "bright spot"), or as a mechanical process (a "filter," "capacity," "processor," "zoom lens," "gradient," "microscope" or "computer"). When we say that we "pay" attention, it suggests that it is a scarce resource. Still other language communicates that we have agency in our attention: we "direct," "hold" or "focus" our attention. Or, we lack agency: we "lose focus" or "wander" in attention. But in the digital age, this language is not all that helpful for understanding how our attention works when we spend most of the day on our screens. We need new language to characterize how we dynamically change our state of attention on our devices.

Our society puts a high premium on the ability to focus, but what does it really mean for us to be focused, engaged or absorbed with something? In Latin, *absorbere* means to "swallow up" or to "devour," like how our attention might be thoroughly captured by a book, a Wikipedia article or a video game. Psychologists view a person's disposition to be deeply absorbed in such external stimuli as a unique individual quality similar to a personality trait like being an extrovert or introvert. This absorption trait has been measured with the Tellegen Absorption Scale,[4] which asks people to rate how much they agree or disagree with statements like "When I listen to music I get so caught up in it that I don't notice anything else." Those who score extremely high on this test tend to blur the boundaries of what they perceive and imagine. When reading about the ocean, they may hear the sound of the waves on the beach, or if they read a mystery, they may hear the killer's footsteps on creaky wooden stairs. They also report more spiritual experiences and a greater sense of presence when viewing virtual reality simulations.[5]

While some individuals are born with such a predisposition to readily become absorbed in stimuli, most of us do not score so high on this trait using the Tellegen scale (though women score significantly higher than men[6]). But even if you don't, that doesn't mean that you are incapable of becoming deeply engaged in a task. You can, but for most of us, being engaged in something can change with the situation—our perceptions and cognitive experiences can shift as new stimuli come along. Our attention can even change moment by moment with the same stimuli—from being focused to mind-wandering and back to being focused again, as we discussed earlier.

We might also shift from using sustained attention in one activity to then doing something else less effortful, perhaps even playful, where we are just lightly engaged.[7] But being in control of one's attention can mean not just holding sustained attention or resisting distractions, but also being able to intentionally switch to different attentional states, like switching from the Big Mind to the Little Mind and back again. Maya Angelou might have been deeply absorbed in her writing with her Big Mind, and then she might have switched easily to her Little Mind, where her attention was lightly engaged with playing cards.

The elusive flow

The epitome of deep engagement is known as *flow*, which describes total immersion in an activity, where according to the psychologist Mihaly Csikszentmihalyi,[8] "nothing else seems to matter." Hungarian-born Csikszentmihalyi used total immersion in chess to help himself mentally survive World War II. At the end of the war, at age eleven he spent time in an Italian prison camp with his family. His father had been consul general in Venice, working for the former Hungarian government, which was implicated in the war. While interned, and even before, to block out the horrors of the war, the young Csikszentmihalyi played chess in the camp, immersing himself and creating a separate world from his surroundings. After seven months, his father was exonerated, and the family was released. Csikszentmihalyi dropped out of school, but later, in 1956, he emigrated to the US, took a high school equivalency exam and enrolled in the University of Chicago to study psychology. His experiences with immersion as a youth led him to embark on a decades-long career studying what he considered "the optimal experience."

Csikszentmihalyi set out to discover why people do activities without any extrinsic reward, such as playing chess, or even more dangerous pursuits such as rock climbing. These individuals all described the feeling that Csikszentmihalyi named flow. When in flow, people feel carried away by some internal current—the activity itself provides the reward, and they are masters of their attention. There is an optimal balance between using one's skills and the demands of the activity. People in flow are curious and playful, they lose self-consciousness, and because they invest so much of their attentional resources in the activity, they don't have any left to think about time passing.[9] Flow is a creative experience that is unique and deeply rewarding in which people are challenged to use their skills fully.

Flow is a subjective experience, and to study what was going on inside people's minds, Csikszentmihalyi used a technique called experience sampling.[10] He would give electronic pagers to his study participants. The pagers were programmed to beep at specified times, and when they did, the participants were instructed to fill out a questionnaire about their concentration, involvement and enjoyment in whatever they were doing. At the time of the beep, people were doing all sorts of activities such as gardening, cooking or business deals, and they may or may not have been in flow. They used the pagers for a week, which provided a good representative sample of what they were experiencing in a typical day. As you can guess, a limitation of these kinds of studies is that the pagers interrupted people. Still, the results helped Csikszentmihalyi understand and define this idealized state. His book *Flow* became a great influence on the study of attention.

When I was an art student, I often got into flow. I would work in my studio. Late in the evening, my shortwave radio would pick up Radio Havana (they had the best songs to work by), and I would dance to Cuban rhythms while painting. I would get deeply immersed and attributed all sorts of meaning to the abstract images I made. The title of one painting I did, *Heyday*, reflects the exuberance I felt during its creation. Time sped by, and often hours would pass before I realized it was 2 a.m. A flow state is not that hard to get into when you're doing something inherently creative and challenging like painting, making music or even skiing. But the nature of the work we do determines quite a bit about whether or not we get into flow states. Now I work as an academic, designing studies, conducting scientific research and writing papers. I have to use analytical thinking, which sometimes requires intense focus. When I work, I switch attentional states, from deep focus to light engagement, similar to Maya Angelou's Big Mind and Little Mind. Once in a while, I might get into flow when brainstorming ideas with others or when writing a part of a paper, but generally not. So, would I trade my academic life for that of an artist, where I was often in flow? Absolutely not. I reap different types of rewards with the kind of work I do now. When I want to go into flow, I know that I can paint or dance. When I want to investigate something about the world, then I turn to science and can expect to use focused attention, but not be in flow.

I have heard similar experiences from others. Recently I had a conversation with a friend who is a manager at a large high-tech firm in Silicon Valley. He told me that he doesn't get into a flow state at his job—it's more like keeping plates spinning. Once in a while when he is in a creative brainstorming session with other people, he says the group might get into flow. But in his earlier career as a coder, he was able to get into flow more often.

Even Maya Angelou describes her writing process as using focused attention but not necessarily being in flow. Discussing her writing process with journalist George Plimpton in an interview for the *Paris Review*, Angelou said that writing did not always come easy for her: "I try to pull the language in to such a sharpness that it jumps off the page. It must look easy, but it takes me forever to get it to look so easy. Of course, there are those critics—New York critics as a rule—who say, well, Maya Angelou has a new book out and of course it's good but then she's a natural writer. Those are the ones I want to grab by the throat and wrestle to the floor because it takes me forever to get it to sing. I work at the language."[11]

Unfortunately, flow is a much rarer experience than many of the readers of Csikszentmihalyi's bestselling book had hoped. In a survey done by Nakamura and Csikszentmihalyi in the mid-1990s in which people were asked to report if they had flow experiences, while some did experience it, 42 percent of Americans and 35 percent of Germans reported rarely or never experiencing flow.[12] And while people have had flow experiences, such as when creating art, woodworking or playing music, in our studies we have found that it rarely occurs in the knowledge workplace. Much of the nature of knowledge work is just not conducive to flow, the optimal creative experience. This doesn't mean that the work isn't fulfilling—it can be deeply fulfilling. Some people do experience flow while on their devices, for example when doing complex coding, and we might even experience flow when doing creative writing on our computers. But the reality is that for most knowledge workers, our computing environments, the nature of our work, and our responsibility for multiple projects and tasks create a high barrier to reaching flow. However, we need not feel bad if we cannot reach flow. We can rather achieve a feeling of balance and well-being by working in sync with our natural rhythm of attentional states.

A theoretical framework of attentional states

I have been fortunate to be able to work as a visiting researcher at Microsoft Research in the summers. Summers are beautiful in Seattle, and in addition to enjoying the lush greenery, I also had the opportunity to take a deep dive into research on attention. Walking into the lobby of Microsoft Research in Redmond, one enters a huge atrium buzzing with activity. There would be striking digital artwork, like a large sculpture using cameras and sensors and AI that changes color when people interact with it. You might overhear people sitting at café tables or on a couch discussing neural networks or the latest visualization tools. At the elevator you are greeted by a robot who helps direct you to where you want to go.

I was inspired by the idea of flow but found that it happens rarely in the workplace. Instead, my colleagues Mary Czerwinski, Shamsi Iqbal and I wondered if there were attentional states that could better characterize what people experience when they use their devices at work. When people shift attention rapidly on their devices, might they be shifting among different *types* of attention like the Big Mind and the Little Mind? Are different types of attention associated with particular activities in the digital world? As my colleagues and I explored further, we found that it was not sufficient to merely describe a person as being more or less engaged, or absorbed, in something. There was another dimension that we discovered to be very important in the mix. Similar to the idea of flow, it also mattered how *challenging* the activity was, i.e., how much mental effort or use of cognitive resources was involved. However, unlike flow, people might still be engaged in something and be challenged to different degrees. For example, creating a strategic plan can be quite challenging. Other activities are not at all challenging, such as scrolling through Facebook or Twitter. We set out to understand what it really means to be engaged with something in the digital world. Like Maya Angelou, whose attention could be engaged differently with a crossword puzzle or with a poem, a person could be very engaged in playing the game Two Dots, which doesn't really require much mental effort at all, or a person could be very engaged in reading difficult financial material requiring a lot of mental effort. In both cases, the mind is engaged, but quite differently, corresponding to different amounts of cognitive resources expended. (In Chapter 10, I will discuss more why one can be so absorbed in such a mindless activity like Two Dots.)

If we consider, then, not only how engaged one is, but also how challenged one is, we can characterize different attentional states that cover a range of activities. We came up with a framework to describe different kinds of attentional experiences in the digital world. Figure 1 shows these two dimensions of amount of engagement, and amount of challenge, in a theoretical framework of attention.[13] These are temporal states: people fluctuate across these attentional states throughout the day, depending on their goals, the tasks, interactions, their inner thoughts and a host of other factors. Each of these types of states has a very different quality that I'll describe next.

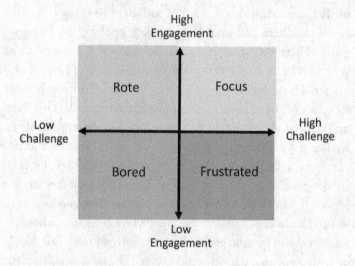

Figure 1. *A theoretical framework of four quadrants representing different attentional states.*

Focus

When people are highly engaged and highly challenged, we call this an attentional state of focus, as shown in the upper right quadrant of Figure 1. Focus represents a temporal state when people feel absorbed in an activity and the activity requires some degree of challenge to a person's skill set. Being highly engaged and challenged in work is correlated with motivation, activation, concentration, creativity and satisfaction.[14] But this is not the same as what we think of as flow. One can be focused, such as when trying to read an instruction manual, without experiencing the conditions of flow—feeling deeply creative, unaware of the passage of time, optimally using one's skills. Rather, our label of focus is better thought of as a type of engagement that could be a *precondition* to flow. It also costs a lot of cognitive resources to maintain focus as the phrase "paying attention" conveys.

Rote

When people are highly engaged, but not at all challenged, we call this a "rote" attentional state, as shown in the upper left quadrant of Figure 1. Rote activity is mechanical and routine. It is easy and can absorb our attention. When Maya Angelou plays cards, her Little Mind uses rote attention. We can be very engaged in a game of solitaire, and our card choices involve very little mental effort. Similarly, we can be highly engaged in digital activities that are mechanical and repetitive, such as playing Candy Crush (a game with over 273 million active users[15] and with over 9 million playing the game more than three hours a day[16]). Because rote activity involves tasks that are not challenging, this type of attention uses fewer cognitive resources. This can explain why people can play a game like Candy Crush for hours each day without feeling expended.

Bored

When people are not very engaged and not very challenged, we call this a state of boredom, as shown in the lower left quadrant of Figure 1. Surfing the internet, flitting from site to site, and barely sticking around long enough to read a few sentences, or flipping through TV channels because nothing catches our interest, is a good example of experiencing boredom. Needless to say, boredom uses few cognitive resources, or put more aptly, it underuses available resources. Our dimensions of low challenge and low engagement are consistent with how boredom has been considered, as a state of low arousal: boring activities just don't provide much stimulation, making it difficult to concentrate on the activity.[17,18] Being still or inactive doesn't automatically lead to boredom. If one enjoys doing yoga or being in a meditative zen state, then that activity is not boring. Earlier I mentioned that in flow, people become unaware of the passage of time. But boredom is the polar opposite: having all those spare attentional resources, we can't help but think about how much time is left before the activity is over and how slowly it is passing. Interestingly, the German word for boredom is *Langeweile*, which translates into "long length of time."

Frustrated

Last, when people are highly challenged but not at all engaged in what they're doing, we label this a state of frustration, as shown in the lower right quadrant of Figure 1. Everyone can recall times when they have been frustrated in their work, feeling like they were banging their head against the wall and not making progress. We may find the activity difficult, yet for many reasons we cannot give up, perhaps because we have a deadline, or we're required by our manager to work on it, or because we have some inner obsession to finish it. Software developers report feeling frustrated when they cannot solve a bug, and frustration can even happen with a difficult puzzle that one just cannot put down but feels compelled to solve. This attentional state can use up a lot of our resources.

How attentional states change throughout the day

Rhythm is part of life. Rhythms appear in nature, as with seasons, day length, moonrise, and tides, as well as in our physiological systems, with body processes such as sleep, temperature, and metabolism, and with the rising and lowering of insulin, the neurotransmitter serotonin, and the stress hormone cortisol. People have different circadian rhythms as well that make some early-morning types, or larks, who are at their best earlier in the

day, while others are late-night types, or night owls, who prefer
to start their day much later. Circadian rhythms influence body
temperature with lower body temperatures in the morning that
rise through the evening. These rhythms also appear to explain
variation in people's alertness and selective attention throughout
the day.[19] Homeostatic rhythms, based on the time since waking,
are correlated with declines in performance as the day wears on,
as shown with memory tasks.[20] There is also some neurophysi-
ological evidence that suggests the visual system is influenced
by internal rhythms of the electrical activity of your brain.[21] In
a laboratory experiment, subjects were shown cues on either the
left or right side of a computer screen and told to direct their attention to the cued side. They then had to answer whether they
saw a small light stimulus. The researchers found that oscillations
of neural activity in the brain influenced whether a person perceived the stimulus at all and also influenced the amount of the
neural response. Thus, the visual system fluctuates along with
neuronal excitability, i.e., with electrical impulses in our brains,
indicating internal rhythms at a very low level. This experiment
suggests then that we don't have continual sustained attention
but that rather we have what the authors describe as "perceptual moments." But it also leads us to wonder, given that there
are various types of human rhythms, whether rhythms of attention might exist over the course of a day as people go about
their daily lives. Does sustained attention follow a daily rhythm
with peaks and valleys?

The rhythms of focused attention

With my colleagues at Microsoft Research, we set out to understand if attention followed rhythms by studying people's actual
behavior in their workplaces. But we faced a dilemma: How
do you find out what is inside a person's head while they are
working? In past studies, I had used objective measures such
as computer activity logs and heart rate monitors, but these

didn't capture people's subjective experiences of their attention. Csikszentmihalyi's technique of using experience sampling was a good method to capture people's subjective flow experience. But we were studying people in their workplaces, and we needed to update the technique to capture people's attention on their computers. We designed probes that appeared as a pop-up window on people's computers and asked a few questions about their experience. These were sent based on their natural behavior: after a person used email for at least three consecutive minutes, after using Facebook for one minute, soon after a person unlocked their screen saver, and if fifteen minutes passed by without any probe. The attentional probes could be answered in a few seconds. When people received the probe, they were asked to think about the activity they were doing *right now*, and to answer two questions on a scale of how "engaged" they were and how "challenged" they were. We also asked them to report their mood, which we'll cover in Chapter 10. We sent thirty-two people probes about eighteen times over each workday for a full workweek. We had to juggle between getting a detailed picture of how attention changes over time while not burdening our participants who had to do their work, and probing people eighteen times a day seemed to be about the maximum we could expect. The irony of interrupting people to ask about their engagement and sense of challenge was not lost on us, but since the probes could be answered in a few seconds, participants were able to get right back to their activities. We instructed our participants that if they were annoyed at the probes, they should answer the questions based on what they were doing immediately before the probe and not to reflect a feeling of annoyance. Thankfully, our participants were good sports, and while a few did complain about the frequency of the probes, they assured us that their annoyance did not influence their answers. We also logged people's computer activity and measured their face-to-face interactions using SenseCams, small wearable lightweight cameras that I will talk more about shortly. Collecting data for a full workweek gave us a representative sample of people's daily attention behavior, and we could also see how attention varied over the week. We studied a range of participants in different fields: administrative assistants, managers, technologists, engineers, designers and researchers.

After collecting the data, we then mapped the responses to the attentional states shown in Figure 1. Surprisingly, our participants were rarely frustrated at work—only seven times did people's responses fall into the "frustrated" quadrant of our framework. Because there were so few, they were not included in the graph. Perhaps one reason that we found so few reports of frustration is that it burns resources very quickly, and people try to avoid that state.

There do appear to be rhythms of focused attention. Figure 2 shows that over the day, people experience the attentional states of being focused, rote or bored.[22] Across all jobs, people showed two peak times of focus: late morning at 11 a.m. and midafternoon at 3 p.m. We discovered that people don't come into the workplace ready to go, focused right from the start. It takes them time to power up into a state of focus. After a lunch break, people slowly ramp up their focused attention again. After 3 p.m., their focus begins to decline—likely coinciding with how their cognitive resources have been expended. Rote attention shows a different type of rhythm through much of the day, starting around 9 a.m. when it begins to rise, and then rote attention continues until around 2 p.m. and then declines. Boredom peaks around 1 p.m., right after lunch. The good news is that throughout the day, on the whole people were more focused than bored in the workplace, but the not-so-good news is that they generally report more boredom than rote attention throughout the day. We will discuss later in the book that boredom does not put people in a good mood.

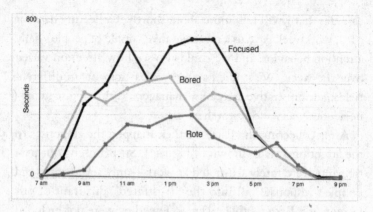

Figure 2. *How different types of attention vary over the workday.*

A description of how attention has rhythms over the day comes from a person I'll call Mira, who was in a related study. Mira works in a large company as a document manager, and described her focus throughout the day in terms of peaks and valleys. She said that she is maximally focused at her "peak" between noon and 2 p.m., when she deals with emails, and checks in with her manager and those she manages. Then, from 2 to 4 p.m., she's in a "valley." She always fears that during her valley period, an unexpected "fire" will happen such as urgently needing to track down certain documents. She explained that she would have to perform at the same level as her peak focus even though this is not what her body or mind feel capable of. Mira is forced to scrape up scarce attentional resources when she is in her trough.

It turns out that people also show rhythmic behavior in what they do on their devices. Since we logged computer activity, we were able to measure precise times (to the second) of people's activities on their computers. We then synchronized these in time with their responses from the time-stamped probes. In this way we could match people's attentional states with each computer activity. We show the rhythmic nature of different computer activities in Figure 3 and can see how they vary over the course of the day.[23] The time people spend in their inbox and calendar peaks about midmorning (10 a.m.) and also midafternoon (2 p.m.) and corresponds roughly to their peaks of focus. Using apps like Word, Excel and PowerPoint also seems to follow the same rhythms. Remote communication and web search is done continuously throughout the day. Facebook checking is fairly spread out over the day, though our statistical analyses show that people do much more Facebook activity after returning from lunch compared to before lunch.

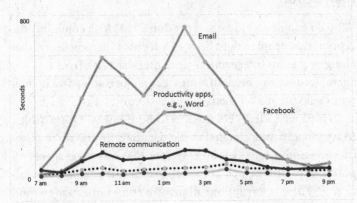

Figure 3. *How people's computer activity varies over the day, based on logging.*

We then took a deeper dive into the data, looking at correlations to see whether what people do on their computers is associated with different attentional states. As the rhythms suggest, we found that when people do email, they tend to be focused. When people surf the internet or switch among computer windows, they are more likely bored. When people are on Facebook, they either feel bored or have rote attention, but they are hardly ever focused. These results seem to confirm our intuitions.

We also found there to be a rhythm over the week: people

are most focused on Monday, when they might come to work with their tank of cognitive resources replenished from catching up on sleep over the weekend. After this burst of focus on Monday, it seems that they take it a bit easy on Tuesday, when they are least focused in the week. Wednesday shows a smaller burst of focus. Perhaps the reason Thursday is the day when most rote activity is done is also to take it easy and replenish resources. This could also explain why on Friday, we see a small burst of focus again.

Attentional states and susceptibility to distraction

Why do people lose focus and get distracted? It's a common conception that people might be deeply focused on something, then along comes an interruption, and afterwards it's hard to focus again, leading to boredom. But what if a person's particular attentional state makes them *susceptible* to distractions?

In a paper called "Focused, Aroused, but so Distractible," Mary, Shamsi and I looked at the data to examine three of the most common types of interruptions that our participants reported experiencing: email, Facebook and face-to-face interactions.[24] These interruptions all involve communication in some way. Email interruptions are generally work-related but could be related to social or personal life, Facebook interruptions are generally social, and face-to-face interactions could be either. Earlier I mentioned that we measured face-to-face interactions with SenseCams, cameras worn around participants' necks that took photos about every fifteen seconds. We applied software that quite accurately detected if faces were in the photos, and if so, we inferred that a person was interacting with someone else in person. But software is not perfect. One error we discovered inadvertently was that our male participants often forgot to turn off the SenseCams when they went to the restroom, and the round shape of toilets was misinterpreted as faces by the software.

We found that when people were bored, they were then more likely to switch their attention to Facebook and face-to-face interactions. Similarly, when people did rote activity, they were more likely to switch their attention to face-to-face interactions. In other words, a rote or bored attentional state provides an easy entry point for distractions. Our results support the notion that the *attentional state one is in* makes one susceptible to distractions. Why might this be? When we're bored, our attention is not goal-directed, and when we're doing rote activity, we might only have a weak goal (scrolling social media posts to see if there's anything interesting). Attention is driven by goals, and without a strong goal, like when you're bored or doing rote activity, then your attention is like a reed in the wind.

Rhythm is the new flow

Our data dispels the myth that we should think about our attention as only focused or unfocused and shows that rather, there are different ways a person can be engaged in something. Why do people ebb and flow in their focus, and why might they switch to other attentional states? During the day, our attention is likely influenced by the level of our cognitive resources, by our circadian rhythms as some research suggests,[25] by the time since being awake,[26] and possibly by hormones, which is still being investigated. But aside from these reasons, there might also be a psychological explanation for why our focus tends to show a rhythm.

To explore this idea, I needed to find an expert on rhythm. I spoke to the drummer Barry Lazarowitz. He has performed in different genres including jazz, folk and rock with musicians such as Stan Kenton, Leonard Cohen, Lou Rawls and Judy Collins, and has played on a Grammy Award–winning record and on the Academy Award–winning soundtrack for the movie *All That Jazz*. He believes that people have an internal rhythm: we inherently resonate with the tempo of sixty beats per minute of a John Philip Sousa march or a Donna Summer disco song because our hearts tend to beat about sixty times per minute and our walking pace is about sixty strides per minute. Other musicians have had similar ideas about internal rhythm. Lester Lanin, a society orchestra bandleader popular in the 1950s and 1960s, knew how people resonated with rhythm and arranged music at a consistent tempo—a two-beat tempo known as the businessman's beat. Even if people didn't know how to dance, they knew how to walk, and a walking pace is typically rhythmic.[27] Lanin's popularity is attributed to the fact that so many people were drawn to the dance floor by his two-beat tempo.

But people also have deeper, longer, internal rhythms, and this is shown by how people can maintain rhythms even after a disruption. Lazarowitz described how the tenor saxophonist John Coltrane, in what many consider his masterpiece, *A Love Supreme*, wrote eight or twelve notes of a simple melodic line, a mantra of sorts, and improvised for thirty-three minutes in a free-form transcendence of the initial rhythm, and then, without missing a beat, came back and picked up the tempo. Coltrane had an internal metronome and was a master of rhythm. But we can all find our own rhythm. We can feel the rising and lowering gauge of our inner cognitive resources. Paying attention to it can let us know when to recharge so that we're not trying for nonstop focus and getting overspent. Our resonance with rhythm can help us restore our psychological balance, which we'll talk about more later. Being in control of our attention is about being aware of our level of resources and switching our attentional states between using our resources and restoring them when we need to.

Flow might seem like an antidote in our digital lives, but the hard truth is that it is especially challenging to find flow in the type of work that many of us do. Even though we may aspire to flow, in our current work environments, it may not be realistic or what we really should strive for. Lazarowitz, who works during the day managing and contracting musicians, also has a similar experience as myself and many others in that the nature of his work facilitates whether or not he gets into flow. In his day job as a knowledge worker, he can be focused but is never in flow when he calls clients, writes contracts and maintains databases. But in the evening, when playing with other musicians feeding off each other's improvisations, he can get into flow. In our everyday use of computers and phones, rather than thinking about experiencing that idyllic but elusive flow state, which in countless hours of study I have found to be rare, we should instead aspire to achieve a balance in our attentional states, which means not overspending our cognitive resources. If we can't get into flow, we still can find our internal rhythm.

So, how do we achieve a balance when we're on our devices? We can leverage our inherent connection with rhythm to maintain a good level in our tank of cognitive resources, switching from being focused to other attentional states over the course of a day. The Pomodoro technique also uses the concept of rhythm, breaking up the day into twenty-five-minute segments of work and five minutes of a break. Interestingly, though, I found no academic study that tested the technique. You can, however, design your own rhythm, based on your sense of cognitive resources, which we'll talk about more later in the book. Focused attention is a king of resource utilization, whereas rote activity and boredom require far fewer resources. While we may think of focus as an ideal state where one can be productive and creative, rote attention (and even boredom) are just as important and play critical roles in our well-being. The idea that light, easy engagement, or even an unfocused state, might be good for us runs counter to our conventional thinking that only deep engagement is worthwhile. At times we can completely pull away from stimulation, and sometimes mind-wandering or being bored is what we need. We can keep our mind lightly engaged as Angelou did with her Little Mind. The change is like switching from running to easy walking, which still keeps us active and alert but gives us a chance to catch our breath and replenish. In our lives outside of our computer and phone screens, we generally know how to seek a balance. When people are bored, they seek stimulation; if they are overstimulated by being in Times Square, they can seek a quiet refuge in Central Park.

Every attentional state has value and purpose in helping us achieve a balance of cognitive resources. We can't be experiencing continual mental challenge nonstop all day using cognitive resources in the same way that we can't be challenged to lift weights nonstop all day using our physical resources. Ideally, we should take breaks and leave our devices to replenish our resources. We also have the power to control how we switch attentional states, and we can try to tap into that innate need to achieve an inner balance, to recover and replenish cognitive resources, which rote, mindless or even boring activity can do. Here is where we can learn to harness our dynamic, kinetic attention to shift purposefully and strategically among different attentional states to achieve a balance, still be productive and experience well-being. But it turns out that not all attention-switching is beneficial for us, as we'll see when we examine multitasking in the next chapter.

CHAPTER FOUR:

Why, How and How Much We Multitask

One morning in the mid-1990s, I came to work in Germany and found my colleagues, all computer scientists, huddled around a computer screen. I went over to see what the buzz was about. They were looking at Mosaic, a completely new browser that opened a gateway to the World Wide Web. The interface displayed images along with text, which seemed light-years ahead of the purely text browsers at the time, paving the way for audio and video, leading Bob Metcalfe, co-founder of the company Ethernet, to claim that "several million then suddenly noticed that the Internet might be better than sex."[1] These computer scientists and I were in awe. We could not have foreseen at the time how radically our lives would soon change in so many ways: our social practices, our work, our leisure time, and especially our attention behavior. Our tools would eventually become inseparable from us. In this chapter I will discuss the changes over the years in our attention behavior as computer technology permeated our lives, including how the foundation for short attention spans is laid at a very young age.

★ ★ ★

I'm a news junkie, and at the time, news was not yet in digital format. My favorite paper, *The New York Times*, was quite expensive to buy overseas. A former student once visited me in Germany and kindly brought me a copy of the Sunday edition that she had picked up in Paris. To give you an idea of its cost, she wouldn't tell me the price but did tell me that I should consider it my wedding present. It felt life-changing when a few years after Mosaic was launched, I was able to access *The New York Times* online with photos, and more so when I could even watch US TV news with streaming video, albeit a postage-stamp-sized image of the newscaster Dan Rather. What started as daily news posts soon became hourly and then minute-by-minute updates. I began to check the news again and again. Online communities were also proliferating, and suddenly it seemed that everyone had a blog, revealing their deeply personal lives in a public forum. How could we not participate?

The digital world was evolving, creating ideal conditions for an explosion in multitasking. We hear so many complaints about multitasking as though it were a new phenomenon, but it certainly did not start in the digital age. In her book *A Prehistory of Ordinary People*, Monica Smith writes that multitasking has been around for over 1.5 million years, since our bipedal ancestors began to build tools.[2] Humans relied on multitasking to survive as they had to continually monitor their environment. Hunters and gatherers would forage for food while at the same time searching for resources to make tools, looking out for their children, and of course, keeping an eye out for predators. While they were selectively attentive in looking for food, they were also vigilant for signals of danger. Since today we no longer need the skill to constantly scan the environment for survival, we should be able to focus deeply on our chosen task for long periods of time. Yet we don't.

People fall along a continuum for how they like to use their time: monochronic, preferring to finish one task through to completion before beginning another task, or polychronic, pre-ferring to juggle multiple tasks at once. A very small percentage of people are "supertaskers," who have the extraordinary ability to shift between tasks without being impeded much by the cog-nitive load. This ability is attributed to a more efficient use of parts of their attentional control network, located in the anterior cingulate region of the brain, responsible for detecting conflicts with goals, and the posterior frontopolar prefrontal cortices, which work at maintaining, switching, and updating goals.[3]

Most people fall in the middle of this continuum between mono- and polychronic, based on a scale called the Multitask-ing Preference Inventory, which asks participants to rate state-ments like "I do not like having to shift my attention between multiple tasks."[4] Using a similar scale called the Polychronic Attitude Index, Carol Kaufman at Rutgers University and her colleagues surveyed over three hundred people to explore char-acteristics of polychronic types.[5] They found that those with a preference for polychronic time use, i.e., those who like to jug-gle tasks, were more highly educated, worked longer hours and were more flexible in their plans. Interestingly, they put more of an emphasis on relationships with other people than on tasks. Polychronic types were also less bothered than monochronic types with what is called role overload, the feeling that one has too many things to do and not enough time to do it. But as it turns out, most people—even those who are monochronic or not strongly polychronic—actually work in polychronic ways, which is most likely due to the demands of the workplace and the na-ture of continuous electronic communications like email, text-ing and Slack—and social media as well. Thus, there is a serious mismatch in the lives of most people today: monochronic types are working in polychronic styles, like square pegs jammed into round holes, which further serves to impede their ability to gain cognitive control of their own attention. As you might imag-ine, monochronic types are the ones who tend to experience role overload, and yet they are stuck switching among multiple tasks, trying to keep up. This is consistent with the many people in our studies who report feeling overwhelmed in their work.

What is multitasking?

In general, activities cannot be done in parallel unless one or both of the activities require little or no attentional resources, like speaking on the phone while walking, as we discussed earlier. But if I'm talking on the phone and trying to answer emails, I'm really not doing these simultaneously. What I am really doing is switching my attention rapidly between them. In multitasking, the mind allocates attention back and forth to different sources. Switching activities can be triggered by an external stimulus, like an email notification, or by something internal, like a memory.

You've undoubtedly had the experience of being in a crowded party, hearing your name mentioned across the room, and then suddenly switching your attention to listen to that person while ignoring those right beside you. This is the cocktail party phenomenon, named so by Colin Cherry in 1953,[6] an example of how our attention can be triggered fast to attend to something else. One time I realized I was double-booked for two important teleconference meetings. It was too embarrassing to cancel one of them at the last minute. So I sat there with two different earphones—one in each ear, one plugged into my computer, and the other plugged into my phone. I switched my attention back and forth between the two teleconferences. When I was asked for my opinion from time to time, the mention of my name caught my attention as in the cocktail party phenomenon. Each time, I cringed and had to ask the speaker to repeat the question. To my knowledge, no one realized I was attending two meetings. Even so, performing two tasks that require effortful controlled processing is just not possible for humans to do well.

Switching attention away from a hard task can be beneficial

at times. Moving on to a new activity can draw one out of a negative frame of mind or can serve to refresh one's cognitive resources. Leaving an unsolvable task to incubate can possibly lead to new thoughts for a solution. On the other hand, too much task-switching at a fast rate, where you are continually forcing yourself to refocus your attention, is often detrimental because of time and performance decrements, and it leads to stress. I know I performed exceptionally poorly on those teleconference calls even though I was able to get away with it.

Multitasking from two perspectives

How do people think about switching their attention among different activities? In our studies, sometimes people would talk about switching their attention from one project to another such as when they stopped working on their departmental restructuring project to turn to the mental health project. But sometimes they described their attention-switching in much finer detail, like when they stopped writing in a document to send an email to their manager. People thought flexibly about their multitasking, seeing it at different scales, sometimes zooming out to view switching their attention in terms of their projects and sometimes zooming in to view switching their attention in terms of finer-grained events. These different perspectives can provide a more holistic understanding about our attention behavior.

An analogy is when we use Google Maps. If I am planning a trip from Los Angeles to Boulder, I can view the trip at different levels of granularity. Broadly, I can zoom out and look at an entire map of the United States, and see the big picture of the trip as more or less a diagonal in the direction north–northeast, crossing California, then southern Nevada, through the center of Utah, and then entering Colorado to proceed to Boulder. But I can also zoom in and see the individual highways, small towns and national forests that I would pass through. With multitasking, we can zoom out to examine how people switch between projects, or what I prefer to call "working spheres," such as writing a research paper or preparing a proposal. But we can also zoom in and change our perspective to think about how people switch their attention between "low-level" operations such as typing a text message, reading a social media post or answering an email. Both of these perspectives can provide valuable insight into the nature of multitasking.

Remember that attention is goal-directed, and when we switch our perspectives from broad to fine-grained views of our tasks, we are also switching our goals from high-level to low-level. When I work, I am constantly shifting between high- and low-level goals, say from the high-level goal of finishing a paper to the lower-level goal of making a phone call that has been lingering in my mind.

Creating living laboratories

After becoming an academic, and realizing how much my own attention was fragmented, I was determined to find out how widespread this experience was. Psychologists know how to measure attention-switching in a controlled laboratory setting, using equipment to measure reaction times, but how does one measure attention-switching in a real-world environment in the course of people's actual work? Studying people in a laboratory can yield valuable insights, but it's just not possible to model all of the things that we experience in our real lives: the daily pressures, conflicts with colleagues, career trajectories, the things that make us laugh. To really understand how people use technology and how it affects them, I had to go where people are every day. I needed to be able to measure how they used and reacted to technology *in situ*—so as to capture details without interfering with their normal lives. I had to create *living laboratories*.

This was a challenge, but with my graduate student Victor González, we drew inspiration from the work of Frederick Taylor, who, in the early part of the twentieth century, became one

of the first management consultants. Born in 1856, and starting his career as a machine shop laborer, Taylor later moved on
to become an engineering consultant, where he developed and
published his technique of the scientific observation of work,
which became known as Taylorism.[7] Taylor timed people's work
activities with a stopwatch and sought ways to improve their
efficiency, for example, finding the optimal size of a shovel for
coal. I couldn't stand the idea that Taylor's work was designed
to squeeze out every last productive second from workers, but
we did find his method useful for our research purposes. We
shadowed people in a range of knowledge work professions and
workplaces, using stopwatches to time precisely how long they
spent on any activity before switching to another. I want to emphasize that we did not intend to optimize their behavior like
Taylor, but rather observe it. For example, when a person opened
their email client, we clicked on the stopwatch and noted the
start time. When the person turned away from email and picked
up their phone, we noted the stop time of email and the start
time of speaking on the phone. It was laborious but precise and
also fascinating, which was puzzling to our participants, one of
whom turned around to me once and remarked, "It's like watching paint dry, isn't it?" We also noted down as many details as
possible about the work, such as the applications and documents
people used, and even which colleagues they interacted with.
Participants may have been self-conscious and behaved differently while initially being observed, and so we disregarded the
first hours of observations. Soon, however, people acclimated
to our presence, but more importantly, they had to react to the
demands of their work, which overshadowed any change they
may have initially made in their behaviors.

After painstakingly collecting this data, my graduate student
and I discovered that people in workplaces averaged only three
minutes, five seconds on *any low-level event* on or off screen before switching to the next one.[8] This included interactions with
colleagues. But if we just looked at attention behavior on the

computer, we found that people shifted their attention on average every two and a half minutes. Switching all activities every three minutes and specifically switching attention on the computer every two and a half minutes seemed unfathomable at the time. But this was nothing compared to what was to be discovered in the next decade and a half to come.

Our attention spans are declining over the years

Shadowing people with a stopwatch was painstaking, and I knew there had to be a more efficient way to collect data in the wild. Fortunately, my interest in understanding human behavior in real life coincided with a revolution in the development of sensor technologies. The innovations were sophisticated and exciting: new sensors such as heart rate monitors worn on straps around the chest and later on the wrist could measure stress. With actigraphs in the sensors, which measure physical activity, we could see how much people moved around the workplace. The wearables could also measure sleep. New computer logging methods could record precisely how long people's attention remained on a screen and when they switched their apps, websites and computer screens. The duration of time spent on a computer or phone screen serves as a proxy for how long one is focusing attention on that screen. When a person switches to another screen, they are making a cognitive shift to focus their attention on something else.

We could then sync together all these different measures collected in the living laboratory based on precise time stamps, and create a holistic picture of how people were using technology in their real-world environments. These new methods were unobtrusive: people could work without having an experimenter observing them. The best part of all was that these measures were objective and exact—to the second.

Precision tracking was a new frontier in measuring behavior. Participants were fully aware of their behavior being measured—

all of our studies were approved by the human subjects review board, all study participants signed consent forms, their data was kept anonymous, and they could leave the study at any time without penalty (no one did). Our participants consented to their computer actions being logged, and we recorded no content— we only collected time stamps of the apps and URLs that they visited. With the exception of a few participants who were not compliant (e.g., not wearing the heart rate chest straps all day or not charging their devices), most people participated fully.

Forty-seven seconds of attention

To understand how people's attention spans have changed with the rise in computing, I have been tracking people's attention over the years, using increasingly sophisticated and unobtrusive computer logging techniques. I studied a range of participants, all of whom are knowledge workers, but in different jobs, and in different workplaces. Most were in the age range of twenty-five to fifty years old, but I have also studied younger college-age students. Our observations ranged from multiple days to multiple weeks. Each study yielded thousands of hours of observation.

The results of all this attention-tracking show that the average duration of attention on a screen before switching to another screen is declining over the years (Figure 1). In 2004, in our earliest study, we found that people averaged about one hundred fifty seconds (two and a half minutes) on a computer screen before switching their attention to another screen; in 2012, the average went down to seventy-five seconds before switching. In later years, from 2016 to 2021, the average amount of time on any screen before switching was found to be relatively consistent between forty-four and fifty seconds. Others replicated our results, also with computer logging. André Meyer and colleagues at Microsoft Research found the average attention span of twenty software developers over eleven workdays to be fifty seconds.[9] For her dissertation, my student Fatema Akbar found the average attention span of fifty office workers in various jobs over a period of three to four weeks to be a mere forty-four seconds.[10] In other words, in the last several years, every day and all day in the workplace, people switch their attention on computer screens about every forty-seven seconds on average. In fact, in 2016 we found the median (i.e., midpoint) for length of attention duration to be forty seconds.[11] This means that half the observations of attention length on any screen were *shorter* than forty seconds.

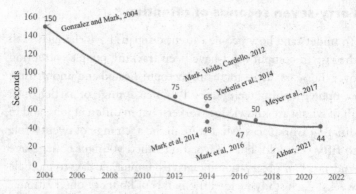

Figure 1. *Average attention duration on a computer screen, 2004–2021.*[12]

Email, which many of our participants refer to as the bane of their digital lives, shows an increase in overall duration over the years. The daily time spent on email jumped from an average of forty-seven minutes per day in 2004 to eighty-three minutes per day in 2016. This statistic does not account for other communication tools used like Slack, so we can figure that even more time is spent daily messaging with colleagues (with likely short bursts of attention because of the nature of texting). In the next chapter I will show the effect email has on our stress.

Thus, our individual attention spans on our personal technologies are getting significantly shorter on average over time. These results held true with all types of jobs: managers, administrative assistants, financial analysts, technologists, researchers, software developers and others. But alongside this shortening of attention spans, other kinds of changes were occurring as well: with social relations, environmental influences, individual habits and people's sedentary behaviors, which I'll talk about shortly, all in tandem with the rapid rise in technology use. Looking back over the last fifteen years, not only were attention spans short when I first set out to study this phenomenon, but they actually have diminished over time.

Work and distraction modes

What did our participants think about their attention behaviors? They described common reasons for their rapid shifting: habit, boredom, feeling overwhelmed with a task, an urge to check in with friends or colleagues, to avoid doing something they just didn't want to do, and more. People often talked about flipping from work mode to distraction mode: one person even described it as having two selves. A millennial in one of our studies who plays music on YouTube while working explained how he is accustomed to seamlessly switching attention back and forth between work and a song's lyrics. One person liked to call their frequent shifts to social media as "snacking." Many participants described their attention veering off from work and losing track of time as entering a "rabbit hole" or "tunnel"—they get caught in an attention trap. One participant, Helen, explained how hard it is to "come out of that zone."

Chloe, a researcher in her thirties, who works in a tech company, described how frequently her attention wanders when on her computer. She said the slightest urge to think about something other than "the cold reality of work" triggers her to look that idea up on the web. Surfing the web and flitting from link to link is stimulating for her and fills a gap in her work life. She justifies her attention-shifting as productive because she learns new things. Yet like many of our participants, she often feels guilty when she realizes how much time she has spent on non-work activities.

Another participant, Ron, a software developer in his early forties, is an evening-type person, and his best performance is between 2 p.m. and 9 p.m. However, he must be at his job nine to five. Because the morning is not his peak performance time, it is harder for him to sustain focus during those early hours, and he is more susceptible to rapidly shifting his attention. He described his morning as cycling through websites, Twitter, news sites and other social media.

Steve, another fortysomething analyst at the same company, said he has little self-control when he uses his devices. Similar to Chloe, when he encounters a hard problem at work, his tendency is to shift his attention—to playing a simple game or posting on social media, which makes him feel that he is accomplishing something easy. Steve also feels guilty when he realizes that he has been spending too much time on nonwork activities.

Like many participants, Steve described his attention-shifting behavior as "nonconscious." In fact, we frequently heard from our study participants that they were unaware when they got into a mode of rapidly shifting their attention—until at some point they realized they had been doing it for some time. This nonconscious type of shifting attention is in contrast to William James's notion of volitional attention, where one is in command.

Rapid attention-shifting has repercussions on our ability to process information. What one looked at previously can interfere with what one is currently looking at and becomes what researcher Sophie Leroy calls attention residue,[13] especially if the current content is not engaging. Emotions can also leave a residue, and an emotional reaction, say a spike of sadness from reading tragic news on a Twitter post, can linger if attention then switches to a work application. Attentional and emotional residue make it even harder to apply focused attention.

Declining attention spans and increasing sedentary behavior

One of the other surprising changes happening along with attention spans shortening is that people were spending more time at their desks and becoming more sedentary over time (Figure 2). Earlier studies observing how knowledge workers spent their time in the workplace (in these studies, the researchers noted the time from watches and not stopwatches), from the mid-1960s to the mid-1980s, before the rise of email, found that people averaged only 28 to 35 percent of their day at their desks.[14][15][16] The rest of the time was spent in scheduled and informal meetings. In 2004, as the internet and email were skyrocketing in use, we found that our participants averaged 52 percent of their day at desk work (working on computers and phone), quite a bit more time than in the earlier studies.[17] In a 2019 study where we collected data from 603 people over a full year, using wearable wrist trackers to detect step activity and small wireless transmitters to detect office location, we found that office workers spent nearly 90 percent of their time at their desks.[18]

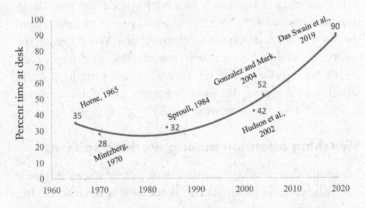

Figure 2. *Percent of time spent at the desk, 1965–2019. Desk work in the González and Mark (2004) study includes both desk phone and cell phone use. Studies 1965–1984 were done prior to email in these workplaces.*[19]

Of course we cannot claim that the rise of email and the internet *caused* the increase in time at the desk and more sedentary behavior. But we found something else happening that might offer a clue as to what is going on: over the years, people also spent less time in formal scheduled in-person meetings (these studies were done before the pandemic), where people might sit together in a conference room or go to someone's office for a meeting. In the period of 1965 to 1984, knowledge workers averaged 34 percent of their day in such face-to-face meetings, but in 2004, we found that the time declined to an average of 14 percent.[20] How can we make sense of this change? We might infer from the data that more of the work that was formerly done in face-to-face meetings was now being done on the phone and computer, whether through email, messaging or video conferencing. With more time at the computer come more chances to switch attention on the screen. But also, with more meetings being done on the computer, especially as we saw during the pandemic with Zoom meetings, there is also less of a transition time between computer work and that meeting, and between one online meeting and the next. (Of course people can also multitask, answering email or surfing the web, during an online meeting.) Even a walk to a conference room provides at least some movement and a short mental respite to detach from the last activity and prepare for the next one. We are losing the ability to catch our breaths between meetings. I thought back on my time in Germany, where we actually took long walks after lunch, and how this provided a nice break and transition before starting afternoon work.

Switching attention among working spheres

We found that people's attention span on any screen in recent years has reached a steady state of about forty-seven seconds. But maybe switching between low-level events isn't so bad if they all involve the same working sphere, i.e., the same project? As an academic, when I work on a research paper, I am constantly switching my attention between writing, email, Slack, searching for information on the web, meeting on Zoom, speaking with colleagues, and doing analyses. Yet, through it all, I am typically using a high-level perspective, thinking about the working sphere—even though I may be switching among lower-level operations within it. As long as these attention shifts all concern the same working sphere, then perhaps switching may not be so problematic. Or is it?

In another workplace study, my graduate student Victor González and I looked at switching attention among working spheres.[21] In our study, we found people dealt with an average of slightly over twelve working spheres per day. In fact, my own number of working spheres always seems to hover around this number. We also found that not only is the time spent on any low-level operation short, but the actual average duration of time spent in a working sphere is also quite short (ten minutes, twenty-nine seconds) before people switched to another sphere of work. In other words, people's days are characterized by shifting their attention among working spheres about every ten and a half minutes. But if we zoom in to examine their behavior more closely, we see of course that their attention on smaller operations (like email) is even shorter.

But let's consider that not all interruptions are the same. Think, for example, of how being interrupted by someone asking for your signature on a document might not be very distracting. Other interruptions can be quite disruptive: imagine that your colleague asks for your help figuring out a scheduling problem. So we decided to remove from the data what we considered to be events of two minutes or less that wouldn't be very disruptive, and then we connected the data over time as though these short interruptions hadn't occurred. Surprisingly, we found that people still averaged only twelve minutes and eighteen seconds in a working sphere before switching. In other words, about every twelve minutes, people are faced with a significant disruption that lasts two minutes or longer!

This is not a good thing. We require time to muster up the cognitively demanding processes that we need for each task. Every time you switch working spheres (or even low-level events, for that matter), you need to access the knowledge of that task stored in your long-term memory, which requires cognitive resources. If it has been some time since you accessed a working sphere, then it will require more resources to retrieve or develop a schema of that task, even if you're just working on some small part of it, like writing an email.[22] If I am returning to a paper that I had set aside for some time, then I need to put in a lot of effort to regain my understanding of what I had already written and what the next steps should be. Even when you are engaged with a current working sphere, after doing something else you still need to retrieve that schema from your long-term memory. It still takes some cognitive resources to get up to speed on it as you need to reconstruct the exact state of the unfinished work. Considering how often people switch their attention, and also considering the effort involved to get back to a task, it's no wonder that our cognitive resources get depleted.

Resuming interrupted work

What happens, though, when people are interrupted? How long does it take to resume work on that interrupted task? There is good news and bad news on this. First, the good news: 77.2 percent of interrupted working spheres are resumed on the same day. But now here's the bad news. It took people an average of twenty-five minutes, twenty-six seconds to return to work again on their interrupted working spheres. And now here's the really bad news. When people get interrupted, they do not just turn to another task and then snap right back to their original, interrupted work. They work on an average of 2.26 *intervening* working spheres before they go back to their original working sphere.[23] Figure 3 shows this general pattern throughout the day. That means that they're working on one working sphere, then they switch to another, then to still another, and then again another, and then finally go back to that original interrupted working sphere. These switches can be due to external interruptions (e.g., a phone call) or can be from the individuals themselves, which we will get to in detail in the next chapter. Remember that each time people switch, they have to retrieve that task schema from their long-term memory, and that increases cognitive load. There is also tension accumulating from leaving tasks unfinished, which adds to stress, which we'll talk about in the next chapter.

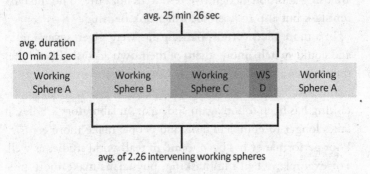

Figure 3. *Patterns of switching between working spheres for information workers throughout the day.*

Mulitasking, stress and performance

Some people may believe that multitasking helps their productivity. However, evidence has long shown the contrary: productivity suffers when people multitask. Nearly one hundred years ago, in 1927, the American child psychologist Arthur T. Jersild demonstrated that when people multitask, performance slows. Jersild studied this to understand how young people adapt to complex situations.

In this specific experiment, he wanted to see what happens when people made a mental "shift" from one element of a task to another. He gave children (in grades six to eight) and university students a list of numbers and asked them to subtract 3 from each number. They then received another list of words where they were asked to name the opposite word (e.g., *cold* when shown *hot*). When the numbers and words were interspersed, and participants had to switch between word and number operations, Jersild found there was a switch cost.[24] It took children longer than the university students to do the tasks, but the same switch costs were found at all ages. Thinking about one task while doing another increases the mental load because people are using additional cognitive resources not only to do the current task but also to keep the other task in mind.[25]

In a more recent study, participants were given several tasks and could switch among them of their own accord. The higher the frequency of switching, the worse the performance on the main task.[26] The result that people perform worse when multitasking has been found again and again in laboratory studies: it takes longer to complete tasks and people make more errors.[27] Poor performance has been found in real-world studies as well. For example, when multitasking, physicians make more prescribing errors,[28] and pilots make more in-flight errors.[29] We all have experience in how multitasking impacts our performance even when we're at home. Imagine you are cooking, texting and trying to keep the kids from fighting.

Another cost of multitasking, as mentioned, is the attention residue from your previous task that causes interference in the current task[30] just as drinking red wine interferes with the taste of a delicate Dover sole. Indeed, we find that in real-world work, the more switches in attention a person makes, the lower is their end-of-day assessed productivity.[31]

But it's not just productivity that suffers. Laboratory studies consistently show that multitasking is associated with higher stress. Multitasking leads to decreased secretion of immunoglobulin A reactivity, a marker of stress,[32] higher perceived mental workload measured by the NASA Task Load Index (NASA-TLX) scale,[33] and higher systolic and diastolic blood pressure.[34] Results from real-world environments are consistent with what lab studies found: higher multitasking is positively correlated with higher self-reported perceived stress.[35] In fact, the faster the attention-switching between devices, the higher the stress, as we found in our own studies using heart rate monitors in the wild.[36 37]

Young children, Gen Z and multitasking

The foundation for multitasking is laid at the very youngest of ages. Children as young as two to four years old already average two and a half hours of screen time a day, and it soon climbs to an average of three hours and five minutes for ages five to eight. While most screen time is TV and YouTube viewing, children ages five to eight spend forty minutes a day gaming.[38] We don't yet know what young children's attention spans are when watching, say, YouTube, but we do know from laboratory studies that young children are more susceptible to distraction than older children, and when distracted, it takes them longer to regain their focus on the original object.[39] Exposure to so much media at such young ages acculturates children to think that long periods in front of some kind of screen is normal behavior.

One thing we should worry about with very young children using digital media so much is that self-control and executive function are not yet mature. These functions develop throughout childhood, reaching similar competencies to adults at around age ten.[40] Perhaps a child's self-control may not matter so much while watching a YouTube video. But it will matter with schoolwork, as more and more instruction is delivered digitally. In the 2020 pandemic year, online instruction was almost ubiquitous and even now is becoming more commonplace. Self-control is a necessary skill for online learning, to be able to search for information, solve math problems, and read and write online, without being distracted. Adults have a hard enough time resisting urges for distraction, but children are thrust into a digital world before some critical mental functions are fully developed to take on the challenge. Meanwhile, children are spending increasingly longer hours on computers and phones, environments not conducive to developing skills of sustained attention.

Social media also sets the stage for young people to multitask. While much has been written about potential dangers of social media for young people (e.g., with cyberbullying or influencing harmful behaviors[41]), it also plays a very important role for developing adolescents: it helps them socially connect to others and allows them to explore different aspects of their identity. Young people construct their own patterns of social media use to fit their growing needs. Gen Z'ers are prolific users of social media: at the time of this writing, 85 percent of teens aged thirteen to seventeen use YouTube, 72 percent use Instagram and 69 percent use Snapchat.[42] Social media use does not wane as people get older, and in the age group of eighteen to twenty-nine, 84 percent use a wide range of social media. During the pandemic, TikTok use rose by 180 percent in this age group,[43] with 55 percent of young people using it.[44] More social media platforms in use means more opportunities for multitasking. In a study where we tracked computer and phone usage among college students for all their waking hours, we found that they checked social media on average 118 times a day.[45] The most frequent social media checkers (the top quarter of our sample) checked social media sites on average 237 times a day, over six times more often than the less frequent checkers in the bottom quarter of our sample (averaging 39 times a day). Indeed, in our studies, just like with older adults, we found that college students also had short attention spans, averaging forty-eight seconds on a computer or phone screen before switching. The ten highest multitaskers in our sample switched their attention every twenty-nine seconds, and the ten lowest multitaskers, every seventy-five seconds, which still astonishes me. The faster that students switched their attention, the higher their measured stress.[46]

Young people commonly use two or more different types of media at the same time, such as texting while doing homework online, known as media multitasking. Heavy media multitaskers were found in a laboratory study to have more difficulty filtering out information not relevant to their task.[47] Simply put, these individuals are accustomed to switching their attention a lot and they are distracted more easily than others even when not on their devices. The communications researcher Susanne Baumgartner and colleagues at the University of Amsterdamset out to discover what happens with media multitasking over a period of months. They had 2,390 Dutch teens fill out a media multitasking survey, where they were asked questions like, "While watching TV, how often do you use social networking sites at the same time?" The teens also filled out a survey about various symptoms associated with inattentiveness that are associated with ADHD according to the DSM-5, the Diagnostic and Statistical Manual of Mental Disorders. The researchers found that young teens who had problems with attention did more media multitasking than teens without attentional problems. But in looking at the effects over months, media multitasking had adverse effects on attention only for younger teens and not for older ones.[48]

Can young people learn to focus their attention better? Gaming is quite popular among young people, and when playing action games like *Monster Hunter Rise*, people have to monitor and keep track of a lot of different activity happening at the same time. Shawn Green and Daphne Bavelier at the University of Rochester wondered whether people who play action games might have better attentional capabilities.[49] These researchers did experiments with young men who were gamers and non-gamers with an average age of twenty-one. In the experiments, participants had to react as quickly as they could to identify target shapes (a square, a diamond) inside circles on the screen and to ignore distractor shapes that appeared outside the circles. In fact, gamers did better at these visual selection tasks—they could better detect shapes that appeared both in the center of the screen and on the periphery. The authors propose that video game players have more attentional resources available. Gaming, then, seems to make people more adept when they use kinetic attention. Does this mean that children or teens should play action video games to grow up into super-multitaskers? I argue that you should pause before you buy your kids *Deathloop*. More recent research questions whether it is really the video games that lead to better attention performance or rather whether people who play them have some innate cognitive abilities that lead them to self-select to play these games.[50] Perhaps they are the supertaskers. In any case, if you are thinking of setting up your child with video games, consider that the number of hours in the day is finite. Playing video games means less time for studying, working and interacting in real life with human beings. Your child (or you) might indeed become faster at reacting to text messages, but you'll both have less time for other things in life that matter more.

There is still a lot to be learned about the attention behavior of young people on their devices. Children and teenagers are so fragile—their attentional processes and self-control skills are still developing. Yet young children get a lot of screen time, sometimes even encouraged by parents, perhaps believing it will improve their reading and motor skills, and social pressure is huge for young people to use Instagram, Snapchat, TikTok, and a host of other social media.

In our digital culture, multitasking starts very, very young. A polychronic world with rapidly shifting attention has become the new normal. One participant in a study who commented that his life is "constant, constant multitasking craziness" in fact has a real basis for noting his increased physiological stress. Attention-shifting results in work becoming fragmented, drains cognitive resources, is bad for productivity, and can lead to cumulative stress, which can negatively impact health. A skilled ceramicist, by the nature of her work, may be able to work sequentially on projects. However, for knowledge workers, a monochronic style seems to be a luxury in our current professional and personal lives. We exist in a world that urges us to multitask, and if we don't, we risk falling behind. Multitasking has become part of our modern lifestyle, and in the next chapter, we will take a deep dive into research on another aspect of attention: how interruptions affect our lives.

CHAPTER FIVE:

The Consequences of Constant Interruption

Not too long ago, one of my doctors who knew of my research confessed to me that when he had to write a grant proposal, to keep himself from logging onto the internet, he bought a round-trip plane ticket from California to Washington, DC. He said that having to procure Wi-Fi access on the plane is an impediment to going online. I asked him if it wouldn't be easier to simply turn off the internet and stay at home? I was envisioning all the distractions on flights: announcements, people talking and moving about, babies crying. He told me that these things did not distract or interrupt him—it was the internet. He explained that he did not have the discipline to keep away from the internet while at home, but as addicts do when they change their environment to remove the substance or any reminder of it, a plane enabled him to create a barrier to getting on the internet. In his book *The Shallows*,[1] about how the internet impacts our reading and thinking, Nicholas Carr also mentioned a doctor (I doubt it could be the same one) who said he was better able to focus when on airplanes. The psychological pull of internet distractions is so strong that these doctors choose to work many thousands of feet above the ground.

It's hard for many people to stay away from the internet where the sources of interruptions keep multiplying. Interruptions and multitasking are partners in crime that disrupt our attention. In this chapter, we will explore how the mind deals with these interruptions.

The costs of interruptions are well-documented. Martin Luther King Jr. lamented them when he described "that lovely poem that didn't get written because someone knocked on the door."[2] Perhaps the most famous literary example happened in 1797 when Samuel Taylor Coleridge started writing his poem "Kubla Khan" from a dream he had but then was interrupted by a visitor. For Coleridge, by happenstance the interruption came at a particularly bad time.[3] He forgot his inspiration and left the work unfinished. While there are many documented cases of interruptions that have had repercussions in high-stakes professions such as with doctors, nurses, control room operators, stock traders and pilots, they also impact most of us in our everyday lives. Work productivity suffers due to interruptions,[4] and the finishing blow, like with multitasking, is that they generally induce stress.

But interruptions can have benefits as well. They can offer a mental break from work, which helps to replenish cognitive resources, they can serve as a social break to connect with others, and they can lead us to generate new ideas. When people were asked to keep diaries of their interruptions and the corresponding emotions they felt, 80 percent reported that interruptions generated positive as well as negative emotions for them, especially if they regarded the interruption related to a worthy endeavor.[5] So while not all interruptions are bad, we do need to learn how to harness our attention so that we don't become overwhelmed by the unwelcome ones.

The tension of interrupted tasks

For her dissertation, Bluma Zeigarnik interrupted people. Her work is significant as it helps explain why we are so bothered by interruptions. Born in 1901 into a secular middle-class Jewish family in the town of Prienai, Lithuania, Zeigarnik was highly gifted and skipped the first four grades, entering school in the fifth grade.[6] Her own life itself was interrupted, however. She contracted meningitis, stayed home for four years, and recovered—at the time only 20 percent of people survived. She yearned to attend a university, but her education at the girls' high school was limited. Among her classes of mathematics, science and literature, her instruction included "God's law" and needlework. She had grit, though. She studied long hours in the library, retook the university entrance exam, and in 1922 was admitted to study philosophy at the University of Berlin, which also happened to be a nexus for Gestalt psychology. The theory of Gestalt psychology holds that we perceive things as a whole rather than as separate constituents (think of the IBM logo—we see letters as opposed to individual horizontal lines). The lectures of the famous Gestalt theorists Max Wertheimer and Wolfgang Köhler captivated her, and she switched her major to psychology.

In 1927, Zeigarnik discovered what would later become famous as the Zeigarnik effect.[7] In her Berlin laboratory, she conducted a series of experiments in which she gave subjects about twenty different tasks: half were then interrupted, and half not, in random order. At the end of the study, subjects were asked to recall the tasks they had worked on. In a paper entitled "Remembering Completed and Uncompleted Tasks," she proved that one remembers interrupted tasks better than tasks that are completed. When a task is interrupted, it creates a state of tension from that unsatisfied need to finish it, which stays with us and serves to remind us—over and over and over again—to return to the task.

While at the University of Berlin, Zeigarnik was a student of Kurt Lewin, who later was considered the founder of social psychology, a field that studies how our social context affects the way we think, feel and behave. Lewin happens to be my favorite psychologist, and his work is so relevant to our lives in the digital age. Like Zeigarnik, he was born into a middle-class Jewish family in Mogilno, Germany, part of Prussia, in 1890. He started out as a medical student at the University of Freiburg, then switched to biology at the University of Munich, where he got involved in the women's rights and socialist movements, before finally settling down at the University of Berlin, where he received a doctoral degree in psychology in 1914. He stayed put there and was very popular with his students, who were not very much younger than him. But Lewin moved once again in 1933, this time due to the rise of Nazism. He settled in the US, joining other European émigrés like Theodor Adorno, Fritz Heider and Gustav Ichheiser, who were at the forefront of developing social theories about behavior. The field of social psychology largely owes its birth to the emigration and confluence of great personalities like these who were forced to flee.

At the time that Lewin was in Berlin, common thinking among psychologists was to view the individual in terms of separate and distinct psychological attributes, such as their perceptions, thoughts and emotions. However, like Zeigarnik, Lewin also became infused with ideas of Gestalt psychology and saw the individual as a Gestalt or "whole," integrated with, and influenced by, their everyday social environment—what he called the "life-space."[8] This was radically different from the current thinking at the time, which did not consider how the environment and context affected people. The notion of a "field" included the person in relation to their surroundings. According to Lewin's field theory, unfulfilled needs create a tension within us, and we reduce tension when we progress towards a goal. If a person's goal is to go to the post office, the drugstore and a flower shop, when the errands are completed, tension is released. If traffic hinders us from getting to any of these places, it creates tension. His field theory explained that everything people did could be explained as striving for tension reduction.

Zeigarnik's work provided support for Lewin's field theory: an interrupted task creates an unsatisfied need or tension to finish it. This tension that stays with us also keeps us thinking about that unfinished task. That's why we remember it—the memory of that interrupted task sizzles on the back burner of the mind. Little could Zeigarnik and Lewin have known how relevant field theory would be to explaining our attention and emotional experiences with our devices today. It is interesting to note that a few years after Zeigarnik graduated with her doctoral degree, she took a position, fittingly, at the Institute of Higher Nervous Activity in Moscow.[9]

External and internal interruptions

Most people tend to think of interruptions as originating from another person or from our devices, such as through a notification. But in our studies of people in their natural work environments, we observed a strange and regular phenomenon which typically looked like this: a person would be working on a task on their computer. Then, for no apparent reason to the observer, this person suddenly stopped what they were doing and checked their email or picked up their phone. There was no discernible stimulus that caused the person to interrupt themselves—there was rather some internal trigger, perhaps a thought, a memory, or habit. These interruptions originate from within ourselves. One of the most surprising results in our research is that we find that people are nearly as likely to self-interrupt due to something internal in them as to be interrupted by something external to them.[10]

We may not even be aware of how often we self-interrupt. Recently, in the middle of reading an article on AI, a random thought suddenly entered my mind to find out how safe it is to eat nonorganic strawberries. I couldn't get this question out of my mind and switched to my browser and searched for *straw-berries* and *pesticides*. I then spent a good chunk of time reading about the topic (there are conflicting views, so this remains an unfinished task). Many of our participants report that these inner urges are disconnected from their work. Even basic human drives can cause us to self-interrupt: a graduate student of mine said that when she gets hungry, she self-interrupts to look up recipes.

What leads people to self-interrupt? Jing Jin and Laura Dab-bish from Carnegie Mellon University set out to answer this question, and shadowed people in a workplace for about one hour each, noting down their interruptions, and then inter-viewed them to ask why they self-interrupted. They found that people self-interrupted for a range of reasons that you might guess: to change their environment to be more productive (e.g., closing distracting windows), to do something less boring, to seek information, to take care of something that they remem-bered needs to be done, or to fill time (e.g., while waiting for an email). Their current task might also cue them to interrupt themselves, like to send an email. People may also self-interrupt just out of habit, such as following a routine that includes check-ing news when starting to work.[11]

Self-interruptions can help people manage stress, like open-ing a steam valve. Lea was a participant in one of our studies, in her late twenties, completing her PhD while at the same time holding a demanding job in a software company. She needed to be ultra-disciplined as she had to manage both work and school projects. However, Lea complained about her difficulty in fo-cusing because she self-interrupted so often, mostly to check social media. Upon more reflection, she explained that she self-interrupts to help herself cognitively cope with such an over-whelming schedule. Lea self-interrupts to switch from focused to rote attention. She has a good understanding of her personal attention rhythm and her level of cognitive resources available, so she can sense when she needs to self-interrupt. However, as she admits, she's not good at getting back on task.

Not too long ago, I was searching for an apartment in New York City for my sabbatical from UC Irvine. I put in a number of inquiries. While there wasn't really much urgency, I kept checking my inbox and the real estate sites to see if a response had come in. My anticipatory stress mounted, and it was hard to concentrate on my work. My first choice did come through. But even after the apartment was booked, it was hard for my mind to settle down and for me to not keep self-interrupting to check my inbox. It can take anywhere from 18 to 254 days to form a habit,[12] and my habit of checking for rentals was developed in closer to 18 days.

I had become conditioned to self-interrupt, which is consistent with evidence that my student Victor González and I found in an early study from 2005. We observed thirty-six people in three different companies for three days each as they went about their daily work, using the Frederick Taylor stopwatch technique that I described earlier. The observers recorded every moment-by-moment activity that each participant engaged in. In addition to timing their activities to the second, we also observed and noted down when people were being interrupted by something external to them (a person, a phone call, an email notification) or by something internal (i.e., with no observable stimulus). We looked then at interruptions within the broader view of people's working spheres. We found that 40 percent of the switching among working spheres was due to interruptions. The other times people switched working spheres were due to completing a task. They experienced gradually fewer interruptions as the day wore on.

Of the interrupting events, 56 percent were due to external interruptions, and 44 percent were due to self-interruptions. We then counted the number of internal and external interruptions on an hourly basis. We wanted to see if there was any relationship between these two kinds of interruptions in people's daily lives. We indeed found a stable pattern where, when external interruptions waxed or waned in one hour, the internal interruptions followed a similar pattern in the next hour.[13] Thus, if external interruptions increased, then self-interruptions in the next hour would also increase. But only external interruptions predicted self-interruptions. Conditioning seems to play a role here. If a person is not getting interrupted externally, then it seems that a person will self-interrupt to maintain a consistent pattern of interruptions (and short attention spans). We have become so accustomed to being interrupted that we do it to ourselves.

When you start getting external interruptions, it's like driving on a country road and then turning onto a busy highway. You were coasting along, and then suddenly have to deal with tailgaters and motorcyclists. In the same way that driving on a congested highway is different from that peaceful country road, when you face interruptions, the cognitive operations you use, and even your goals, change. Since the most active goal in our mind governs our attention,[14] to stay on task we need to perform a cognitive dance of trying to maintain endogenous (internal) control of our goals to keep on track with our project, while dealing with exogenous goals, such as answering the Slack messages of your colleagues and getting them the information they need from you. But we know from Zeigarnik's work that we tend to remember those unfinished tasks, however minor. Thus, our primary goal can get buried under the mental clutter from all those unfinished tasks.

Recall from Chapter 1 that to resume an interrupted task, people have to rewrite their internal whiteboard, reconstructing their task schema, goals and thought processes, tapping into that limited pool of cognitive resources, which are best saved for actually doing the task. It takes time and effort to reconstruct our mental model of the task.[15] Interruptions can linger in your mind, and this can create static interference as you try to work on your current task. It is no wonder, then, that at the end of a busy day, especially with external interruptions, you feel drained.

The cost of interruptions

In 2005, I was on a Fulbright scholarship, living in Berlin. At the time, I was living in the former West Berlin and was commuting to the psychology department at the Humboldt University campus, located in the former East Germany. The Berlin Wall had come down over fifteen years earlier, but as I commuted eastward, the change in context was striking: the neon signs and bustling traffic of vibrant West Berlin faded into the Stalinist architecture of the former East. Whereas West Berlin showcased edgy fashion on the streets, East Berlin dress seemed to be stuck in the 1950s. I was struck by the irony of studying twenty-first century technology use and attention in a laboratory located in this time capsule, in the same city where it all began with Bluma Zeigarnik.

In this laboratory, I measured the disruption cost of interruptions—how much time they actually took away from work. Working with a dedicated student, Daniela Gudith, and postdoc Ulrich Klocke, we set up a study to simulate an office environment. We gave forty-eight participants a simple task of answering emails, all covering the topic of human resources. In one condition, a set of participants did the task without any interruptions. In a second condition, another set of participants was interrupted by questions (via phone and text messaging) related to the topic of human resources. In a third condition, still other participants were interrupted by questions (also via phone and text messaging) about a completely different topic than human resources (e.g., ordering food for a company picnic). To find the time cost of dealing with interruptions, we then subtracted the time spent handling interruptions from the total time to perform the task in each of the conditions.

We found a surprising result: any interruption, whether of the same or different context from the main task, caused participants to do the email task *faster* than if they had not been interrupted.[16] When interrupted, they used fewer words in their emails, yet there were no differences in politeness or accuracy. Perhaps when people are rained on by external interruptions, they work faster (and write less) to compensate for time they know they will lose while handling interruptions. Time at work is finite. If you know you have to leave the office at 5 p.m., say, to pick up your child from day care, then you proactively work faster to compensate for dealing with interruptions. It also turns out that people resume a task faster when they get more interruptions, compared to when they get fewer interruptions.[17] Together, both results suggest that with frequent interruptions, people speed up their work and perform more efficiently. Perhaps tasks with frequent interruptions are remembered better and thus people resume them quicker. However, before we become too sanguine about these results, we found that work efficiency did come at a price. We measured the participants' mental workload and stress using the NASA-TLX scale, which provides a good measure of cognitive resource utilization. This scale was developed at NASA to measure mental workload for people in environments such as aircraft and spacecraft cockpits, and has been validated with a large number of mental tasks like short-term memory tasks, mental arithmetic and dual tasks.[18] Using the scale, people rate their experiences along various dimensions of workload and stress from very low to very high. The NASA TLX measures showed that when interrupted, people reported experiencing significantly higher mental workload, frustration, time pressure, effort and stress. Experiencing interruptions all day, every day, can certainly take its toll in terms of more drained resources and increased stress—a high cost.

How often we are interrupted

Email was not always the interrupting demon that it is today. When I was a graduate student, I might have gotten one or two emails a day, and these were entertaining—usually jokes that students circulated. At Columbia, my graduate university, computers were located in a common room. My advisor and I would work side by side on our computers, and rather than interrupt him verbally with a question, I would send him an email. A bit later, he would then reply back with an answer—interchanges all without a spoken word. But then email use snowballed to what it is today.

Over the years in our studies, the number one cause that participants reported for interruptions (both external and internal) was email. If email really was such a problem, we wanted to find out exactly how often people are interrupted by it. In a first study, we logged computer activity of thirty-two people over five days to get a precise measure. We found that our study participants averaged checking their inboxes seventy-four times a day,[19] replicated a year later in another study where we logged the computer activity of forty people for twelve workdays and found that they checked email an average of seventy-seven times a day.[20] One dedicated person checked their email 374 times a day. We could also get a fairly good estimate of how often email checks were due to external or internal interruptions by whether people used email notifications. Most participants—41 percent—checked email without notifications, i.e., they self-interrupted to check it, and 31 percent of our participants primarily checked email from notifications, which would be external interruptions. The remainder—28 percent—did have notifications turned on but reported that they checked email about equally due to external or self-interruptions. Sometimes people might check their email without interrupting their tasks, say, first thing in the morning or after a lunch break. But nevertheless, we found that people do tend to check their email throughout the day—a lot, mostly due to self-interruptions. What our participants told us about email being interruptive was spot-on, proven scientifically.

But of course, email is not the only source of interruptions. The most common social media that was used by our participants in the workplace at the time was Facebook. In 2016, when the study was done, 68 percent of US adults were Facebook users, and this usage rate has been steady, but since 2018, this has been surpassed by YouTube as the most common social media used, at 73 percent.[21] When we logged social media use for five days, we found that those people who were active Facebook users averaged 38 visits daily—one person even checked it 264 times a day! Not only do people check Facebook a lot, but they do so in short bursts of about eighteen seconds—it really is like snacking on social media.

Escaping the email zombies

In 2010, a *New York Times* article described emails as zombies: you keep killing (deleting) them, and they keep coming.[22] I was determined to find out if by turning off email, people could be more focused when working with digital media. What if we removed the zombies entirely? It took me six years to find an organization willing to cut off email for some of its workers, but I finally found a large scientific research and development organization who agreed to participate, where senior managers felt that email overload was a serious problem.

I almost didn't get permission to do this study. I was invited to give a talk at this organization and while there asked if I could pitch the experiment. The executive committee met in a conference room with a long table, and I stood in front by the projection screen. The director of the organization was an ex-military captain seated at the head of the long table, facing me, and the different department heads were seated along the sides. It was obvious that they deferred to her opinion and kept glancing at her. As I gave the pitch, she started to shake her head no, and I watched all the other heads around the long table start to shake their heads no. Grasping at straws, I blurted out that an office was like a military unit. If a soldier was taken down in the field, then the team would have to reconfigure. What if email wasn't available? Could team members quickly reconfigure to communicate? The analogy had worked. Suddenly the ex-military captain, thinking tactically, started nodding. Taking her cue, the other heads began nodding in unison. While reconfiguring communication is an interesting prospect, what I was really interested in was finding out whether, without email, people would be able to focus on their work for a longer duration. Would work become less fragmented? Would people be less stressed?

With clearance to do the study, and working with Stephen Voida, my postdoc, we first logged participants' typical computer activity and email use in their normal work for three days as a baseline measure. The next week, we cut off their email for five days, a full workweek. To directly measure stress, we asked our participants to wear heart rate monitors while at work. The heart rate monitors measured physiological stress using heart rate variability, i.e., how much the time varies between your heartbeats. If the variation between consecutive beats is low—in other words, if the beats are quite regular—then your autonomic nervous system signals that you are in a stressed fight-or-flight state. But if there is high variation, then your autonomic nervous system is at ease and able to respond to changes. Think about when you're really relaxed. The slightest sound might cause you to jump, but then you'll calm back down again.

While cut off from email, participants could still meet with colleagues or receive phone calls. Though their email was blocked, participants still persisted in trying to check email due to sheer habit, but finally broke their habits by around the fifth day. We discovered that when email was cut off, people's attention spans were significantly longer while working on their computers—in other words, they switched their attention less frequently. The fact that people could focus longer shows that email *does* cause attention spans to decline. But perhaps the best result was that without email, the heart rate monitors revealed significantly less stress by the end of the week.

In interviews, the contrast in how participants described their work with email ("ruining my life," "interfering with my happiness") and without email (a "freeing experience," "feeling liberated," "could work at a human pace") was clear-cut. This last comment led us to title our paper "A Pace Not Dictated by Electrons."[23] We found there was also a social benefit to not having email. When email was cut off, our participants replaced digital interactions with face-to-face interactions. Though they could phone others, they frequently chose to walk to others' offices, and sometimes even to other buildings to meet people. They described that they enjoyed their social life at work more, which email seems to have replaced.

Some managers of the participants in the study (but who were not in the study themselves) changed their behavior as well. One study participant described how her boss became much more impatient when he couldn't reach her by email—she said he would enter her office when he needed something and "wave a paper in front of me like a crazy man." Another participant, Rich, described that before his email was cut off, his supervisor interrupted him often, delegating work to him via email. When his email was cut off, the supervisor suddenly stopped delegating work though he could easily have walked down the hall and done it face-to-face. Even though the study showed that part of the hierarchical delegation of work broke down without email, the director was happy with the rest of the results and was especially satisfied that people could reconfigure their communication networks without email should the need ever arise.

In 2012, when we published the paper, we were optimistic about the results that cutting off email lowered stress and recommended that organizations batch email, i.e., send it out two or three times a day. However, in a later study that I did in 2016, we tested whether reading email in batches really was associated with less stress. Unfortunately, we found that not to be the case. In this study, conducted at Microsoft Research with Mary Czerwinski, Shamsi Iqbal, Paul Johns and Akane Sano, using computer logging of email and heart rate monitors to measure the stress of forty people for twelve workdays, we found that people who read email in batches showed no difference in stress levels compared to people who checked their email continually. What did have an effect on stress though was the duration of time spent on email: people who spent more time daily on email were more stressed—even after controlling for their job demands and job autonomy.[24] A few years later, at UC Irvine, colleagues and I replicated this result with sixty-three people using a thermal imaging camera to measure stress. Again, we found that reading email in batches didn't lower stress, but we found a twist: people who scored high on a personality trait of Neuroticism actually were *more* stressed when email was batched.[25]

The study suggests then, that without email, we increase our focus on our work, reduce the cognitive load of dealing with the email, save cognitive resources by not having to resist email distractions, create a more relaxing workplace environment with less stress, and perhaps foster more fulfilling social interactions. Cutting off email should be a no-brainer. However, individuals alone cannot solve the email problem by simply cutting off from it, as then they are unfairly left out of the communication loop. Email is a much bigger problem that needs to be tackled at the organizational and even societal level, which I'll get into later in the book.

Gender differences in interruptions

Try out a thought experiment where you imagine who might be better at managing interruptions: men, women or neither. What do you think? If you imagine that women are better at managing interruptions, you are correct. In our studies, women were responsible for managing more working spheres daily on average than their male counterparts. Yet female workers also experienced fewer interruptions and were less likely to self-interrupt themselves compared to their male colleagues. Further, though not a big difference, women were more likely to resume interrupted work (87 percent) than men (81 percent) on the same day. Altogether, the data suggest that the women in our study were more focused and more resilient after interruptions than the men were. When I present this result, people often propose that there are evolutionary reasons why women stay on task more than men. After all, they say, women were the gatherers in early history (though it's not clear that these actually were women's roles). However, my own interpretation is based on our current times and what participants have described. Women in our sample frequently explain that to be considered on an even playing field with their male counterparts (especially by their bosses), they feel the need to perform above and beyond them.

Gaining agency over interruptions

The organic chemist August Kekulé, while struggling to solve the shape of the benzene molecule, is said to have daydreamed of a snake in a circle biting its tail, which gave him the idea of a ring shape for the molecule. This is a great example of how, through following his internal thoughts, Kekulé was able to use his mind-wandering to find a solution.

Think of your attention as a flashlight that can be trained on one spot or diffused to illuminate a larger area. When attention to the external environment is diffuse, we can be alert to and process more signals, in what researchers Yoshiro Miyata and Don Norman describe as a state of processing driven by interruptions.[26] This can be beneficial, for example when we are attentive to important events or tasks, such as keeping an eye out for that incoming time-sensitive budget while we're working on something else. With attention diffused and pointed inwardly, our minds can also be open to new insights, like Kekulé's was.

There is, of course, a trade-off, as Miyata and Norman describe. It's true that when we are focused closely on something, we can miss important information in the environment. But if our attention is too diffuse, we use too much interruption-driven processing and may not accomplish much in our task at hand. We need to strike a balance and remain flexible, adapting to our environment and our situation. Ideally, we would want to be able to dynamically adjust that flashlight's beam. In other words, we need to harness our ability to use our dynamic, kinetic attention to be responsive to important things, whether externally or within ourselves, to apply sustained focus when we need it, and to direct our attention to less challenging things when our cognitive resources are low. To be able to narrow or disperse our field of focus as our task and emotional needs change is to have agency in our attention. We want to be able to control that flashlight.

How can we effectively manage that trade-off? First off, it can help to know that there is in fact evidence that having control over interruptions, at least external interruptions, helps people to be more productive. In a laboratory experiment conducted by researcher Daniel McFarlane, subjects were either able or unable to control when they were interrupted. They were instructed to play a Nintendo-like video game (though with a serious premise: catching bodies as they fell from a building) and were interrupted by a task where they had to match colors or shapes. When the subjects were given the choice of when to allow themselves to be interrupted (at the risk of missing a falling body!), they performed the best. People had the worst performance when they had to handle the interruptions immediately.[27] This experiment shows that being able to have control over when to act on the interruption is thus best for performance and productivity. When you can redirect your attention purposefully, you can also better manage your cognitive resources.

A good time to intentionally redirect your attention is when you reach a break point in a task[28] such as finishing writing a chapter or completing a budget—natural places to pause. At break points, fewer cognitive resources are being used than when you are working full throttle. In the middle of a task, memory load is high, and interruptions are most disruptive. This is exactly what researchers Piotr Adamczyk and Brian Bailey at the University of Illinois found in a laboratory experiment. When people were interrupted after finishing a task of searching the web, editing or watching film clips, they performed better and experienced less annoyance, frustration and time pressure than when they were interrupted at random points in the task.[29] You can make it a priority to pause work at a natural break point, say, when finishing writing a section of that report. It is also easier to resume work after a break point.

There is a way to off-load that very tension that Bluma Zeigarnik discovered a century ago with unfinished interrupted work. As interrupted tasks pile up, you carry that tension around with you, and it becomes more and more of a drain on your resources. You certainly want to limit the stress by the end of the workday as there are carryover effects of bringing stress from the office into your personal life.[30] Those unfinished tasks churn around in your thoughts, and what you can do to reduce that churning is to externalize your memory of that unfinished task. What this means is to record information about the interrupted task in some form external to your mind, like writing down a note or recording a voice memo about your most important unfinished tasks, their priority, their state of completion and a plan for the next step. Try to do this as soon as you can after the interruption, or when you have a long break or at the end of the day. Do this for your most important tasks. Otherwise, when you keep thinking of that unfinished task, you are rehearsing it in your mind so that you won't forget it—it is the Zeigarnik effect in full swing. But when you write it down, you are transferring all that unwanted tension from your mind onto something outside of yourself.

Michael Scullin and colleagues at Baylor University did an interesting experiment that supports the idea that off-loading unfinished tasks onto an external memory can relieve tension. They studied fifty-seven participants who came to a sleep laboratory. Half were instructed to write down their unfinished tasks: everything that they needed to finish tomorrow and in the next few days. The other half were instructed to write down only the tasks they had finished that day and in the last few days. Those who wrote down their unfinished tasks fell asleep significantly faster than the other group. Interestingly, the more detailed the to-do lists of unfinished tasks, the faster people fell asleep.[31] This finding can be explained by the Zeigarnik effect: as people lay in bed, unfinished tasks agitated around and around in their minds, stirring up tension. So why didn't the people who wrote down their completed tasks fall asleep faster? One explanation is that perhaps their unfinished tasks (which they didn't write down) remained in their minds and created tension.

Interruptions are part and parcel of the digital world. We can sequester ourselves and turn off notifications, which can help us shore up cognitive resources in the short term, but people, especially knowledge workers in our current times, who cut themselves off from office and social communication penalize themselves by not getting important information. Further, re-sisting or responding to interruptions drains cognitive resources above and beyond the resources needed to conduct work. When we enter the digital world, we open ourselves up for an onslaught of interruptions from a myriad of sources—bots, pop-up ads, automatic notifications, other people, and above all, from our-selves. Recall how Lewin saw individuals as inseparable from their environments, what he called their life-space. In his terms, the digital world is now part of our life-space. We need to learn how to exist in this life-space and be in control. We can take action by finding our own break points to pause work, by harnessing our kinetic attention so as to develop control over our attentional flashlight, and by externalizing memories of our unfinished tasks to reduce the Zeigarnik effect and that tension described by Lewin. To be interrupted is part of life, and in the coming chapters, we will learn about underlying forces in our broader life-space that pull on our attention, and how we can develop agency so that we can better preserve our precious cognitive resources, utilize our attention more effectively, and not leave our tasks too far behind.

Part Two:

The Underlying
Forces of Distraction

CHAPTER SIX:

The Rise of the Internet and the Decline of Focus

Before smartphones were introduced, to do a digital detox, all I needed to do was to stay at my mother-in-law's house, as she did not have Wi-Fi. I was never able to abstain for long, and I would set out wandering her small Austrian town, looking for a hotspot. I might have looked odd walking the streets carrying my open laptop, checking for the signal bars to appear. One day in 2006, I found a hotspot and set myself down at the edge of someone's front yard to do my email. Soon two elderly Austrian men came out of the house carrying lawn chairs, set them up, and sat down right in front of me. They didn't say a word, just carefully eyed me, a foreigner exhibiting extremely odd behavior. From my perspective, I just wanted to get through my email before I would be asked to leave, and from their expressions, it would not be done kindly. They kept watching me in silence, and I kept doing my email. Finally I pointed to myself and said, "California." Suddenly they burst into laughter and said, "Schwarzenegger," vigorously nodding to me in approval of my state's Austrian-born actor-turned-governor. I knew I could stay and finish my email.

How did we get to a point where it is so hard to untether from the internet? And how did we arrive at a situation in which, once we're online, we find it so hard to stick to one site even for reasonable stretches of time? Why does our attention wander so much when we're on the internet?

Before the movie *Summer of Soul* won an Academy Award in 2022, I received an email from a friend recommending that I see it. I immediately typed in *Summer of Soul* on the internet. The movie documents the six-week-long 1969 Harlem cultural festival. I was astounded that I had never heard of this festival, which featured the likes of Stevie Wonder, Mahalia Jackson, Sly and the Family Stone, and Nina Simone. I started reading the Wikipedia article and then clicked on the name *Mahalia Jackson*, which took me to another Wikipedia page to read about her history. She struggled as she held a string of different jobs, and I was struck by her resilience. I began wondering more and more how Jackson got her big break as a singer. The words *Apollo Records* jumped out at me on the page, and I clicked on that link. As I read, my eyes were drawn to the link to *Apollo Theater*, perhaps because the word *Apollo* was fresh in my mind, and I clicked on that link. I was now reading more broadly about Harlem, music and theater, and the words *Harlem Renaissance* stood out to me, and so I quickly clicked on that link. I continued doing this for some time, clicking on different links, following my interest, before I realized how far I'd gone down the rabbit hole. Afterwards, I analyzed what I had been doing. My mind had traveled through an associative trail of ideas linked together in what outwardly might seem to be haphazard but were strongly linked together in my mind. Following that associative path of ideas, I had rambled deep through Wikipedia. My experience illustrates one powerful influence that affects our attention—the very design of the internet itself. To fully understand the issue, we need to start at the beginning with an ingenious idea called the Memex.

The Memex was proposed in 1945 as an idea for a personal desktop device where people could store and retrieve all their personal information. The impetus for the Memex idea, the forerunner of the internet and the entire digital world that followed, was simple: we can't get to information because it's not organized in a way that makes sense for humans. The creator of this powerful idea was actually an unassuming person. Vannevar Bush was born in 1890 and embodied the formality of the turn-of-the-century culture. The son of a reverend, he dressed immaculately, was hardly ever seen without a tie in public and spoke in a measured tone. He was not a fan of the humanities or social sciences—they were not hard science, and he was an engineer to the core. Viewed from the perspective of today's high-tech culture, he seems so anachronistic. Unlike modern tech entrepreneurs, he didn't eat vegan like Biz Stone, do yoga like Sergey Brin, meditate like Jeff Weiner, or walk barefoot and take LSD like Steve Jobs. Vannevar Bush was pretty strait-laced, at least outwardly. Inwardly he was wildly unconventional.

Revered by the scientific community and the public alike, he had won the highest civilian medals in the US, Britain and France. He conceived of the US National Science Foundation, invented the analog computer, and founded the company Raytheon. But his idea of the Memex was not consistent with his scientific rigor. It seemed like speculative, magical realism.

For someone who had a disdain for the social sciences, it was paradoxical that he titled his groundbreaking article about the Memex "As We May Think" when it was published in *The Atlantic* in July 1945.[1] Germany had recently surrendered in World War II, the Philippines was liberated and the United Nations Charter was signed. The world was cautiously tiptoeing towards optimism. For the last five years, the US had heavily invested in research for the war effort. But now the war was coming to an end. What to do with all that scientific talent? The US along with much of the world was starting to turn to the future. For Bush, the answer was obvious: there needed to be new institutions to insure the continuation of scientific research.

Some years earlier, in 1938, Bush had invented an instrument for referencing microfilm at high speed, a kind of automatic library called the rapid selector. On the surface, the idea of the Memex was just a continuation of this earlier invention. But the real genius of the Memex was not the medium that was being used, but how information would be stored and located. Bush had a vision to use what he called "associative indexing," where documents would be linked together. If you accessed one document, you would be able to retrieve another one that was connected to it. You could sit at your desk and be able to retrieve all your information—your records, your books, your photos, your messages. It would augment human memory.

Systems of indexing at the time were "artificial." The Dewey decimal system, the most common one used, organized information by topic. At the time of its invention by Melvil Dewey in 1876, it was an innovation, an improvement over the prevailing system at the time, which shelved books, believe it or not, according to height and when they were acquired.[2] While shelving books from biggest to smallest might look aesthetically pleasing in a library, imagine how hard it would be to find a specific book you had in mind. The Dewey decimal system was a big leap forward, as it organized knowledge into a hierarchy. Information was classified into static categories such as history and geography, and then into subcategories of world history, European geography and so on. But people don't automatically think this way, plus these categories are arbitrary. People who searched for a book had to twist their thinking to fit rigid categories determined by other individuals.

Vannevar Bush argued that conventional indexing systems should be redesigned to function the way human memory does. According to semantic network theory, developed by Canadian psychologists Endel Tulving and Wayne Donaldson, our memory is structured as concepts that are associated with each other. If a person thinks of pizza, their mind may easily connect to concepts of cheese, beer or Ray's pizza parlor. A structure of associations makes it easier to retrieve information. When documents are linked together by relationships, if a user accesses one document, then it is easy to think of connections to other related documents. Today, Wikipedia's network structure enables such quick associations in our minds: when I look up Leonardo da Vinci, it links to the *Mona Lisa*, which in turn links to the Louvre, to the Right Bank of Paris, and so on. Before the internet, it would have been infeasible to follow such connections, as one would need to go to a library, look up a book's classification number, search the shelves for the book, read a passage, find a reference to another book, search for that, and so on.

But with the electronic Memex model, it would be easy. Bush's vision planted the seeds for the internet today, where information is organized by, and for, the masses. The Memex idea was revolutionary, bringing us from the nineteenth-century era of Dewey's information retrieval system into the modern computer age. But the Memex remained only an idea and was not put into practice. A lot more innovations were still needed for it to be technologically possible.

Then, a few years later in 1949, along came Edmund Berkeley, who wrote a book with a title that sounded more like science fiction: *Giant Brains, or Machines that Think*.[3] He had been an actuary at Prudential Insurance but left when the company wouldn't allow him to work on projects that advocated against nuclear war. So he became a writer, and with *Giant Brains*, he expanded the notion of accessing information from only your own personal repository as in the Memex to that of an entire society. Slowly the cornerstones were being laid for the conceptual foundation of the internet. Berkeley wrote presciently,

> We can foresee the development of machinery that will make it possible to consult information in a library automatically. Suppose that you go into the library of the future and wish to look up ways for making biscuits. You will be able to dial into the catalogue machine "making biscuits." There will be a flutter of movie film in the machine. Soon it will stop, and, in front of you on the screen, will be projected the part of the catalogue which shows the names of three or four books containing recipes for biscuits. If you are satisfied, you will press a button; a copy of what you saw will be made for you and come out of the machine.[4]

While Vannevar Bush's Memex was an idea as profound and important as the internal combustion engine, it was Ted Nelson in 1960 who developed the crankshaft, so to speak. Nelson was the practical creator of hypertext, the name given to interconnected documents and images that could also include summaries, annotations and footnotes.[5] Nelson was another unlikely person to have played a role in propelling the internet forward. He had studied philosophy and sociology at Swarthmore and Harvard. These fields encouraged him to think broadly—he conceived of the underlying file structure that provided the programmable design for hypermedia, i.e., the computer networking of information. He envisioned a body of information that, in his words, "could grow indefinitely, gradually including more and more of the world's written knowledge."[6]

The digital world was taking off. Around the same time that Nelson was working, Doug Engelbart, a computer scientist at Stanford Research Institute in Menlo Park, had an idealistic vision of mobilizing the collective intelligence of humanity to solve the world's problems. Computers would be the way to amass information from as many people as possible in the world and offer it freely. Not knowing about Ted Nelson's work, Engelbart presented a demo of the first hypertext system, the NLS ("oN-Line System"), which he demonstrated famously in 1968, later called the "Mother of All Demos" by journalist Steven Levy.[7] At the time, computers were the size of a room and were used as super-calculators—the idea of using hypertext on a personal computer was groundbreaking. For most people, it was unfathomable to think that in the next two decades, personal computers would become commonplace in people's homes. But these databases were still just storing personal information, and for the vast majority of people, their data was not publicly shared. In 1969, the Advanced Research Projects Agency Network (ARPANET) was developed, enabling networked connections among four host sites: UCLA, the Stanford Research Institute, UC Santa Barbara and the University of Utah. It would take over two more decades for Engelbart's vision to be realized.

Then, in 1990, a software engineer working at CERN (European Organization for Nuclear Research), in Switzerland wrote a proposal to his manager requesting to work on a side project. His manager turned him down the first time, believing that the project wouldn't be worthwhile. Later, his manager relented, which was a good thing, because that project of Tim Berners-Lee was to write software for hypertext that would share information, and it became the World Wide Web. Shared documents could be viewed on any individual's browser, and this program became the keystone for enabling the wide-scale sharing of information from anyone, anywhere in the world. The interlinking road and superhighway structure of the internet was paved.

By the mid-1990s, the internet had exploded. Its technical design was based on a decentralized network structure, which meant that the architecture was open and democratic, allowing anyone, individuals as well as large companies, to contribute and link to other information. People did. And the world changed.

The internet grew exponentially until, in 2000, the dot-com bubble burst. People had procured computers and network access and now were looking for new ways to use them. There was no shortage of ideas. In 2001, Jimmy Wales and Larry Sanger had a vision to create a modern-day Library of Alexandria and launched a free online encyclopedia called Wikipedia where anyone could contribute and monitor the content. It also now seems inevitable that social networking sites such as Friendster and Myspace were launched, as previous social online communities such as LambdaMOO and the Internet Relay Chat were quite popular and had been active since the 1980s. Then, in 2004, a college sophomore in his Harvard dorm room wrote a program for students to rank their classmates' appearance. This did not go over well with the Harvard administration, and it was shut down. But the student persevered, and Facebook was launched. Facebook opened the doors to a new paradigm of social interaction, and soon the internet was awash with social media sites. More social media meant more choices for linking to and interacting with people and information. From their graves, Melvil Dewey was horrified, and Vannevar Bush was smiling.

Joyous associations

Vannevar Bush's idea of associative trails of thinking could be traced back to the eighteenth-century Scottish philosopher David Hume and then on to the twentieth-century British philosopher and logician Bertrand Russell. Russell was a pacifist and had ideas that were radical enough to get him fired from several universities. His teaching contract at City University of New York in 1940 was canceled in a ruling by the New York Supreme Court stating that he was morally unsuited to teach as he advocated for the right to sex before marriage and for homosexuality. Ten years later, Russell would go on to win the Nobel Prize in Literature for a body of work that promoted humanitarian principles.

Russell had great insight into how we think by association. To Russell, a word that we read or hear evokes an expansive meaning of that word with all its associations.[8] Our minds are flexible. Seeing an event, hearing or reading a word, or even a memory, can light up the pathways in our minds to think about other related concepts. Recently, I saw a cat heading into busy traffic on Varick Street in New York City, and as cars dodged it, I immediately associated this cat with my own cat Buster. I also immediately thought of "accident," "cars," "bicycles," and "children." Fortunately the cat was rescued by its owner. Concepts don't just have one-to-one associations but are linked together by many-to-many associations.

The theory of semantic memory describes human memory being organized as a network of such interconnected concepts. When you think of rain, you associate it with an umbrella, or when you think of Disneyland, you think of California. Even seemingly disparate concepts can be associated together, for example, if you happened to experience them in the same situation. If you lost your smartphone at a Yankees game, then every time you hear about a Yankees game, it might evoke a memory of your smartphone. How well one concept evokes the idea of another concept depends on how closely linked the concepts are in your memory. If you hear just the word *stadium*, it may not lead you to think of your lost smartphone as the specific word combination of *Yankee Stadium* would.

The node and link structure that Vannevar Bush envisioned for organizing information in his Memex is patterned after the idea of human semantic memory. The structure of the internet is a simulation of Tulving and Donaldson's semantic network model of the mind, and with its vast network of nodes and links, has no prescribed order in which to view it. When I was reading about Mahalia Jackson, I could have clicked on any link and traveled down any path. When information is organized in a network structure, you can traverse the links and content any way you like. Similarly, the idea of human semantic memory is that it's flexible, and we can retrieve things and make associations any way we like—either serendipitously or based on context and on what we encounter in the environment,[9] as I did with that cat on Varick Street.

In the mid-1990s, with the web growing in popularity, I did an experiment that showed how the node and link structure of hypermedia on the web encourages people to think of associations. With colleagues at the German National Research Center for Information Technology in Darmstadt (which, strictly speaking, translates into English as "gut city"), we conducted an experiment with hypermedia. We had forty-eight people come to a conference room in groups of three. They were instructed to brainstorm ideas for a "library of the future." The conference room had an electronic whiteboard where the groups could write down ideas for what such a library would look like. Half the groups used the whiteboard as a regular board without its electronic functionality, and could write down their ideas in any way they liked. Most wrote them in lists. The other half could use the same whiteboard with added computer functionality that enabled them to organize their ideas in a hypermedia format. When people circled an idea on the whiteboard, the computer automatically recognized the idea as a node, and when they drew lines between ideas, the computer automatically recognized these as links. This enabled people to select and move the ideas all around the whiteboard with the links remaining intact, and create a hypermedia structure. I remember this experiment well, as I was eight months pregnant, it was an extremely hot summer, and the experiment took place in a room with no air-conditioning and packed with computers that heated the space up like a steam bath. But the sweating was worth it, as we made a nice discovery: people who had the opportunity to use hypermedia to organize their thoughts created ideas with more depth, elaborating on them more, and with more relationships and associated concepts among them. They had double the number of ideas compared to the groups who didn't have the hypermedia functionality. They also found unexpected relationships between the ideas. Independent writing experts, blind to the experimental conditions, judged the hypermedia group as having generated more original ideas, likely due to the deeper elaboration.[10] These results suggest that using hypermedia facilitated more associations among the ideas, which in turn led to more ideas overall, like a spark spreading flames throughout a dry forest.

Of course, reading a book or magazine can also spark our imagination, but because of its node-link structure, the internet allows our minds to be flexible. By comparison, the linear format of a book constrains us to follow the content in a particular sequence, page by page. When we surf the internet, we have the freedom to pursue any associative path. Sometimes the content on a web page inspires our thinking, or our inner thoughts may drive us to click on new links; the two processes work in tandem. The internet structure sets our imagination in motion.

Mind-wandering through the internet

What happens with our attention when we surf the internet? Our attention may start as goal-directed, as mine did when I looked up *Summer of Soul*. But then my attention shifted as I made associations and clicked on new links, setting my mind off on unexpected paths. When we surf the internet without a specific goal, our minds are open and opportunistic, allowing us to freely make associations in our inner semantic network, pursuing any direction, primed by the information on each web page.

Mind-wandering happens when our attention is disengaged from the external environment. When we mind-wander, we generate thoughts unrelated to our task at hand—these could include thinking about our past experiences, our future goals, or just something completely out of the blue. People mind-wander a lot. A study using experience sampling probed 2,250 people at random times in their natural environments and found that people's minds wandered about 47 percent of the time they were sampled.[11] Though not technically the same, internet surfing does have parallels to mind-wandering. First, mind-wandering is usually not goal-oriented, similar to when we surf the internet and let ourselves be open to skipping among concepts freely, facilitated by the links we see. Another parallel with internet surfing is that mind-wandering often occurs without us even being aware that our thoughts have meandered.[12] We can be so focused on following a path of concepts on the internet that we don't even realize that we've been in an attention trap for hours.

Your computer is a trove of priming cues

The internet offers us so many entry points to access content in our mind's network. Priming happens in our minds when the exposure to some stimulus that we see or hear facilitates us to respond to another stimulus. In cognitive priming, the exposure to a context or word activates concepts in our memory that are related semantically or are associated together with the initial word (like *needle* and *thread*). With simple stimulus-response tasks in a laboratory (after seeing the word *sparrow*, we then respond faster when we see the word *robin* compared to if we see the word *chair*), the effects last just a few seconds. But there is evidence that when material is thought about and processed more deeply, priming effects can last longer, over two minutes, even when other words intervene.[13] So, for example, I went to the Wikipedia Winter Olympic Games page. As I started to read it, all sorts of related ideas sprang to my mind, like ice-skating, bobsledding and ski jumping, and when I saw the link "alpine skiing," I was drawn to click on it. If you're reading a topic and primed with all sorts of ideas about it, then links can attract attention like a neon sign.

Priming can lead us to think about and sometimes even do things automatically as a response to some cue, activating our inner goals without us even making a conscious choice to do so.[14] Advertisers have known about this for a long time—exposure to concepts can affect what we bring to mind and also the choices we make. This is shown in an experiment where subjects were first asked to assess statements that included names of product brands ("Irish Spring is a laundry detergent"). Afterwards, when asked their brand of choice for various product types, they were more likely to choose a name mentioned in one of the earlier statements.[15] The reason is that evaluating those statements brought those brand names to the forefront of subjects' minds. When we see a beer commercial on TV, we are primed to think about beer and might then grab a beer during the commercial break.

When a link on a web page primes a person to think of an idea, to what extent is the person consciously making that association? The psychologist John Anderson has spent decades studying associative memory and claims that the activation of concepts that are associated in the semantic network of our minds is an automatic process.[16] Being primed by an idea on a Wikipedia page and then clicking on a highlighted link is likely a mixture of automatic and controlled thinking processes.[17] It's like we arrive at a buffet and may not have thought about chocolate cake beforehand, but once we see it, the sight of that luscious slice lights up our minds and links to associations of that chocolate taste or a memory of eating cake at our child's birthday party. We may consciously (or impulsively) put that slice on our plates, but there is an entire iceberg of automatic associations underneath that action urging us to take it. Similarly, it may be hard to resist clicking on a link to another Wikipedia page. When I analyzed my internet behavior while reading about the movie *Summer of Soul*, I realized that when I clicked on links, it was quite spontaneous.

Of course, we may also be driven by sheer curiosity to click on links and not necessarily by being primed. But it can be hard to separate the two—they may go hand in hand. The psychologist George Loewenstein explains that curiosity is an urge to fill a gap in our knowledge, and we are drawn to information that can help us resolve our curiosity.[18] Even a small amount of information can arouse our curiosity, says Lowenstein—and this could be links we encounter on a web page. We then act—sometimes impulsively—to quench that thirst for curiosity by clicking on the link, consciously or not. Our inquisitiveness is satisfied and we are rewarded. In fact, fMRI studies show that curiosity triggers an expectation of a reward, as shown by activation in the caudate nucleus and lateral prefrontal cortex, regions of the brain associated with anticipating rewards, and with an intrinsic value of learning.[19] When we see a link on a web page, it ignites our curiosity. Knowing it's a gateway to new information, we anticipate a reward, and we click. So as we traverse the internet, reading content, it activates associations and/or stimulates our curiosity, we select links, read more content, our mind is further aroused, we click on new links, and we easily fall down the rabbit hole. Curiosity is the drug of the internet.

The design of the internet and attention-shifting

The internet seems to work like magic, but so does our memory. The structure of the internet, in its hypermedia format of nodes and links, parallels how knowledge in your brain is theoretically organized, and also mirrors how people flexibly associate concepts in everyday life. The design unleashes the floodgates for distraction—ideas on the internet are as irresistible to pursue as your own thoughts.

To stop our unhindered mind-wandering through the internet, three things are needed. First, we need to be aware of our behavior, which is not so easy, because it means bringing automatic behaviors to a conscious level. Later in the book, we'll learn how you can develop a meta-awareness of your behavior to help make you more aware of why you might be roaming around the internet. Second, we have to be motivated to want to stop the behavior. And third, we need to have enough cognitive resources to resist those urges.

The internet, by making so much interconnected information available, has created what Andy Clark, author of the book *Natural-Born Cyborgs*,[20] refers to as the cyborg mind. We might think of a cyborg mind as having electrodes implanted to boost memory storage or increase processing speed. But Clark argues that it can also mean an extension of our own minds. Humans have long used technologies to extend their memory, from writing to taking photos. But the internet surpasses all of these as a computerized extension of our minds, where we can bookmark text, images, video and audio so that we don't forget them. Further, we have them at our fingertips from our phones. In fact, studies have shown that when people use the internet to conduct searches, they have a hard time differentiating whether the knowledge has come from the internet or from themselves.[21] It is becoming harder to distinguish our own memory from the internet's body of information. Our reliance on the internet might even be reducing our own memory capacity, as one study suggests. Doing internet searches for six days actually decreased some brain functions, reducing the functional connectivity and synchronization of brain regions associated with long-term memory retrieval.[22]

The internet's pioneers dreamed of making the world's information easily available. With any great innovation, there are unintended consequences, both good and bad. Automobiles led to the development of road and highway infrastructure, which eventually led to suburbs, which enabled more living space but also introduced economic, social and environmental impacts like vehicle emissions of greenhouse gases, which cause global warming. Implicit in the internet pioneers' visions was the idealistic assumption that people would contribute meaningful information to the internet and seek information purposefully, and that this information would be beneficial to humanity. Likely they did not conceive of the lure to spend countless hours with internet surfing or social media, or noxious behaviors related to the dark web, echo chambers or cyberbullying. And just as the first cars did not have seat belts or airbags, there were no safety features built into the internet to prevent scamming, misinformation or targeted ads, either.

The media theorist Marshall McLuhan writes, "Technology leads to new structures of feeling and thought."[23] He described how the development of the print medium led people to arrange their perceptions to conform to the printed page. In the digital era, technology has similarly led to new structures of attention. The organization of the internet, with its nodes and links and ever-changing content, has shaped not just where we pay attention but also the frequency at which we shift our attention. People arrange their perceptions to conform to and process the stimuli afforded by digital hypermedia. In an ironic reciprocal arrangement, people are adding to and developing the structure of the internet, and in turn, the structure of the internet is influencing and shaping a new type of kinetic, shifting attention. McLuhan is right—the internet has led to new structures of thought, coinciding with how our attention spans on our devices are shortening over the years.

Internet use may be associated with more than just our changing attention spans. Changes in how the brain is structurally and functionally organized is part of normal human development, and that organization can change throughout the lifetime.[24] Just as it affects memory, some research even suggests that using the internet may change the brain's functional responsiveness, especially in areas related to complex reasoning and decision-making.[25]

Vannevar Bush's Memex idea removed the hurdles for finding information, but also set the stage for joyriding through the web. What Bush didn't foresee was how his simple design of associative trails of information would later evolve to powerfully influence our distractibility. As the internet is digital, nonlinear and has discrete elements, our attention has come to mirror this and is easily fragmented. The internet was built by ordinary people—anyone, anywhere could add to the internet, and they surely did. The improvisatory nature of the growth of the internet has given rise to the improvisatory behavior of its users.

By the time I started examining multitasking behavior in the 1990s, I realized that I was tackling a huge phenomenon. In trying to understand how our attention functions while on our devices, it was like I was trying to understand a sailboat's path based solely on wind when other factors like ocean currents were also affecting the vessel. The internet pioneers' idealistic visions have been supplanted by new visions from companies that have invented ways to keep us scrolling for their profit. We will next talk about how these new visions are realized and how they affect our attention.

CHAPTER SEVEN:

How AI and Algorithms
Influence Your Thoughts

I am being pursued by a pair of boots. These boots have followed me around for the last month, appearing in the most unexpected places. They show up first thing in the morning and are sometimes the last thing I see at night. When I read *The New York Times*, the boots appear, when I go to Facebook, the boots are there, and when I go to shop for headphones, the boots are taunting me. When I see them, I cannot help but be drawn to them. I am not paranoid, but I know it is not by chance that these boots trail me. There is a motive to it. They know that I desire them. It seems that I cannot escape them. The only way to stop their pursuit of me is to buy them.

It is not just you browsing the internet. The internet is also browsing you. The structure of the internet is not the only technological mechanism that affects our online behavior—our attention is also tampered with by algorithms. The algorithms that we encounter daily in the digital world are nearly perfect manipulators of our attention.

Humans are no strangers to algorithms: natural selection, or survival of the fittest, can be modeled by an algorithm. The word *algorithm* comes from the name of the eighth century Persian mathematician Muḥammad ibn Mūsā al-Khwārizmī, which in Latin became Algoritmi. An algorithm, at its root definition, is simply a set of instructions. It is not a stretch, then, to say that, given genetic adaptability, humanity itself is based on a natural algorithm. Everyday activities rely on algorithms, such as cooking from a recipe, following GPS directions or assembling an IKEA bookshelf. Computer algorithms are used in designing traffic flows, navigating self-driving cars, business decisions, diagnosing diseases, setting bail and determining criminal sentences. Algorithms might be designed to benefit a group (using a decision model to select a project) or perhaps an organization (who to hire at a company or admit to a university) or even an entire society (to identify extreme weather events), but they are also applied on a much more personal, individual level—to program people's attention.

Because people have a limited capacity of attentional resources, internet companies who specialize in offering social media, messaging and e-commerce are intent on capturing as much of your attention as they can. There is intense competition to occupy your mind's real estate. These companies invest a lot of financial and human resources in developing sophisticated algorithms to sway you to invest your attentional resources in their offerings.

Your distraction is being paid for

There is indeed a scheme behind this relentless hounding of me by those boots. Let's analyze what is going on. Not too long ago, I visited a shopping site and clicked on these boots to take a closer look. The shopping site is part of an ad network, a broker between advertisers and publishers. The ad network runs software on the shopping site that records what I viewed and places this information on my computer in a cookie—data stored in a file on my web browser, or else in a profile that is stored on the ad network database.[1] Whenever I go to other sites on the internet that are part of the same ad network, they recognize me from my browser, and they know that I took a look at the boots.

So I am being tracked, and the boots follow me around the internet in what is called "ad remarketing." The more I see them, the more commonplace they seem, and I know that the more we are exposed to something and our familiarity with it increases, the more we like it.[2] This also helps explain why I am so distracted by those boots. Most of us have heard a song played over and over again on the radio and then found the tune stuck in our minds. In fact, brain activation, as measured through fMRI, shows that the more familiar a song is, the more emotionally attached we become to that song.[3] The power of brand familiarity on purchase behavior has also long been known in advertising.[4] That's why we see repeated ads for beer or mouthwash on TV. But what is also happening in the digital arena is that those boots keep being presented to me in different contexts. I recently clicked to read a *New York Times* tribute to the Rolling Stones drummer Charlie Watts, and the boots appeared. In this context, my attention (and imagination) was primed by the association with the Rolling Stones to think of the boots as hip rocker boots. The algorithm that instructs those boots to tail me is playing with my mind.

We discussed in the last chapter how the internet structure of nodes and links has inadvertently been designed to distract us. Of course, we cannot talk about our attention spans on the internet without addressing intentional distraction via targeted advertising as well. Manipulating people's attention is not new—advertising has been around since the Babylonians in 3000 BC.[5] Its incidence rose in the industrial revolution as the print medium, especially newspapers, became more popular. The goal of advertising was to first attract people's attention, and then to convince them that they needed a particular product or service. This basic idea has not changed in the age of digital media. Advertising started out by appealing to a general public. For example, lest one believe that natural supplements only came of age in the 1960s, in nineteenth-century England "Eno's fruit salts" were advertised to appeal to all for the removal of "foetid and poisonous matter from the blood."[6] Attention-grabbing advertisements started out as a one-to-many broadcast—one size fits all. Everyone saw the same Coca-Cola advertisement.

But not everyone is the same, and clever advertisers have long believed that business could be boosted by customizing ads to appeal to what people were personally interested in. Advertising became targeted. An example of more tailored advertising was to asthmatics in the 1890s, ironically to sell Joy's cigarettes.[7] Starting with television, a slew of patents were filed describing how advertising could be configured to television viewers depending on factors like their location, or when they watched TV.[8] But targeting advertisement for television and radio audiences is pretty crude compared to what is possible in the digital age. There is a lot more detailed information that can be gleaned from internet users because they leave digital traces of their online behavior. Targeted advertising patents for online sites started as early as 1993, twenty years later 2900 patents had been filed,[9] and they have since skyrocketed. Spending in digital ads exploded to nearly $400 billion in 2020.

Targeted ads also grew in sophistication. Creators of ads deploy algorithms to discover things about people so as to personalize the ads more precisely. The company selling those boots knows quite a bit about me: what styles of clothes that I buy, what sites I visit, what I like to read online, and more—enough to chip away at my resistance to the boots. Computer algorithms know even more than this—about people's habits and desires, and of course their attention behavior. Targeting information means gearing specific content to people at the right time in a context that would make them most attentive. Unlike TV ads, digital ads can be relentless, popping up in different contexts, each of which can prime a person to think about that product in different ways. Seeing a leather jacket on a web page where you are reading an article about climate change may turn you off to it, but seeing it on your Facebook page can prime you to think about how your friends might compliment you if you bought it.

Targeted online advertisement started in the mid-1990s, beginning with ads placed on particular consumer websites aimed at certain audiences, and then later incorporating user demographics (e.g., age, gender), a person's location (based on the IP address), behaviors (what sites they looked at), and even values that can be inferred by what a person browsed online (whether a person reads *Huffington Post* or *Newsmax*). Algorithms also began to incorporate social information about people from their social media use and networking sites. Companies now know how you are influenced by your friend network: how often you go on social media, at what times, what you look at once there, which friends' posts you read, which ones you like (or love, care, or are angered about), which videos you watch, which stories you share, and what you yourself post. The proliferation of mobile devices increased the precision of information that companies could get about the user. If a person does vigorous exercise and moves around a lot, then their smartphone sensor data might record and interpret them as a runner. That person then might be shown an ad for running clothes. Context can be used strategically to make the advertising more relevant. A high-tech winter jacket might be shown to a person living in Minnesota in November but not to someone who lives in southern California (unless the company knows that you bought airline tickets to Aspen). When the product fits the location context, it is more likely to grab a person's attention. You may not realize it, but you are collaborating with the algorithm because you provide it with a lot of data about yourself. You are unintentionally complicit with the algorithm in capturing your attention.

The algorithms that target your attention are based on psychometrics, a field of study that measures people's behavior, attitudes and personality. Psychometrics has been around since the late nineteenth century and was developed by the Englishman Sir Francis Galton, a sort of Renaissance man who is known for inventing the correlation statistic but who also has a tarnished legacy as he promoted eugenics. In early psychometric studies, people's cognitive abilities were measured first with physical tests, and then with surveys, which is how IQ scores came about. But surveys and tests are no longer needed when sensors can unobtrusively detect people's physiological signals and tracking can detect digital traces of their online behaviors. Companies such as the marketing research firm Innerscope collect biometric data of people when they view ads in a laboratory, for example, by using biosensors, eye tracking and facial expressions to determine how much they sweat, what exactly they look at on the ad, and what emotions the ad elicits. When a person sweats, it means they are aroused, and their facial expressions will help interpret whether the person is excited or stressed by the ad. The marketing company Numerator uses an algorithm based on consumers' behaviors, attitudes and purchases to classify people along three hundred and fifty psychographic variables and provides this information to companies to help sell products.

Online advertising leverages these advances in measuring personality. In what was trumpeted as the new age of bottom-up advertising, the firm Cambridge Analytica claimed they were able to map the personality of every person in the US from their online behavior—unbeknownst to them—and used the Big 5 theory to describe five basic personality traits: Openness, Conscientiousness, Extroversion, Agreeableness and Neuroticism. For instance, Cambridge Analytica found that people in New

York are generally more neurotic than people in California (in a later chapter we'll go into more depth on the Big 5 and show how much that one trait, Neuroticism, can influence your focus and susceptibility to distraction online). Working for clients specializing in political ads, Cambridge Analytica targeted individuals based on their psychometric profiles. The data was used to potentially influence elections in the US and abroad, such as the UK Brexit vote, allegedly. But unfettered greed can have a backlash. The company was shut down and will always be remembered in infamy after it used personal data of Facebook users, including their friends' networks, without their consent.

But once such particularized details about people are collected, how do you analyze this information to make sense of it? The era of Big Data solved all that. Every time you visit Amazon, the content you are viewing, your search patterns and your profile are all crunched together with data collected from millions of other users. Amazon conducts similarity searches to find out what might grab your attention based on what other people do who are similar to you. The algorithm is continually updated. That is the power of the internet: there are hundreds of millions of data points that can be collected about what you and everyone else online does—in real time—and patterns can be discovered from it. The algorithms incorporate this information—who you are, how you feel, what you do when and where—and then use it to capture your attention.

Reading your mind to distract you

At this point, you might be wondering what else can be inferred about you based on your online behavior. When you take a survey and answer questions about yourself, you know exactly the information that you are giving out. But what information can be gleaned about you just by looking at your digital footprints? It turns out quite a bit.

Digital phenotyping refers to collecting data that people produce in their online behavior and using it to measure things about them, such as their mood and cognition. The Greek root *pheno* means "to appear," and phenotype refers to what you can observe about an individual based on the expression of their genes such as freckles, type of earwax, or whether you have a high- or low-pitched voice. But we also express more than just our personalities when we go online, even unwittingly. Think about all the things you do while on the internet. You provide demographic information such as your gender, age, location, e.g., in your social media profiles. You perform web searches, you like your friends' posts, and you post content yourself. Your posts can be mined for a host of different things and reveal more about you than just the meaning of what you wrote.

Researchers at the Chinese Academy of Sciences and Nanyang Technological University discovered that among other data, your linguistic patterns—the patterns of words you use—in your social media posts can reveal your subjective well-being. It's not just what you say—using positive words like *happy* or *awesome*—but how you say it, such as the types of pronouns you use, which is called the structure of your language. They collected posts from 1,785 users of Sina Weibo, a Chinese social media site similar to Twitter, and these participants agreed to have their Weibo social media data downloaded. They asked these users to fill out two well-validated questionnaires: one was the Positive and Negative Affect Schedule (PANAS),[10] to assess a person's affect (how positive or negative they feel), and the other was the Psychological Wellbeing Scale.[11] Together, these questionnaires provide a good picture of a person's subjective well-being. The researchers collected each person's gender, age, the population density of where they live, interactions with other users who follow them, their privacy settings, and the length of their username, as well as the linguistic patterns of their posts. They found that this combination of features correlated quite well with a person's emotional state and psychological well-being.[12] The correlations, which indicate the extent to which variables are related to each other, were both .45. In the field of psychology, a correlation of .45 is impressive—human beings are quite variable, and there are not many measured psychological phenomena that correlate so strongly. More specifically, these researchers discovered different word patterns that correlated positively or negatively with subjective well-being, such as the more that people used the first-person pronoun *I* in their posts, the less positive they felt. That makes sense, as an unhappy person might direct their attention inward towards themselves. This result illustrates how a company that is selling products to de-stress, like spa bath salts, can find out who to target their ads to by using basic information from Twitter posts. If you are in a particular frame of mind, you might be more likely to pay attention to that ad as it might be exactly what you feel you need. But assessing your subjective well-being can be pretty innocuous compared to even more personal information that can be discerned by what you do online. Whether you have major depressive disorder can also be predicted from your publicly available data on Twitter[13] or even from your Instagram photos.[14]

The above studies used demographic information, and the content and photos people posted. But it turns out that even the minimal information of Facebook likes alone can predict your personality traits to a reasonable extent, with correlations between your Facebook likes and the Big 5 personality traits ranging from .29 to .43[15]—again, these are impressive correlations. Facebook likes can also predict to a fair extent people's intelligence, use of addictive substances, age and political views.[16] In fact, if the algorithm analyzes just three hundred of your likes, it knows your personality better than your significant other.[17]

Algorithms can be engineered to affect our attention through leveraging knowledge about our personality, which, as we already saw, companies can discover through our internet behavior. For example, neurotics tend to be more susceptible to stress and fear than non-neurotics.[18] A neurotic will likely pay attention to an image that evokes fear such as a burning house or flood in an insurance ad. Extroverts are more social than introverts, and so if it is discovered that you're an extrovert, a company might target ads to you for a party cruise. This idea is supported by a study that showed that extroverts were more likely to click on the ad "Dance like there's no tomorrow" showing partiers, whereas introverts were more likely to click on the ad "Beauty doesn't have to shout," which showed an individual looking into a mirror.[19]

A lot of data about you and your physical activity can be collected just from your smartphone, and you may not even realize it. In Chapter 3, we discussed how people exhibit rhythms in their attention. You also have rhythms in other behaviors that can say a lot about you too, including your smartphone use: how regularly you use it day to day, how your twenty-four-hour circadian rhythm affects its usage, and even how regular your usage is on an hour-by-hour basis. Researchers from Dartmouth, Stanford and Cambridge University tracked the smartphone usage of 646 college students for seven to fourteen days, collecting data such as the person's physical activity, the ambient sound picked up by the phone, their location, and how much they used their phone. All Big 5 personality traits except for Neuroticism (it is unclear why) could be predicted by these types of rhythms of smartphone usage.[20] Just like with your internet behavior, the data that smartphones collect about you unobtrusively—and it's quite a bit—can be incorporated into algorithms to effectively target your attention.

But algorithms are not just designed for e-commerce ads. Knowing information about you such as your personality and your subjective well-being is also used more broadly by social media and messaging platforms to tailor notifications to you. Not surprisingly, Facebook has filed plenty of patents that are geared to using algorithms to better capture your attention. One patent, for example, is entitled "Determining user personality characteristics from social networking system communications and characteristics."[21] Your personality traits will be used in algorithms to feed you ads and news stories that are more likely to attract your attention. The more you are presented with information that you like and is of interest to you, the more you will pay attention to the notifications, and of course the more time you'll spend on Facebook.

Targeting our most basic instincts

When we receive a Facebook notification that a friend has a new post, our curiosity leads us to click on it. Such social notifications tap into that fundamental property of human relationships—curiosity about others. We receive a notification that our friend has posted something with 143 likes, and then we're off to find out more about it. We expect to feel positive when we see it.

While some notifications require controlled attention to respond to them, others leverage involuntary or automatic attention. Many algorithms are designed to capture our attention because they elicit integral emotions from us such as happiness, surprise, fear or disgust. These types of basic emotional reactions occur spontaneously and automatically without cognitive processing and are called lower-order emotions.[22] Notifications that touch lower-order emotions demand our attention, triggering impulsive responses to click on them. If you see an ad with an image of a totaled car, and especially if you have teenagers, then this will induce fear and horror in you—lower-order emotions that you can't help but feel. If you receive targeted notifications going after your lower-order emotions when you are low in attentional resources or in a bored or a rote state, when you are more susceptible to distraction, you can't help but respond to them.

Anger is one such lower-order emotion that is used to capture your attention. In 2021, former Facebook employee Frances Haugen testified before the US Securities and Exchange Commission.

Among other revelations, she described how Facebook leveraged the fact that people's attention is drawn to posts that are controversial. Facebook weighted posts according to the emojis used, and it promoted posts to the top of users' feeds that had elicited the "angry" emoji. Haugen testified that Facebook's AI program was tweaked to deliberately provide content to people that could be harmful. Eventually, Facebook stopped weighting and including the angry emoji in its algorithm, and it gave more weight to the emojis of "love" and "sad." Facebook claimed that discounting angry emoji posts resulted in algorithms feeding people less misinformation and presumably less disturbing posts, though this has not been tested by scientists outside of the company.[23]

Some posts, however, still reach the masses, such as a BuzzFeed ad with a quiz to test intelligence—most people want to know how smart they are. Your ability to withstand distraction is affected by several things, as you know, such as when you're low in cognitive resources, or if something involves a person in your friend network. Our attention can still fall prey to one-size-fits-all advertising.

Why you are glued to TikTok

To further explain how your attention is captured using algorithms, let's look at the case of TikTok, the popular social media platform. TikTok has a very sophisticated algorithm, called a recommender engine, and it's what helps keep you in an attention trap, glued to those short, mostly fifteen-second videos. The algorithm quickly discovers what engrosses you and tries to keep the momentum going. But before we discuss how any video is recommended to you, we need to back up a step, because to recommend something to you, TikTok needs to collect the right data about you and needs to know what's in that video. For every video that's uploaded to the site, key words, images and descriptors about the content are collected. For example, if you're watching a dance video of someone dancing to "Then Leave" by BeatKing featuring Queendom Come, the engine collects words that describe what the actor is doing (dancing), what the song is ("Then Leave"), and even the genre (rap music). But that's just the high-level view, because in fact, the recommender engine is collecting far more details such as where the actor is dancing: in a bedroom, outside in nature, in a closet, or on a roof. Details of the dancer are included such as "female," "male," "baby" or even "dog," since animals can also be stars on TikTok.

TikTok also collects data about you for the algorithm: things like your gender, your age, your profession, where you live, what you're interested in, and much more. The search engine you use generates lots of details like your IP address and your location to use in the algorithm as well—it then can determine what region of the country you're in, the political orientation of your region, and so on. You will be clustered together with users who are similar to you, and the more people who use Tik-Tok, the more data the company has to work with, the better the recommendations, and the longer your attention is captured.

TikTok even collects information on how much you use the site. How many videos do you watch at a time? How long do you spend on TikTok at a stretch? You can easily pass through one hundred twenty videos, which would only be about thirty minutes of your time, and the more videos you watch, the more information TikTok gets about what you like. The engine will also look for trends such as how many people are watching a particular video, where they're trending, and whether you watch videos of trending topics.

Even though you don't realize it, TikTok's engine also collects data about your context, or what they call a scenario— where and when you're watching TikTok videos. What videos do you like to watch when you're at home? What about when you're far away from your home, say, on vacation? Knowing your scenario can say a lot about your preferences. For example, you might like to watch faster-paced hip-hop dance videos in the morning, and slower-paced videos in the late evening. If TikTok knows your context, say, that it's evening and you're at home, then it will send you videos that you will especially like to watch at that place and time. The right content in the right context increases stickiness to the site.

Despite the fact that my husband and I have watched movies together for years, I can't always predict what movie my husband might enjoy (usually black-and-white, depressing films), and I sometimes get it wrong (sometimes he likes color and action films). TikTok doesn't get it wrong, or at least not for long. If you suddenly decide to watch another kind of dance genre, TikTok's engine is agile, quickly adjusts, and then sends you videos of the new dance genre.

The recommendation engine learns through what is called a feedback loop. It sees what you watch, learns about you, your behavior and context, and then feeds that information back into its engine and makes tweaks. So the loop is this: observe, tweak, present another video, and repeat—all done in the blink of an eye. The more you watch, the more the algorithm knows about what you like or don't like, and the better able it is to fine-tune its targeting and present you with content that will draw your attention.

So now that we know the mechanics, we can turn to the psychological reason for why TikTok holds your attention. I wanted to speak with someone about how their TikTok obsession affects their attention and through my network found Rachel. A professional flutist working on her PhD in music, she seemed an unlikely person to get carried away with TikTok. At thirty-one, she is also a bit older than the typical TikTok user. When she has a lull in her day, she says, she wants to do something mindless. She goes to TikTok out of a combination of boredom and curiosity for quick entertainment. But when she's on TikTok, she described how the content can get funnier and funnier, and she gets sucked in for longer than she planned. Because the stories in the videos are so condensed, within the first five seconds she can usually "heart" (like) a video.

Let's take a look at what happens to Rachel's attention in the fifteen seconds of a TikTok video. Many TikTok videos are constructed like a condensed version of a film in that they have plot development. But they usually just show the first three of the five stages of classic plot development: the introduction, building the tension, and the climax (the last two stages are the falling action and resolution). Many TikTok videos captivate audiences because they end with a surprise. Sometimes there is foreshadowing to create tension, but almost always there is a plot twist in the last second or two, such as people suddenly changing into crazy outfits. Watching Billie Eilish fit an entire ukulele head in her mouth is the climax of one of her TikTok videos (this video does have a plot resolution with her laughing afterwards). Other videos can be plotless, like a Boston terrier dancing salsa to the song "Suavemente." The short video length holds our attention because it reaches the climax so quickly, within fifteen seconds.

When some behavior is positively reinforced, with a reward like laughter, there's a pretty high chance that you'll do it again. B. F. Skinner, the behaviorist psychologist, figured this out in his discovery of operant conditioning. Skinner put animals such as rats into cages (called Skinner boxes). When the rat figured out that when he pressed the lever in the cage, he received a food pellet, a positive reinforcement of that behavior, he kept pressing the lever to keep getting the reward. When you watch a TikTok video that makes you laugh, your laughter becomes the reward, and this feeling reinforces and strengthens your behavior to keep watching more videos. TikTok videos usually tap into your lower-order emotions like laughter or anger or even sadness. When you watch a person dancing down an escalator or see a cute baby smiling to music, you can't help but feel positive. The more videos you watch, the stronger the reinforcement to continue watching.

There is also another reason why our attention is so captivated by TikTok. The laughter caused by watching the video triggers an endogenous opioid release in those parts of the brain that process rewards, and in fact, repeated experiences of laughter over time can lead to neuroplastic changes in the brain.[24] Laughter can also reduce stress.[25] So within fifteen seconds, TikTok videos can reward us with laughter and potentially reduce our stress, and the more time we spend on TikTok, the more we are bonded to the app to reap the rewards. Of course, not all TikTok videos induce laughter—some can induce other emotions like anger.

Time flies when a video is short, fast-paced, has a high degree of "interestingness," and has a surprise plot twist. But time really flies by if the videos on your feed are those that TikTok knows will captivate you. To get a better understanding of how TikTok worked, I watched a lot of videos. I made a serious framing error as I expected to spend only short amounts of time doing it. But every time I started to watch TikTok, I found myself anchored to the screen for long stretches. I knew I had way better things to do, but time flew by, and I found it so hard to pull myself away.

The TikTok recommender engine model is a black box, using an algorithm only known to the company. But we know it works so well because of its feedback loop. You watch a video, and then the algorithm takes over and keeps learning more about your attention. Watching something that makes us laugh is not bad in itself, but it can be when we cannot get out of a behavioral loop and fall into an attention trap, and we've got more important things to take care of.

You can't hide from Instagram

I did not have an Instagram account, and in order to research it, I signed up for it using a fake name. When signing up, it asked if I want to connect with my contacts on Facebook and I declined, so I did not give it my contact list. But then, on the next screen, it sent me suggestions of people to connect with. Of the top twenty suggestions, some were popular people like Selena Gomez or Michelle Obama. But of the rest of the fifteen or so suggestions, seven of them were people I did have a connection with—five Facebook friends, and two who were not Facebook friends but people I knew. One connection in particular struck me as odd. It was a person I had interviewed in New York City in person a few months prior, and the only electronic connection I ever had with this person was a brief email exchange. There are millions of Instagram users, and this was no coincidence.

So I looked up a friend, an expert on online privacy, Bart Knijnenburg, who is a professor at Clemson University, and asked him what was going on. He suspects that it could be the IMEI (International Mobile Equipment Identity) number of my phone (i.e., its unique identifier number assigned by the manufacturer) that is being used to identify me. Likely Facebook, which owns Instagram, also tracks my phone's IMEI. What Bart can only guess—and this is really iffy—is that perhaps at one point, this person who I interviewed may have searched for my profile on Facebook. The algorithm finds your contacts even if you don't want it to.

Instagram—which is part of Meta, and so this point applies to Facebook too—knows the power of social influence over your attention (we'll get into that more in the next chapter). It knows that you're going to be curious about and pay attention to feeds of your friends. Even if you try to hide from your connections like I did, the Instagram algorithm will find you. It's like those boots that keep pursuing me wherever I go online.

The strengths and motivations of algorithms

When you are on the internet, you become part of a digital ecosystem that involves interacting with others, with information, and above all with algorithms. Whether you realize it or not, you are contributing to the development of algorithms. Nearly every action you take on the internet and nearly every digital trace you leave feeds information that is used by algorithms, and like a spouse, partner or enemy, the more they know about you, the better they can predict your behavior.

But algorithms can be wrong. When Mike Ananny, now a professor at University of Southern California, was installing the Grindr app on his smartphone in 2011, he was surprised to see that another app was recommended to him: Sex Offender Search, which enables users to search for sex offenders who live in their area.[26] Grindr is a social networking app for gay and bisexual people that is geared to helping find partners or matches in your location. This association between apps was made by the Android Marketplace algorithm. Ananny is not a sex offender. But some set of instructions incorporated into the marketplace algorithm linked people who download Grindr with the idea that they might also be interested in an app that searches for sex offenders. Algorithms that target our attention can mess up.

But when algorithms work well, what chance does a person have to resist information presented to them that is so customized to match their personality and emotional tendencies? Of course, turning off notifications will shield you from some effects of algorithms. But your best defense against algorithms is to understand how they work, how you cede control of your attention to them, and how your kinetic, rapidly switching attention is driven in part by them as they can lead you to impulsively direct your attention to them. By leveraging your personality traits and online behavior, companies know with high likelihood what videos you will watch, which friends' posts you will read, what you will find interesting when shopping and what you are likely to buy. While a shoe salesperson might give up in trying to sell me something inside of a store, that pair of boots that follows me around on the internet never does. The more I see them, at some point I might just cave in and buy them. Algorithms are designed to manipulate attention—like guided precision missiles, they know exactly how to attack and destroy your attention focus. While my cognitive resources may run low and make me vulnerable, algorithms never lose their power.

CHAPTER EIGHT:

Our Digital Social World

The metaverse, in the public eye after Mark Zuckerberg in 2021 announced it as the future for his company, is a concept that has actually been around for a long time. The idea of the metaverse—where people could enter virtual spaces and interact and access information—comes from the 1992 sci-fi novel *Snow Crash* by Neal Stephenson. Separate metaverses have long existed in the form of early virtual worlds on the internet. In the late 1990s, I was researching one such metaverse, a virtual world called OnLive! Traveler, one of the best I had seen. You opened the application from your laptop and spoke with others using your computer microphone. The system used spatial audio, which meant that it mimicked how we perceive sound in the physical world. If you moved your avatar (which could be a wolf, fish, goddess or other sort of image) closer to another in this virtual environment, then their speech would get louder. If you were in a group, you would hear mumbling unless you directly turned your avatar to face the person speaking. The lips of the avatars moved in sync with one's voice. Being in this environment was fascinating to me. You could meet people from all over the world. I was learning how people behaved and interacted in an early metaverse.

One day I opened OnLive! Traveler and saw something new called Japan World, and clicked on it. Suddenly I was transported into a different 3D simulated landscape and saw three avatars in the distance. I moved my avatar closer to them and introduced myself. These Japanese users backed their avatars away from mine, but then I noticed they each made an unfamiliar movement with their avatars. I realized that they were bowing to me. Though not a design feature built into the system, the Japanese nevertheless had figured out how to mime a bow with their avatars. As we spoke, they moved their avatars a bit closer as if they were straining to hear my English and then moved back again to keep their social distance. I realized how powerful social conventions were—we were each transferring our country's norms into a virtual world, and I was seeing cultural differences (I felt like an aggressive American when I moved too close to them). As I studied people interacting in this virtual world and others, I observed a variety of social conventions used, such as when groups signaled that they were open for others to join in by moving their avatars to make a space for them, politely explaining why one was leaving the world, and keeping a social distance (as the Japanese did). Sometimes people developed unique social conventions, such as turning their avatars upside down to signal that their conversation was private. These virtual worlds were more than just physical computer systems—they actually were social systems.

Many of these conventions came about ad hoc—there were no written rules or instructions on how to behave in the virtual worlds, except to be civil. Studying these virtual worlds made me aware of how our behavior on the internet is very much guided, even driven, by our social natures. People naturally adopted common conventions about behavior that guided them in how they used the system, as I wrote in a paper with Barbara Becker.[1]

Email, Slack and social media like Facebook are also social systems. Despite the vast differences in perspectives and backgrounds of its users, these media provide a shared framework for communication. Everyone has a common understanding that there are some basic social conventions used with them. For example, there are expectations with email that we should respond to a message (though not everyone follows this), and often there is social pressure to respond fast. If someone is much higher up on the social hierarchy than ourselves, we might send them email, but we probably wouldn't text them. Because email, Slack and social media are systems made up of people, they incorporate social dynamics, i.e., people can be affected by others' behaviors. We can be socially influenced to participate, we trade in what's called social capital, we build online identity, and those with power can affect others in interactions. Of course, people are different, and some are more influenced by such social forces than others.

If we look at these media as social systems, then it can help us understand why we spend so much time on them, why we have such a conflicted relationship with email, and why we jump to answer a text message. When we interact with others, we expect to get some kind of social reward—whether it be status, friendship or resources. To explore how our social natures affect our susceptibility to distractions, we need to dig deeper into examining human social behavior. In this chapter, we'll look at how our basic social natures contribute to explaining why our attention is drawn so strongly to email, texting and social media, and why we are so easily interrupted even by ourselves.

But first, let's take a look at two historical examples showing how media other than the internet—such as radio and books—can socially influence our behavior, even indirectly. In 1932, a struggling Hungarian man, Rezső Seress, was determined to make it big as a songwriter. This poor chap refused to get a nine-to-five job but wasn't getting published, and his girlfriend left him on what happened to be a Sunday. So he wrote a song with melancholy lyrics, "Gloomy Sunday," where the narrator describes his sadness on the passing of a lover. There was an upside for Seress: the song became an international hit. However, the lyrics were so disturbing that hundreds of suicides in the 1930s were attributed to this song, and the BBC banned it from the radio until 2002.

Granted, the world was looking bleak at the time, with the rise of fascism in Germany and with the world in the throes of the Depression. But there was plenty of circumstantial evidence that listening to the song might have pushed people over the edge (for example, some victims had a copy of the sheet music in their pockets). However, even before radio and newspapers were the mass media of the day, the writer Goethe showed how social influence can occur indirectly. In 1774, Goethe published his novel *Die Leiden des jungen Werthers (The Sorrows of Young Werther)*. Goethe was hopelessly in love with Charlotte Buff, who was engaged to someone else. In the novel, which is partly autobiographical, the main character, Werther, takes his own life due to being tortured by his unrequited love. Like "Gloomy Sunday," this was another tale of lost love that ended in suicide, and to which a spate of suicides in the eighteenth century was attributed. The book was banned in three countries.

Today, social influence through social media is often much more direct and targeted, by spreading misinformation; influencing health, like eating behaviors[2] and vaccine attitudes;[3] and even affecting financial decisions such as cryptocurrency trading.[4] Anyone can start a social trend like losing weight, designing unusual foods and drinks, and creating new fashion, where influencers take the reins as opposed to clothing companies and retailers. Popular fads like flared yoga pants got their start through Instagram.[5] Written expressions that originated in social media like *hashtag*, *LOL* and *BRB* have drifted into everyday language use.[6] But our distractions and attention can also be socially influenced by the internet on a much more subtle level, in ways that you may not realize.

Our attention can be socially influenced

People can exert a social influence that can be so strong that it can lead others to do things even against their rational judgment, as demonstrated in a classic study by the social psychologist Solomon Asch[7] in 1956. Asch became fascinated with the power of influence based on his own experience. As a young child in Poland, one night at a Passover dinner, he watched his grandmother pour an extra glass of wine, which he was told was intended for the prophet Elijah. As Asch later recounted, he was so thoroughly convinced that Elijah would come to the dinner table that when he became a psychologist, he decided to study how far social influence could change people's behavior.

In Asch's experiment, a person first sat alone in a room and was asked to judge whether two lines of clearly different lengths were similar or not, and the individual always gave the correct answer. However, when the same person sat in a room with other people, who were secretly part of the experimental team, and who one after the other stated that the lines were the same, the unwitting person followed the group opinion and reported the lines to be similar in length. Asch's experiment demonstrated how a group could pressure one to conform. Interestingly, when a modern version of the same experiment was done later with robots, it did not work[8]—apparently people are not socially influenced by and don't feel the need to conform to machines, which is quite reassuring. But on the internet, we don't know who is human or a bot posting on social media.

On the internet, we are aware of the social presence of others even though we may not be directly interacting with them.

Digital traces of others signal their presence—their posts, images and comments. When we post on Twitter or Facebook, we are aware that there is an audience out there who is consuming our social media and likely someone who needs something from us, if only a reply. That awareness is also found when reading email: some people are so acutely cued to the presence of others that they report hearing an "inner reading voice" of the email sender. This is actually not uncommon in general—81 percent of people surveyed report hearing voices at least sometimes as they read text.[9]

Young people are very vulnerable to social influence. The speed of online interactions amplifies the urgency and demands of a message,[10] and this heightens peer influence to stay connected. On top of this, being able to access social media anytime and anywhere on mobile devices reinforces the fast cycle of responses, keeping up peer pressure, and we know this is related to young adult alcohol and drug use.[11] Of course, what people do on social media leaves a lasting record, as you probably know from the fact that most companies now screen the social media accounts of job candidates, looking for any evidence of unseemly behavior.[12]

There is a neural basis that can explain, at least partly, how social media exerts influence on young people. This is shown through imaging the brains of people when they view the number of likes they receive on their accounts. Likes provide social validation or endorsement by peers. The area of the brain associated with the reward system is the nucleus accumbens, and in adolescents, this area has heightened sensitivity. In an experiment conducted by researchers at Temple University and UCLA, sixty-one high school and college students of ages thirteen to twenty-one were brought to a laboratory, but before they came, they were asked to submit to the experimenters Instagram photos from their own accounts. Participants were told that their peers would be seeing these photos on an internal social network (in reality they didn't—the experimenters manipulated the number of likes, giving half the photos many likes, and half the photos few likes). Based on fMRI images, the nucleus accumbens in the brains of these young people showed greater activation when they saw their Instagram photos with many likes compared to few likes.[13] The brain activation increased with age for the high schoolers, but not for the college students, suggesting that there is a peak age of sixteen to seventeen for peer influence.[14] This study shows how receiving lots of likes activates their reward system, and young people may keep self-interrupting out of a greater desire to receive social rewards. In fact, my studies of young people suggest this to be the case—we found that heavy social media use goes hand in hand with high multitasking. But it's a particular kind of social media use that's related to multitasking. Those people who experienced more interruptions, switching their attention faster, used more social media that involved two-way interactions, like Facebook, whereas those who switched their attention less tended to use sites that involved primarily one-way interaction: video streaming sites like YouTube.[15]

It is not just young people, but those of all ages, who are driven to keep up with social media, because we feel social pressure to keep up with interaction. In a public forum like Facebook or Twitter, expectations are heightened for interaction since the whole public sphere is waiting for a response. The rewards we get from interactions—likes, shares or comments—further reinforce the attention we give to these media.

The attention we give to our in-group

Social influence can happen in strange ways on the internet. It turns out that just knowing a relatively small bit of information about where a stranger on the internet is physically located can affect how much social influence they have over us.

My graduate student Erin Bradner and I did a study that

demonstrates this. We had ninety-eight subjects come to our laboratory, and they were all given three tasks to work on with a partner. These measured three different types of social behaviors: cooperation (with the Prisoner Dilemma task, used in game theory, and which measures whether a person decides to cooperate with the partner or not); persuasion (using the Desert Survival Task, which measures the extent to which the partner could persuade the subject to change their ranking of items to use for surviving in a desert); and deception (with the Paulhus Deception Scales, which measure the extent to which the subject answers questions truthfully or not that the partner asks them, e.g., "I always obey laws, even if I'm unlikely to get caught"). They interacted with the partner either through video conferencing or text messaging, like they might do on the internet. In reality, the partner was part of the experimental team. The confederate wore a wig and glasses so that no one would recognize her—indeed, she looked quite different with the disguise. Half the subjects were told that the partner was in the same city as them in southern California, Irvine, and half the subjects were told that the partner was across the country in Boston. The backdrop in the video conferencing was exactly the same, the text messages were exactly the same, and the confederate was the same in both conditions. The only thing that was different was where the subject believed the person they were interacting with was located. It turns out that when subjects were told that the partner was in the distant city, they cooperated less, were less persuaded by, and gave more deceptive portrayals of themselves to the partner.[16] It didn't matter if the partner's image could be seen on video or if only text was used—the same results occurred. This finding shows how even the subtlest of social information that we discern from others on the internet, such as where someone is located, can have potent effects on our behaviors. Apparently distance still matters on the internet even though we can exchange messages with people across the globe nearly instantaneously.

In this experiment, the partner's proximity may have signaled they were in the same in-group as the subject. Being far away may have signaled that they were in an out-group. People have an innate tendency to categorize themselves into an in-group and to distinguish themselves from others in the out-group, likely to enhance their self-esteem.[17] You may not be as likely to cooperate with someone in an out-group and may be less persuadable by them and even deceive them more. In-groups can be formed by sharing properties other than proximity, of course. One person who posted for years in the online subreddit Atheism described how identifying with an in-group on this site helped him in his real life: after thirty years of living in a conservative Colorado community where atheism is anathema, only now could he finally begin to open up about his beliefs to others in his hometown in person.

In our everyday use of the internet, you might be less likely to answer an email from someone who you believe is not in your in-group—say, someone outside your organization or from another country. Conversely, you're probably more likely to answer an email from someone you believe to be in your in-group, like someone in the same job, a fellow hobbyist or resident of the same city. I know this is true for myself—if I can't find clues from an email sender who I don't know, to indicate we might share something in common, then I usually pass over that email.

Managing our online identities

Our identities in the digital world can be even more rewarding than our identities in the physical world. Someone working at Target in the physical world can be a star on YouTube. A case in point is Tony Piloseno, who, while in college, worked at a paint store, and became famous as a TikTok star where his videos showed unusual ways to mix paint. Some of his videos amassed over one million views. In one video, he smashes fresh blueberries into white paint and it looks like a blueberry milkshake. The video went viral, and he got fired from the paint store,[18] but now he has his own paint brand, works at another paint store and continues to maintain his identity as a paint-mixing artist on TikTok.

We put a lot of attention and time into constructing our identities online. Our relationship with the internet can well be described by Shakespeare's famous line in *As You Like It*: "All the world's a stage and all the men and women merely players." Sociologist Erving Goffman echoed Shakespeare in 1959 when referring to people as actors in a social setting: "In their capacity as performers, individuals will be concerned with maintaining the impression that they are living up to the many standards by which they and their products are judged."[19] However, in our digital age, the internet is our vast stage. Though Goffman was referring to our everyday life in the "real world," on the internet we also manage the impressions we want others to have of our online selves. In a face-to-face setting, we're pretty good at impression management. For example, you can choose what to wear to a party, and you might carefully pick who to mingle with when you arrive. But we also do impression management online, and because we're human and because the internet easily allows us to create false impressions, we can overdo it. For example, it was found that people inflated their self-importance in their Facebook status updates and for the most part were not aware of it.[20] TikTok offers a video editing tool to make it easier to manipulate images, and this feature has gone viral, with people using it to alter their appearances. Even Zoom has a feature called "Touch up my appearance."

Constructing our identity on the internet can be complicated. Young people especially, but also the rest of us, have to navigate context collapse, where we have many different and distinct groups of friends on social media. How you present yourself to your work colleagues on LinkedIn can be quite different from how you present yourself to your parents or friends on Instagram. You don't want to post a drunken photo of yourself meant for your college friends when your grandmother is also in your friend network. There are multiple presentations of ourselves that we have to manage. Building an online identity and maintaining it can be rewarding but can also be a time sink. In the early metaverses that I visited, identity did not seem so consequential. But online identity is much more significant today (for example, in screening job applicants or dating), and if a single all-encompassing metaverse ever comes to fruition, our online identity will most likely take on much greater importance.

The economy of social capital

Social media platforms like Instagram, TikTok or Facebook tap into our basic human desire to reap rewards through interacting with others. The internet is a marketplace of social capital. Social capital is the benefit we get from being in a group: we exchange resources through relationships—these can be social, intangible or tangible resources. You respond to email or Slack because you expect that someday your colleague will help you in return. In the physical world, I might run to the grocery store for you, but then I would also expect that you'll return the favor for me someday when I'm in a pinch. If an acquaintance invites you to an important event at their organization, you would likely reciprocate in some way. Social capital is valuable to us because it helps us sustain and grow relationships. It is like a sales credit you can redeem sometime in the future.

Joan, a financial analyst who participated in one of our studies, sees answering email as an investment: "I always respond right away to emails from admins in my department because I know there are times when I'll be depending on them for quick action to my emails." Her comment reflects why we want to maintain a balance of social capital with colleagues, friends and sometimes even strangers in our online interactions. You'll answer email right away from someone you suspect may, say, offer you a job in the future. Because social capital is such a powerful social mechanism, we remain on alert and respond to messages from people who we feel can offer us resources, whether it be friendship, information or social connections.

Our desire to gain social capital keeps our attention drawn to social media. On social media, people garner different types of resources, which the sociologist Robert Putnam calls bonding and bridging social capital.[21] With bonding social capital, people receive emotional support through their close ties on social media. On the other hand, bridging social capital refers to the information that people glean through access to, and interaction with, a large set of diverse people—these can be acquaintances or friends of friends. A site like Facebook offers benefits from both bonding and bridging capital because people can benefit emotionally from their small close-knit circle of friends, but also because they can get information from a wider diverse Facebook friend circle.[22] The more diverse types of people that you have connections with, the more different, and potentially valuable, information you might have access to. A person with 2,000 Facebook friends has a large account of bridging social capital they can draw on, for example, when asking the question of where to find an apartment. The large circle of friends offers what the sociologist Mark Granovetter called the strength of weak ties—a finding that shows that people are more likely to get jobs through contacts with whom they have weak social connections as opposed to close friends.[23] Gaining more bridging social capital resources has a cost, though, on our attention: it comes with more notifications and more people to keep up with.

Accumulating social capital resources takes effort. We're not going to get it just by scrolling through Facebook. We reap more benefits when we actually contribute information and interact with others, compared to if we just passively read posts.[24] We may not realize, though, that our desire to build up social capital resources can drive us to invest time on email and social media. And of course it can draw our attention away from other work we need to accomplish.

Social power influences our attention online

Our attention and distractions on the internet are also influenced by the power that exists in our relationships. Bertrand Russell, a keen observer of social behavior, explains, "The laws of social dynamics are laws which can only be stated in terms of power."[25] Humans have always been affected by power—wanting to amass it or being subservient to the power of others. Power is the capacity to control others or to have knowledge that others don't have. We may have power over others in ways that we don't realize. Someone who knows the geography of London may have power over a visitor trying to navigate their way around the city. Power relations can be equal, or unbalanced, where some people have power over others. Parents have power over their children; managers have power over their employees; celebrities have power over their fans; a potential employer has power over a job applicant; and John Gotti had power over the Gambino crime family. But possibly John Gotti's mother even had power over him.

Power is built into social hierarchies. We are all naturally part of social hierarchies, albeit informally—with our colleagues at work, neighborhood block association, book club, sports team, friend group, and of course our high school class was a big one. People want to achieve status in their social groups, and no one wants to lose their footing in the social stratum. When people have social power over others, they have control over some type of valued resource that those with less power want. This resource could be money, a job, or even influence—someone you just met may have the power to introduce you into a social circle that you are longing to be part of. So not surprisingly, social systems like email and social media also involve power relations. Basic human motives of striving for power and wanting to maintain our position in some social hierarchy are reflected in the attention we give to the internet.

The idea of power can be primed and activated in our memory, which suggests that we can respond to it in nonconscious ways.[26] Cues of power relations can occur in our email or social media, which in turn can prime us to think about status. Consider someone's email signature that has "Director" in it or a Twitter handle with "PhD," or an email using a very formal tone. In fact, power is reflected not just in these types of signals but also in how we actually write emails. An analysis of email use in two academic departments by Niki Panteli from the University of Bath found differences in how emails were written based on a person's status. Emails sent by people of higher status (e.g., professors) were terser and more formal, using signatures, whereas emails sent by those of lower status (e.g., support staff) tended to use greetings and were more personal and friendly.[27] A study by Eric Gilbert, now at the University of Michigan, also shows differences in power and status in the writing in emails, in this case reflected even in the phrases people use.[28] Utilizing the Enron corpus of over half a million emails, Gilbert found that people of lower status use polite and deferential language like "thought you would" in their emails directed to those with higher power, whereas those higher in the hierarchy use phrases like "let's discuss" to those lower in status. Even on Twitter, social power can be discerned, interestingly enough, with how emoticons are used: people with higher social power use them more often.[29] So, whether we consciously realize it or not, we all communicate power when we use media regardless of whether our status is high or low.

But there are other signals of power on the internet, and not just in our messages. The number of followers a person has on Twitter or YouTube or Facebook conveys if they are an influencer and how much power they have. We want to move up the social hierarchy and achieve more power, and if a celebrity follows you on Twitter, well, you've won the lottery.

Power in relationships plays a key role in where we direct our attention. You can probably guess that people of lower status pay more attention to people of higher status than the other way around.[30] You probably spend more time anxiously checking for that email from your manager than your manager does checking for your email. We jump to answer messages from people who have some power over us. Those in power have the ability to control the outcomes of others.[31] We respond to email and Slack and text messages from those who have power over us because we may then be able to have some influence over our own fate. We thus stay on high alert—we keep monitoring our inboxes for key messages—because missing them can have consequences. Power relations can even affect multitasking— participants in my studies report that they prioritize and switch to tasks not only based on deadlines but also if others involved in that work have some type of power over them, such as their manager or an influential colleague. The internet is an entire web of social relations, with all the consequent complexity of power built in. Having low power can psychologically chain us to the internet as we hope to move up the social stratum, but also, having high power can psychologically chain us to the internet to maintain power.

Our attention to online relationships

On the internet, we create patterns of relationships, like friend networks, much like in the real world. Social media platforms give us the building blocks to do so, and how we structure our networks in turn affects our attention. We choose who to include, and how many to include. But there is a limit on the number of people we can *meaningfully* interact with. Robin Dunbar, a British anthropologist, found that the number of people with whom humans can naturally maintain stable interpersonal relationships is about one hundred fifty, and this number holds not only in developed societies but also across a number of different modern hunter-gatherer societies, such as the Inuit.[32] (Dunbar also found that the number of people within this circle with whom we can have deep emotional relationships is only about five.) According to Dunbar, the number of one hundred fifty is based on both a theory of the limits on the neocortical processing capability of the brain and, of course, the limits on time that people can invest. Now, we might imagine that online social networks can expand people's capabilities and reduce time constraints. It's quicker to send a text message to a friend to discuss a problem than to spend time on a phone conversation or meet up for a drink. It takes time to coordinate social plans, to travel somewhere, and of course face-to-face conversation lasts longer than electronic messaging. But it seems that we can't overcome our biological and time constraints even with online networking. A study of nearly two million Twitter users found the number of people with whom one can have a stable interpersonal online relationship to be similar to the Dunbar number—between one hundred and two hundred people.[33] Dunbar also examined the frequency of contact within people's friend networks on Facebook and Twitter and validated the original average number of one hundred fifty people.

So, how can we make use of the Dunbar number? It can help us focus on social connections that are more worthwhile for us. Of course, it's not easy to limit our relationships to a cluster of one hundred fifty people and disregard others. But you should think about the types of social capital you are exchanging and what benefits you are receiving. To help manage your attention, you need to first change your expectations of the benefits that your social network can provide. Remember that a social networking site like Facebook is not designed to develop new friendships but rather to maintain old ones. So don't expect that you can invest your time to develop close or even stable relationships with one thousand people. Sure, you might get rewards from time to time through bridging social capital (the resources you get from a diverse set of people), but consider carefully the trade-off of rewards that your network size brings you compared to the time that you invest in it. A smaller network compared to a large network brings more advantages, as a study of the online career network XING showed: the highest success in getting job offers came through a network of one hundred fifty people,[34] which coincidentally happens to be the Dunbar number. I'm not suggesting you unfriend anyone (though you might), but rather I'm asking you to think about the costs and benefits you get from your relationships and time spent on social media. Consider the framing errors from Chapter 2: people can often be poor judges of what choices will bring benefits and how much of their time they expect to spend with their choice. Invest your limited time with those whose relationships you really value and can benefit from. Consider that a large network likely means more time invested, and you may not reap the rewards for the time you put in. Before you jump to check social media, ask yourself what you really expect to gain in terms of social rewards. You can most likely reap social rewards by investing far less time than you do. Have you already received sufficient rewards (at least for today) such that you don't need to spend more time there? Think of your time spent on social media as providing increasing marginal returns.

The pressures of online social systems are particularly potent for young people. Pulling out of social media for many is like cutting off a lifeline to their world. For example, one young person in one of my studies expressed how she couldn't free herself: "I tried to quit it before, but it's almost like a necessity because all my friends and my coworkers are on there."[35] And so young people check their accounts again and again, to receive rewards, seek affirmation, achieve and maintain their status in their social circle, participate in peer evaluation and comparison, and of course to feel socially connected. To make a real difference, actions to help young people pull out or reduce time on social media need to be taken at a broader societal level, which I'll talk about in the last chapter.

If the metaverse ever comes about, that will be the biggest online social system of all, and if we are concerned about our attention now, then we really need to be prepared for it. Sadly, the early virtual worlds like OnLive! Traveler didn't last too long. The metaverse will be a much larger empire of tech companies, and because the plan is for it to encompass nearly everything we do online, it will be even harder than today to resist its social dynamics. Being human means being susceptible to social influence, feeling driven to build and maintain our identity and connect with in-groups, wanting to gain social capital, and wanting to achieve social status. It is this interconnected digital world, and the corresponding social forces and dynamics bound up with it, that lure our attention to keep up with it and distract us from other goals. But we also have individual differences and unique personalities, and we'll next look at how these influence our attention behaviors when on our devices.

CHAPTER NINE:

Personality and Self-Regulation

We are all born with a certain set of qualities that distinguish us and make us unique. Being the life of the party is natural for some, while for others, staying at home to watch a movie is much more preferable. Some people are curious and adventurous, and others prefer familiar routines. Some people can be prone to negative thoughts while others seem to never worry. An individual can even have different personality traits that don't seem to align. The brilliant pianist Vladimir Horowitz, who was emotional and interpretive in his piano playing, was so routinized that he ate the same dinner of Dover sole and asparagus every night, even to the extent that the food had to be airlifted daily into Moscow when he played there.[1] Our personality influences how we act—we can make changes in our behavior, but we can't help who we are to begin with. Not only do the design of the internet, algorithms and social forces influence attention behavior in the digital world, but an individual's personality itself also plays a role.

Some people are very good at controlling their emotions, thoughts and behavior—in other words, they are adept at self-regulation. Our ability for self-regulation doesn't determine, but can influence, our digital behaviors. Hardly anyone has done more to bring the idea of self-regulation into public awareness than the personality psychologist Walter Mischel. He was a professor of mine in graduate school at Columbia, and I fondly recall discussions that I had with him when I took his class covering delay of gratification. What impressed me was how he listened to students and took our ideas and opinions seriously. This gentle professor with a searing intellect moved mountains in the field of psychology. Whereas most people may dream of one lasting contribution in a field, Mischel's work actually created two paradigm shifts, each a major shakeup of an accepted way of thinking about psychological phenomena.

In one significant change, he introduced a new way to think about self-regulation. He is well-known for studying self-regulation through his marshmallow studies, named so by the popular media because he used, well, marshmallows as a reward. When he was at Stanford in the 1970s, Mischel would have young children come into his laboratory, ask them to sit at a table, and then would place a tasty-looking marshmallow in front of them. The children were told that they could either eat the marshmallow now or, if they waited fifteen minutes, they could have a second marshmallow. This seemingly simple choice of whether or not to eat a marshmallow right away, i.e., whether they could delay gratification, turned out to have profound implications and predicted a number of life outcomes, even decades later. Children who were not able to resist that single marshmallow grew up to have lower SAT scores, less job success, higher rates of obesity, and a host of other poor outcomes. Children who could resist the marshmallow and wait were much better able to concentrate later on in their teens.[2]

Mischel's work has been replicated numerous times over the decades.[3] Who could have imagined that the ability to resist a tiny marshmallow could predict life outcomes forty years later?[4] When I was a graduate student, I recall discussing with Mischel why a young child's behavior in this simple experiment might predict outcomes later in life: What psychological mechanism might be responsible? One idea was that children who could delay gratification might be better able to imagine or visualize things in their mind, to help them occupy those fifteen minutes waiting for that treat.

Mischel's other great contribution arrived with his 1968 book *Personality and Assessment*.[5] Up until then, and even now, there is a deep assumption among personality theorists that personality traits such as Extroversion are relatively stable. Mischel challenged this notion, showing in his studies that personality can change with context. There are cues in any situation that can guide people on how to act. I may be an extrovert among my family but become quite introverted if I find myself among a group of strangers. This insight was inspired by Mischel's own experience when he fled with his parents from the Nazi occupation of Vienna in 1938. He was ten when they came to the US. His parents settled in Brooklyn and opened up a five-and-dime store, and Mischel helped out after school, making deliveries. This Austrian immigrant ended up becoming his class valedictorian and went on to get his PhD in clinical psychology. But it was his parents' story that influenced his thinking about personality. While in Vienna, his father had been a confident individual who worked as a chemist, and his mother had been a neurotic, but in the US, their personalities underwent profound reversals. Working at the store, his father became depressive, while his mother worked as a waitress and became confident.

Their countries changed, their lifestyles changed, and their dispositions changed. Mischel used this observation to challenge a long-standing assumption of consistency in personality, and he developed a theory that personality is situational. The other camp maintained that personality is relatively stable across situations, especially after one reaches the age of thirty.[6]

The two camps with their contrasting theories—personality as situational versus personality as stable—were in a stalemate until the idea of a unifying theory of personality was proposed by Mischel and Yuichi Shoda.[7] The notion here is that there can be both a stable underlying personality system and personality states that change with the situation. So how one responds to a situation does have a pattern as it is guided by an underlying deeper personality system. A person who acts quite extroverted in Greenwich Village might be less extroverted when visiting Greenwich, Connecticut.

Personality can be thought of as a system that characterizes how people think, experience emotions, and behave in the world. Perhaps the most commonly used theory of personality today, the Big 5, has an interesting history. Its development originated with an idea called the lexical hypothesis, which proposed that personality characteristics that are meaningful should become part of people's language. Words like *abrasive*, *garrulous* or *personable* should reflect traits that describe people. So it should be possible, then, to derive personality traits from language, which is exactly what two psychologists, Gordon Allport and Henry Odbert, tried in the 1930s. They went through Webster's dictionary and found 17,953 words that described aspects of personality. They then winnowed the list down to about 4,500 adjectives that described observable behaviors. This was still too many words, so in 1948, the psychologist Raymond Cattell used a brand-new technology, the computer, to find similarities in these words and clustered them into sixteen traits. Such distinct traits could be used to explain and assess personality. Mischel, though, argued in 1968 that personality assessments couldn't predict personality because it was situational. This put a damper on the research because Mischel was so influential in the field.

Other psychologists picked the project up again, starting in the mid-1970s, among them a team led by Paul Costa and Robert McCrae, who found that personality could be described in terms of five core traits, now known as the Big 5.[8] These were Extroversion (prefers being with people or alone); Agreeableness (gets along with others or is difficult); Conscientiousness (diligent or laissez-faire); Neuroticism (anxious or emotionally stable); and Openness (open to new experiences or cautious and closed-minded). Mischel was still a bit skeptical about the Big 5 traits, believing them to be a taxonomy that didn't really explain why people feel and behave the way they do.[9] One can describe a person as neurotic, but it doesn't explain why a person might get depressed when they move to another city. Also, it doesn't explain how personality might indeed be shaped by people's societal and cultural roles, which, according to Mischel, would show how the situation influences personality. A test to measure the Big 5 traits was developed in 1998 by Oliver John at Berkeley and Verónica Benet-Martínez at the University of California Davis.[10] Despite Mischel's continued criticisms,[11] the Big 5 survey came into widespread use. You can take the Big 5 survey yourself to find your own personality profile.[i]

You might be wondering whether, following Mischel's thinking of the importance of context, personality might align with a person's culture. People tend to stereotype personalities of people in different countries. We might think of the British as reserved, but it turns out that they are among the highest scorers in the world on the Extroversion trait.[12] We might think of the Japanese as being shy and introverted, but there is no difference on their Extroversion scores from Puerto Ricans. We might also think of German Swiss as being highly Conscientious, but their scores are not much different on this trait than people in Chile or Spain.[13] But there are some gender differences across cultures, with the strongest differences shown in American and Euro-

---

i   https://www.ocf.berkeley.edu/~johnlab/bfi.htm

pean cultures. Women tend to score higher in Agreeableness, Neuroticism, and Openness to feelings (a facet of the broader trait of Openness), whereas men tend to score higher on Extroversion and Openness to ideas (another facet of Openness).[14] Despite what anyone may think, however, stereotypical personality traits based on culture is unfounded. Personality may be expressed differently in certain contexts, but it cannot be generalized to a whole country. When we consider how personality affects our digital behavior, we should realize that we are all in this together irrespective of our country and culture.

Personality and internet use

Personality can explain a lot of behaviors. For example, you may not have guessed that personality partly explains even what genres people like to read: Openness predicts reading literature and suspense but not romantic fiction.[15] Neuroticism is tied both to gaming addicts, and also strangely enough to people who are non-gamers.[16] Using the internet for unethical academic behavior (like plagiarism) is associated with people who score low in Agreeableness, low in Conscientiousness, and high in Neuroticism.[17] The Big 5 also explain some internet behaviors. Extroverts have more Facebook friends, for example.[18]

But aside from these specific online behaviors, whether personality affects how much people use the internet or how much they use social media has long been controversial. The findings have been mixed, with some studies showing, for example, on the one hand, that Extroversion is negatively related to how much someone uses the internet, while other studies show no relationship. Similar confusion has been found with the other four personality traits: the results seem to be all over the map. One problem with these past studies is that they mostly used samples from different college student populations. Students who attend Harvard may use the internet very differently from students who go to Cal State Fullerton, and so the results may not be comparable. Further, college students are not necessarily a diverse sample as they tend to be white and middle class. Also, most of these studies were done within a ten-year period since the mid-2000s, a time when the internet had been changing fast.

One year while on sabbatical, I looked up my old graduate student colleague Yoav Ganzach, who is now a professor at Tel Aviv University. Both Yoav and I were interested in personality, and we discussed the idea of how personality might influence internet use. We set out to try to resolve the controversial findings. To overcome the potential bias from unique college student samples, we wanted to examine a large, representative sample of individuals. It was hard to find such a sample, but after searching around for some time, we decided to use data from the National Longitudinal Survey of Youth, a program of the US Bureau of Labor Statistics that follows individuals over years and collects survey data on topics such as employment, education, and health, but also internet usage. The sample is representative of the diversity in America, including African Americans, Hispanics, and other ethnicities, as well as economically disadvantaged whites who might not show up in a college survey. Our sample was comprised of 6,921 individuals who had an average age of twenty-six, older than the typical college student. People were asked how often they used the internet overall, and how often specifically they used the internet for different types of activities: communication, entertainment, education and shopping. All respondents had also taken the Big 5 personality survey.

Now that we had our data, we set out to correlate personality traits with these different types of internet activity. We found that the higher people score on Extroversion, Conscientiousness and Neuroticism, the more time they spend on the internet.[19] Extroverts seek information outside of themselves, and so not surprisingly, they spent more time than introverts on communicating with others, on internet entertainment, educational activities and online shopping. But conscientious people who like structure and planning presented counterintuitive results. We were surprised to discover that they spent more time on entertainment and shopping sites compared to people who are less diligent. One would think that conscientious people who have strict game plans in their work may not have the time to spend on entertainment and shopping. But there is a method to their madness. Conscientious people rely on online sites for taking breaks in their work (as opposed to taking physical breaks like walks) because online sites offer minimal time disruption for their work time, which I'll talk about shortly. So conscientious people may use entertainment and shopping activities strategically to balance out stress since they are such hard workers. This brings us to neurotics, the royalty of worriers, whose results showed they spend more time on the internet than non-neurotics. Their behavior may be explained as an attempt to relieve anxiety. We found that neurotics also spent more time communicating with others, more time in educational activities, and more time shopping. Neurotics may thus seek retail therapy.

This study does seem to suggest, then, that our personality is tied to how much we use the internet and to the types of online activities we do. However, when we look next at how personality affects our attention spans when we use our devices, the story becomes a lot more complicated.

Neuroticism and Impulsivity

In another year, and another beautiful summer in Seattle, I thought it would be interesting to examine how personality might affect our multitasking on our computers. Together with my colleagues Mary Czerwinski and Shamsi Iqbal at Microsoft Research, we thought very carefully about the different Big 5 personality traits. What first came to mind is that Neuroticism would be tied to rapid, kinetic attention-switching. Neurotics tend to reanalyze past events over and over again in their minds, like part of a music track on continuous replay. This type of continuous instant replay in the mind uses cognitive resources—a lot of them. When resources are being used up by worrying about the past, then there are fewer attentional resources available to devote to the current activity. Those who score high in Neuroticism in personality tests also tend to perform worse on selective attention tasks where they have to pay attention to some things and ignore distracting stimuli,[20] much like the Stroop task. One might expect, then, that neurotics may have more trouble focusing their attention when on their devices.

We also reasoned that another personality trait that could influence multitasking behavior is Impulsiveness, which is the opposite of delayed gratification. Impulsive people have difficulty restraining themselves from acting on their urges. In the same way that they would not be able to resist that marshmallow in front of them, an impulsive person might be unable to resist clicking on that email notification or even checking email without any notification.

Impulsivity has different facets that can manifest in different ways in our behavior. One way is in the short term, as in grabbing that marshmallow right away. This type of impulsive behavior is called Urgency. Another facet of Impulsivity is called Lack of Perseverance, the tendency to give up too easily on a task. If you're a person who gives up pretty quickly on writing that report when it gets hard, or when number-crunching gets complicated, then you might score high on Lack of Perseverance. We decided that both aspects of Impulsiveness could perhaps explain short attention spans on our devices. Scoring high on Urgency would suggest that one is not able to control responding to external or internal distractions, and scoring high on Lack of Perseverance would suggest that one might readily give up on the task at hand and switch attention, perhaps even without any external distraction. You can take the UPPS Impulsive Behavior Scale (UPPS) survey to see how you score on Impulsivity.[ii]

To see if personality had any relation to attention-switching, we recruited forty participants (twenty females, twenty males) in a high-tech organization in various work roles. We gave individuals the Big 5 personality test. We also measured individuals' impulsiveness using the UPPS survey,[21] focusing on the two facets of Impulsivity described above. Last, we also measured each individual's perceived stress using the Perceived Stress Scale.[22] Our participants were asked to work as they ordinarily did in their day-to-day usage of computers, and for twelve days, we logged their computer activity, which enabled us to measure how long people's attention was on their computer screens. Participants were informed that their computer activity would be logged and they could turn off the logging anytime they wanted (no one did). As in other studies, we did not record any content, just the time stamps of the applications they used and URLs they visited. We could tell when the computer entered sleep mode, which indicated that a person was not online, and so we disregarded that data. The upshot was that we had precise measures in seconds of how long people spent on each computer screen, which is a good proxy for the length of their attention span, and to what they were paying attention.

As we guessed, we found that the higher a person scored in the Neuroticism personality trait, the shorter was their average attention duration on a computer screen, as we reported in a paper called "Neurotics Can't Focus."[23] A lot of things can create interference for Neurotics on their current task at hand, as they are worriers. We also found that the higher a person scored in Urgency, the shorter was their attention duration on their computer screen—and this was a very strong correlation. But we did not find any relationship between the trait of Lack

---

ii   https://www.impulsivity.org/measurement/upps-p/. I recommend taking the long-form version of fifty-nine questions.

of Perseverance and attention duration. So if you are someone who tends to give up when the going gets tough, chances are it doesn't necessarily affect your attention span on your computer.

Since Neuroticism and the facet of Urgency in Impulsiveness are tied to more frequent attention-shifting, this suggests that there may be an underlying personality trait that we might call distractedness. We examined the data using a statistical technique to see if there was an underlying structure in the data. We found that Neuroticism, Urgency and also a person's perceived stress comprised this common thread. We called it Lack of Control, which suggests then that there could be a personality trait of distractedness, a trait correlated with short attention spans on the computer.

In fact, the idea of distractibility as a general personality trait has been proposed, and may be related to ADHD symptoms.[24] Researchers found that those who experienced ADHD symptoms as a child were often more distractible in a laboratory study. But I emphasize that while ADHD symptoms have links to extreme Neuroticism and Impulsivity, our participants did not score in the extreme ranges of these traits. So an underlying personality trait of distractibility that we found in our study participants should not be confused with ADHD.

Conscientiousness and email

We all know people who are conscientious, a personality trait that seems to be highly desirable for productivity. But when it comes to email, this personality trait can actually backfire. We reasoned that conscientious people might be the ones who are quick to check and respond to email because it represents work. Because we had logged all the computer applications that our participants used, we could zero in on their email use. We closely examined everyone's day-to-day email behavior, looking at the time-stamped computer logs. We found that there are two basic types of email personas: those who check it continuously and those who check it once or a few times during the day. We expected that conscientious people would be more likely to be continuous email checkers, and that is exactly what we found. In fact, it explained their email checking behavior to a striking extent.[25] A conscientious person is thorough, careful and disciplined and wants to make sure that they catch every email coming in, so they remain a sentry on inbox duty. So if you're a person who is constantly checking your email, even without any notifications, chances are you might also score high in Conscientiousness.

Last, it is worth mentioning that Openness is another personality trait that influences digital behavior. In an earlier study where we compared people who were being interrupted versus not being interrupted, we found that people who score higher on the personality trait of Openness perform better in environments with interruptions.[26] The higher one scores in Openness, the faster one completes work amid constant interruptions. A possible explanation is that people who are more open to new experiences are more agile and flexible and can return back faster to an interrupted task.

Personality and fighting distractions

There is a huge market promising to solve the distraction problem, and not only in self-help books: tech companies have also entered the race to develop software to block distractions. There are essentially two main software approaches: one that makes users aware of how much time they spend on various sites, and one that blocks a person's most distractible sites, forcing them to quit cold turkey.

It is ironic to rely on technology to help us overcome distractions from technology. But how well does such blocking software actually work? Given that I spent years studying multitasking and distractions, I was of course very interested to see if technology could offer a solution to help people become less distracted. It turns out that a person's personality type affects the relative success of such blocking software. In another summer's visit to Microsoft Research, Mary, Shamsi and I conducted a study where we tested whether software that blocks distractions could actually help people improve their focus on their devices.[27] We recruited thirty-two people in an organization to partici- pate in a two-week study. In the first week, study participants worked as they normally would. In the second week, we asked them to install blocking software on their computers, and we let them choose to block those sites that they felt were distract- ing for them (about 90 percent of the sites chosen were social media sites). We also asked them to fill out the Big 5 personal- ity survey. At the end of each week, we asked them to fill out the Cognitive Absorption Scale,[28] which measures work perfor- mance and ability to focus. At the end of the second week, the measures showed that people reported being significantly more focused in their work and assessed themselves as being more productive. That was good news. However, they also were less temporally dissociated during this work—this means that they became *more* aware of the passage of time. Perhaps it's no wonder, as we took away their favorite pastime of social media. Remem- ber, though, that when people are in flow, they feel unaware of time passing, so this suggests that they were not in flow while working but were focused.

But unexpectedly, after using the blocking software, on aver- age, people did not change their assessment of being in control of their attention. Why would that be? After all, they did report being more focused. It turns out that sometimes overall averages can deceive—putting one foot in scalding water and another foot in ice water averages out to putting your feet in lukewarm water and yet describes neither experience. Upon closer ex- amination, it turned out that the average result of reporting no change in the control of attention really didn't reveal what was going on. There were actually two different basic personality types: people with high self-control and those with low self-control. People who were in the high self-control group scored low in impulsiveness and high in Conscientiousness. Conversely, people in the low self-control group scored high in impulsiveness and low in Conscientiousness, and it is known that high Impulsivity is related to low self-control.[29] Once we figured out that there were these two groups, we found a surprising result. First, as we expected, those with low self-control reported that they experienced less mental effort when their distractions were blocked—we can interpret this as the software relieving them of the effort of using cognitive resources to block distractions. So of course they should feel less mental effort. But unexpectedly, people with high self-control actually reported that their workload *increased*. Why would people with high self-control feel that their workload increased? We were at first puzzled by this, but then it made sense. These are people who have very good self-regulation skills. When they go to sites such as social media, they are able to check in, and can then check back out again. But by taking away their ability to take an online break, these conscientious people worked continuously. One person said they felt 10 percent more productive but also much more tired. Another person with high self-control was so immersed in her work that she missed the last commuter shuttle back to her home, which had never happened to her before.[30]

The body as well as the mind can respond to distractions. We discovered in this study that self-distraction habits in the digital world can be so ingrained in people that muscle memory takes over. Andrew, a study participant with low self-regulation, reported that even though he used the blocking software, he noticed his fingers would habitually start to type Facebook.com before he was even aware that he had the intention to go on Facebook. This implicit sensorimotor skill happens without conscious deliberation, similar to how a pianist might sit down at the piano and instinctively start to play a well-learned piece. The idea of a schema can explain this. If you recall, a schema is an internal representation in our minds of a pattern of behavior, and in this case, the schema is the routine action of going to Facebook. When the fingers start to type the beginning of Facebook.com, the muscle movement activates a schema that we have stored in our minds. This illustrates how the unconscious mind can influence distractions.

At the end of the week, only two people continued to use the software (it was free). We asked the others what they thought. Twenty people said they would use it, but it needed to have modifications, like giving them more information to help them learn to self-adjust on their own. Some people reported they would never use it as they felt too controlled by it.

Blocking software might seem like a solution for some, but is there a consequence of off-loading our self-regulation onto technology? Later I will discuss the downside of deferring the work of developing our own agency onto software. I will argue how it is critical to develop our own skills to self-regulate.

Self-regulation and poor sleep

Insufficient sleep affects people globally, in all nations, age groups and genders, and has been referred to as a public health epidemic.[31] You may not be aware, though, of why the poor sleep you got last night affects your ability to focus today. Self-regulation is affected when our cognitive resources are depleted, and when we are sleep-deprived, our resources are low. It thus seems to follow that our poor sleep habits (or insomnia) would affect our attention focus in the digital world. We know that when people don't get enough sleep, they have trouble paying attention the next day. But exactly how poor sleep affects our attention on our devices needed to be tested. College students are notorious for poor sleep habits, and to test how it affected their attentiveness, there was a population at hand to study—

at my university. With my graduate students Yiran Wang and Melissa Niiya, we logged the computer activity of seventy-six undergraduate college students for seven days at the University of California Irvine and asked them to keep sleep diaries. This study was done before we could rely on wearables to accurately track sleep, and at the time, sleep diaries were the gold standard for measuring sleep used in clinical studies. The computer logging enabled us to see how long their attention span was on their computer and smartphone screens. We confirmed that the shorter the sleep duration the night before, the shorter was their attention duration on their computers and phones the next day. Not getting enough sleep saps our resources, and executive function then doesn't have much fuel to resist distractions and invest in attention focus.

Not only a single night of bad sleep, but the accumulation of multiple nights of poor sleep can also affect attention. This cumulative loss of sleep is known as sleep debt. If someone needs eight hours of sleep to be refreshed, but is only getting, say, six hours each night, then sleep debt adds up. The debt climbs steadily with each day of sleep loss. Think of your sleep like investing money in a bank account. When you have had consistently good sleep, then you have a lot of reserves in your account. You will start your day raring to go. You can also bank sleep to repay what was withdrawn like when you sleep long on weekends. But if you consistently fail to get enough sleep, then you accumulate sleep debt.

For these seventy-six students, we found that as sleep debt increased each night, the time they spent on Facebook the following day correspondingly increased.[32] This relationship held irrespective of the students' age, gender, school workload and deadlines. Why might sleep debt lead people to go on Facebook? First, one night of bad sleep may not affect a person that much. But not getting good quality sleep over time, i.e., accumulating sleep debt, robs one of their attentional resources increasingly more each day. With fewer resources, the self-regulation ability to resist going to a social media site like Facebook erodes. Second, if you're beat, it's a lot easier to engage in lightweight rote activities like Facebook or Instagram or Candy Crush than doing work that requires hard focus. When you're exhausted after a long bike ride, it's easier to coast downhill rather than make an uphill climb.

Personality, self-regulation and attention in the digital world

As we now know, self-regulation uses cognitive resources.[33] If you have just spent the morning in Zoom meetings that are mentally exhausting, then you will have a harder time resisting checking Reddit during the afternoon. Similarly, if you have accumulated sleep debt, it will be hard to focus. Practicing self-regulation can also deplete the resources needed to resist temptations or distractions. If a person is exerting a lot of emotional energy to resist eating carbs that day, then they would likely have poorer self-regulation to resist buying those shiny boots that have been following them around on the internet.

Mischel's marshmallow studies showed how children who could delay their gratification to get the second marshmallow had better self-control and were also much more attentive and better able to concentrate later on in their teens.[34] It sounds like self-control is set from an early age, but before you get too dismayed about your personality disposition, keep in mind that environment as well as genetics contribute to self-control. While Mischel studied children of Stanford professors and students, a later study looking at lower socioeconomic status children found a smaller effect of predicting self-control over years.[35] This strongly suggests that environmental factors are at play. In fact, other studies showed that parenting style, such as closely overseeing a child and correcting a child's misbehavior, can promote self-regulation.[36]

Our research shows evidence that personality can play a role in influencing kinetic attention. Neurotics are distracted by inner worries, real or perceived, and their rapid attention-shifting appears to fan out to multiple places like email, Facebook, Instagram, news or online shopping. On the other hand, conscientious people seem to display attention-switching between fewer targets such as the task at hand and their diligent checking of email. In the same way that individuals are prone to different dispositions, they also appear to have different patterns of how they allocate their attention when they use their devices.

In our digital age, we have put ourselves in a precarious position: we are on our devices for much of the day, information and other people continually compete for our attention, and consequently we multitask, are constantly interrupted, and experience high stress, often self-imposed. Can we blame our distractibility on our personality and self-regulation, then? Not fully. Personality can help explain some things about our digital behavior: how often we are likely to use the internet, what sites we might choose to visit, how frequently we might shift attention on our devices and the qualitative nature of that shift, but personality is only part of the story. Even though we are predisposed to certain traits, we can most certainly overcome some of the weaknesses presented by them. Remember, though, as Mischel wrote, personality can be modified by the situation we are in. A neurotic sitting in a quiet park may have a long attention span when reading a newspaper, but not so much when on their computer or smartphone. On the other hand, a conscientious person may have longer sustained attention on their computer or smartphone because it represents work, but may focus less when in a conversation. Our attention to our devices is not just related to personality, though—our attention is also influenced by the role our devices play in making us happy (or not), as we will see next.

CHAPTER TEN:

Happiness and Our Devices

In Greek mythology, heroes often searched for Elysium, the ancient Greek version of heaven, a place for those who were granted immortality by the gods. In *The Odyssey*, Homer wrote that in the Elysian fields, no one needed to work, and the gods provided beautiful weather: no storms but just cool, breezy winds. While it may sound like it is foretelling a modern Florida retirement community, the Greeks' Elysium was located at the end of the earth, and once there, one would experience complete unending happiness. To a large extent, people have always been in search of Elysium. Also, paradoxically, myths can serve as inspiration for scientific study. The field of positive psychology, spearheaded by Martin Seligman and Mihaly Csikszentmihalyi, was developed in order to gain a scientific understanding into the circumstances for when we feel optimistic, hopeful and content, and how these and similar attitudes can be cultivated.

Experiencing such types of positive emotions can bring so many benefits—especially to our physical health: they have even been associated with a longer life span. In a classic study in 1930, nuns who were members of the School Sisters of Notre Dame and living in various US cities were asked by their Mother Superior to write their autobiographies when they were in their twenties and thirties. Sixty years later, the writings were evaluated by researchers for the amount of positive emotion they expressed. The researchers also looked at the nuns' longevity. Those who expressed the highest and most varied positive emotions lived up to ten years longer than those who expressed the lowest amount of positive emotions.[1]

Being able to use our digital technologies effectively, manage our attention and experience positivity is at the heart of this book. I have shown how much people multitask and are interrupted, and that high stress accompanies both. Our devices are here to stay, and in our interconnected world, it's just not feasible to give them up for long. So how can we feel positive when we use them? A common narrative is that when using our personal devices, we should strive to achieve flow, that deep psychological state of immersion, which has been likened to finding Elysium. However, as we discussed earlier, the nature of information work may just not be conducive to flow for most people, and there are other ways to experience flow such as when creating art or playing music. We can, though, learn to use our personal devices in a way that does not induce stress, where we feel positive, psychologically balanced and productive.

In this chapter I will describe the role of our emotions in the digital world, their relationship with our attention, and how our emotional experiences can help explain why our attention can be captivated by mindless activity on our devices. I will show how doing mindless, rote activity makes people happy, helps them recharge their cognitive resources and thus can help explain why people are glued to activities that draw them away from work. You may not have thought that playing Candy Crush can actually help us achieve a psychological balance in our workday, but that might soon change.

The solace of rote activity

The illustrator and author Maira Kalman, known for her illustration of the book *Why We Broke Up* along with many others, loves to iron. To Kalman, ironing is mechanical and meditative and helps her clear her thoughts. She does her writing at the kitchen table, and sometimes she intersperses it with polishing silver. Ironing or polishing silver is mindless, rote activity, like Maya Angelou's solitaire and crossword puzzles. As Kalman describes, "When there are so few things you can control it can be extraordinarily soothing to find little things to be in charge of, and that give you solace."[2]

Kalman is not the only artist or writer who indulges an unusual, undemanding habit during her creative work. Well before the internet, artists had ritualistic rote activities that provided a respite, and by clearing their heads, sometimes even inspired them. Beethoven, while composing music in his head, would pour water over and over his hands—enough to spill through the floor to annoy the tenant downstairs. Every so often he would stop his compulsive hand-washing and write down parts of a score.[3] Gertrude Stein, whose writing omitted punctuation like commas or periods so that it read without pauses, did in fact incorporate pauses into her composition. She would briefly stop her work and gaze at cows. With her companion Alice B. Toklas, they would take a drive through the countryside of Ain, France, where they lived. Stein would set up a campstool, write and at intervals take breaks to watch the cows. Every so often Toklas would nudge a cow into Stein's field of view so she had ample opportunity to observe it.[4]

Ironing, hand-washing, watching cows—these all involve rote, mindless attention. Rote activity has its advantages. It occupies the mind without using up much cognitive resources. Its easy engagement keeps people's minds open while they put hard-to-solve problems aside, making room for new ideas to appear or half-baked ones to progress. For these artists and writers, rote work was intentional, and even purposeful, distraction. This type of rote activity is also easily accessible on our devices in the form of apps like Tetris or simple games like Wordle, and has a similar function. It turns out that rote activity serves more of a purpose for us than we might realize.

How are emotions related to attention?

Let's take a closer look at emotions. While the exact idea of what counts as an emotion has long been debated, a common notion that has crystallized among emotion researchers is that emotions are responses to some event, which could be internal (a thought or memory) or external (a phone call from a friend).[5] But not only are emotions reactive to things like events or other people, they can also elicit actions. When people encounter a conflict, they are faced with a dilemma of whether to approach it or avoid it. From an evolutionary perspective, do you run from the bear or stay and fight? Do you stand up to your irascible colleague or walk away? When a person feels positive, they are more likely to face that grouchy person, or any situation where a conflict is involved.[6] Positive emotions give you ammunition. If you can make peace with that colleague then it may lead you in turn to feel even more positive. One of my favorite sayings is from the philosopher Khalil Gibran, who expressed the recursive nature of positive feeling and action in his poem "On Giving": *"For those who give with joy, that joy is their reward."*[7]

With this in mind, we can dig a little deeper into trying to understand why people seek out rote activities that can make them happy. Let's first review some of the things that we do over the course of a day that can deplete our cognitive resources. As mentioned, long, sustained attention is cognitively demanding. When we have a day with a lot of Zoom meetings, we have to pay attention and interact. Next, multitasking, or switching our attention to different activities, also cuts into our limited resources, and we know that it causes stress. Also, recall that practicing self-regulation also expends your resources, which leaves less available to cope with negative events. If you spend your day trying to resist going to Twitter or Facebook, that chips away at your precious resources.

If you are feeling blue, say, from experiencing a negative event, such as getting passed over for recognition at your job, a paper rejection, or a conflict with your child or spouse, that can also drain resources and cause you to feel fatigued. In fact, the more we are drained of resources, the more a negative event can have an impact on us.[8] So if you are feeling exhausted, then you are less able to cope with a future negative event that might arise. But positive emotions can serve as armor to shield us from those unwanted events.

The idea that positive events might help counteract the effects of negative events was tested by Swiss researchers. In a Swiss workplace, seventy-six people were instructed to fill out diaries for two days, and did this on three separate occasions, with six months in between each time. They were told to record the positive and negative events that they experienced for that day, and to write down the events as soon as they experienced them. At the end of each day, they then filled out a questionnaire that measured their fatigue. The authors found that when people experienced negative or adverse events that day, also experiencing positive events helped them recover their expended resources.[9] One explanation for this finding is that positive events redirect people's thinking away from these nagging worries. (This might be less true for neurotics, who tend to replay their negative experiences over and over again in their minds.) So this study suggests that experiencing positive events can help replenish our resources when we have a bad day. Rote activities, which are associated with feeling positive, and which are easy to do, might also help us build up our resources. They allow us to pull back, escape a bit from our stressful work and refresh. If you are feeling anxious or stressed, then you might be drawn to doing rote activities on your computers and smartphones, because social media and games are easily accessible. If you are in the countryside like Gertrude Stein, you might be drawn to watching cows.

When people feel positive, they generate a wider repertoire of actions that they can take in a situation. So, say you're stuck in a meeting with a difficult person. If you feel positive, you'll likely think of more choices for how to handle that person. If you have a noncooperative child, and if you happen to feel good, then you'll probably have more ideas of how to deal with your child. This is explained by the broaden-and-build theory, in which positive emotions are believed to increase cognitive resources, which in turn widens the scope of attention and the breadth of actions that people can take. There is evidence to support this. Researchers Barbara Fredrickson and Christine Branigan of the University of Michigan showed film clips to subjects in a laboratory, designed to either evoke positive emotions (e.g., from the feel-good movie *Penguins*) or negative emotions (e.g., showing a climbing accident from the movie *Cliffhanger*). After viewing the film clips, subjects in the two different groups were asked to imagine a scenario associated with the emotion they were feeling, and to write down all the actions they would do right then. An example of a scenario is being outdoors in nature. One might take a walk, bird-watch, sit on the beach, pick flowers and so on. After films that elicited positive emotions, subjects reported significantly more actions they would take compared to after watching the negatively charged film clips.[10] This study showed that positive emotion can thus widen one's perspective with a larger choice of actions to take. So if you're feeling positive and need to meet with your irascible colleague, then you should have more options for how to deal with that person.

Positive emotions can also help us bounce back after we experience negative events, as Fredrickson and her colleague Robert Levenson showed in another study. Subjects were shown film clips to evoke negative feelings. But if afterwards they were then presented with film clips to evoke positive feelings, it helped them revert back faster to their baseline emotional level.[11] They didn't continue feeling negative. Together, both results suggest that positive emotions can help us be resilient and take action to build back up our resources that might have been depleted. Positive emotions can offer us a psychological break, allowing us to step back, recover and gain back our energy.[12]

Happiness during the workday

We might expect that people would be happiest when they are highly focused in their work. And there is a long line of research that shows that people feel positive emotions when they are engaged with something. Attentional states that describe engagement—called variously flow, cognitive absorption, cognitive engagement and mindfulness—have consistently been associated with positive mood.[13][14][15] Boredom, as you might imagine, has also consistently been associated with negative emotions. So we might expect, then, that when people have sustained focus on their work, they are goal-directed, and must be happier than when doing mindless tasks like Candy Crush. Well, it turns out that this is not what my research found.

In Chapter 3, I described how people displayed changing rhythms of attention throughout the day. Mary Czerwinski, Shamsi Iqbal and I had used an experience sampling technique, where people reported how engaged and challenged they were *right now*. Thirty-two people in our study were given eighteen probes, i.e., short surveys, to fill out each day for a week. In the same probes, we also asked them to report their emotional experiences. Their reports in the probes yielded a good picture of what they were feeling throughout the workday.[16]

The probes were based on a model of affect from the work of James Russell, a psychologist who specializes in studying emotions.[17] Emotions are made up of many affective components. Two of the most important ones, which have been shown to contribute more to the emotional experience than others, are the basic underlying states of valence and arousal. Valence is a term used to measure the quality of feeling or emotion, which can range along a continuum from extremely positive to extremely negative. Arousal, which you can think of as how much energy you feel, also falls along a continuum from extremely high arousal (when you feel pumped up and ready to go) to extremely low arousal (when you feel zapped of energy). The impetus for developing this model is that people have a hard

time distinguishing between different types of feelings: sometimes emotions can be ambiguous. We may feel negative but
find it hard to pinpoint whether we really feel sadness, shame
or anger. It's a lot easier to disambiguate feelings if just two decisions need to be made: how positive or negative we feel, and
how much energy we have. For example, you might feel super
happy bursting with high energy when you just received a raise,
or you might feel angry and drained when you just had a proposal turned down that you worked so hard on. Both of these
measures have been validated with studies in neuroscience and
physiology. Activation has been found in brain regions that correspond with people's different subjective feelings associated with
positive or negative valence.[18] Arousal has also been validated,
showing physiological signals of measures like heart rate, skin
conductance and EEG, to correlate highly with people's subjective feelings about how aroused they feel.[19] [20]

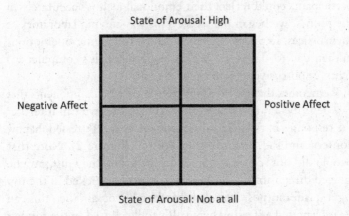

Figure 1. *The experience sampling probes that were presented to participants to measure their emotions throughout the day. Participants were asked to click on that part of
the grid that best reflects their emotions at that moment.*

Figure 1 shows the probe we used in our study that popped up
on people's computers throughout the day. The probes showed

a grid that had a horizontal and vertical axis: the horizontal axis represented valence, and the vertical axis represented arousal. Participants were instructed to click on that part of the grid that best represented how they felt *right now*. If they felt extremely positive and had a lot of energy, they would click in the extreme top right corner. If they felt somewhat positive with a moderate amount of energy, they would click in the middle of the top right quadrant. In other words, they would click the exact place on the grid that matched how they were currently feeling. These dimensions of valence, the *type* of feeling, and arousal, the *amount* of feeling, were continuous measures to match the notion that people's emotional experiences fall along a range. Participants could thus click anywhere on the grid to capture as accurately as possible how they felt along these two dimensions. Our study participants had a chance to practice with us and ask questions to make sure that they understood how to report their feelings on the grid. When we were sure that the participants could reflect their emotional feelings accurately in the probes, we began the study. This was a living laboratory at their offices, so people experienced the full gamut of emotions in their day-to-day work. We also logged people's computer activity unobtrusively, with their consent.

Remember that valence and arousal are two components that can describe a range of emotions. Therefore, we can interpret the responses in the grid as basic felt emotions of stressed, happy, content and sad, according to Russell (Figure 2). Note that people did not see these names on the grid—they just saw the labeled dimensions, as in Figure 1. If people clicked in the top right quadrant (positive valence and high arousal), then this can be interpreted as feeling happy. If people clicked in the top left quadrant, (negative valence and high arousal) then this would be interpreted as stress. Clicking on the lower right quadrant (positive valence and low arousal) indicates feeling content, and clicking on the lower left quadrant (negative valence and low arousal) indicates feeling sad. More broadly, if someone clicked anywhere on the right half of the grid, then they were indicating that they were feeling positive (either happy or content) and if they clicked anywhere on the left half of the grid, then it meant they were feeling negative (either stressed or sad).

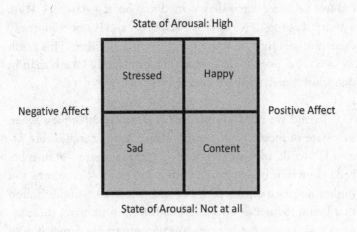

Figure 2. *The interpretation of moods for the four quadrants of Russell's model.*[21]

Effortful and effortless engagement

Let's now return to what was mentioned earlier, the long line of research that shows that when people are highly engaged with something, such as reading, then it is associated with a positive mood. Despite these past findings, when we looked at the results, we were surprised: people were happiest when using rote attention, happier than when they were in a state of focus. Rote attention, as a reminder, is given to the engaging but unchallenging activity that we do every day: playing solitaire, but also browsing Twitter, shopping online and scanning Facebook. Remember that if people reported that they were engaged in something, we also asked them to note how challenged they were in what they were doing. Past studies that showed engagement to be associated with positive emotions did not differentiate whether people were challenged or not, like we did. Being engaged with rote activity like Kalman's ironing is different than being engaged while doing a challenging activity like writing. As in past studies, though, we found that people did feel negative when they were doing boring activities. Rote activity that uses few cognitive resources and is not cognitively demanding is thus associated with feeling positive. This result suggests that people are happier playing Candy Crush than in doing sustained, focused work.

Why did we not find our participants to be happiest when in a state of focus? First, we found that when people were focused at work, they also tended to be stressed. Stress in turn has been shown to be associated with lower positive emotions and higher negative emotions.[22] Second, while past studies found that being focused is associated with feeling positive, these attentional states have been measured on a single dimension of engagement without considering that there might also be different amounts of challenge, i.e., that paying attention to some things might be more cognitively challenging than others. If we unpack then what it means to be engaged in an activity, it can involve challenging experiences such as reading difficult material, or not so challenging experiences such as watching YouTube videos. When you use sustained attention with difficult activities, then it creates a cognitive load, and we know from laboratory studies that you can't keep sustained focus for too long, as your performance then starts to decline. This is explained by the depletion of resources.[23] Using rote attention, on the other hand, uses few attentional resources. I enjoy doing simple crossword puzzles. I can solve them quickly. I get quick gratification. In a digital multitasking environment, these rote activities are quite effortless and bring enjoyment. Plus, they are so easily accessible. So a reason why we spend so much time on rote activities is that it's hard to pull away from something that makes you happy. But unfortunately, for most of us, we can't spend the day just on rote activity.

Is it possible that rote activity doesn't *cause* people to be happy, but maybe they do effortless tasks because they're already happy? The strong association we found doesn't confirm that rote activity *causes* positive feelings. However, I argue that it does. Maira Kalman describes that her rote activity brings her solace, and I have heard from many of our study participants that they turn to rote activity when they need to relieve stress and feel better. My own experience is that rote activity is a way to back off and replenish, and since I started studying our attention with our devices, I realize that it does relax and calm me.

Happiness with Facebook and face-to-face activity

If I asked you what you think makes people happier, Facebook interaction or face-to-face interaction, how would you answer? I ask this question regularly of people, and most say face-to-face interaction. But the result will surprise you. If you recall, in Chapter 3, we discussed how when people were on Facebook, they felt they were doing rote activity or were even bored.[24] In a study I did with Mary and Shamsi at Microsoft Research, we asked thirty-two participants to wear SenseCams for a week so as to take pictures every fifteen seconds of what they were seeing.

After applying face detection software, we could determine when people had face-to-face interaction. We also used the PANAS scale, a well-validated scale that measures subjective mood by asking people to rate how they feel for twenty different types of emotions such as interested, enthusiastic, anxious or distressed.[25] We asked people to fill out the PANAS scale first thing in the morning when they arrived at work, and again at the end of the day before they left. If someone started the morning very positive, but had a grueling day, then the scores on the PANAS scale would reflect their end-of-day mood showing a change from feeling positive to negative. We also probed people's emotions in the moment using experience sampling, as shown in Figure 1, based on Russell's model of emotions. They also reported how engaged and how challenged they were.

So how positive did people feel with Facebook versus in-person interactions? We first examined emotions at the time the interactions occurred, as measured through the experience sampling probes. We found that at the time, they reported being happier when they were face-to-face with people compared to when they were on Facebook.

But when we looked at their mood at the end of the day, we found that the more time people spent on Facebook, the happier they reported being at the end of the day. Yet the amount of time spent in face-to-face interactions over the day did not show any relationship with their mood change at the end of the day.

How do we reconcile these differing results? Consider that the probes are capturing emotions in the moment, which may not last long. The PANAS end-of-day surveys, on the other hand, reflected all the ups and downs over the day. So even though people might have been happier at the time during a face-to-face interaction, it seems possible that over the course of the day, those happy moments didn't lead to a cumulative higher positive mood.

There also seemed to be another underlying reason. We wondered if their attention might play a role. We looked at people's reported level of engagement right after each type of interaction. People reported being more engaged during face-to-face interactions, compared to being on Facebook, which we would expect. It seems reasonable that face-to-face interactions are more demanding of our attention, but at the same time, people may have less control over their attention once they are in one. Face-to-face interactions involve different stages. There is the opening stage, where you greet someone. Then there is the interaction itself, and finally there is a closing stage with parting rituals ("I'll follow up with you tomorrow"). If you are stressed, have a pile of work on your plate or have deadlines looming, then the last thing you will want is to be a prisoner in a face-to-face interaction. Unless you are prone to rudeness, it is very hard to cut off an interaction once you've gotten past the opening stage. On the other hand, people can choose *when* to go to Facebook (though many may lose control once they are on the site). If you are working hard, then Facebook affords a convenient way to take a break and do some rote activity, which of course can help you replenish your resources and make you feel more positive.

Negative emotions when multitasking

We are attracted to people who express positive emotion. We gravitate towards the person in the break room who smiles at us. When we peek in a person's office to see if they are interruptible, a sour expression on their face leads us to quietly retreat. You may recall from Chapter 4 that much of the day, people multitask, and when they do, they experience stress. But organizations are social settings, and often when people multitask, they are around others in the workplace. How does the stress that people experience when multitasking and being continually interrupted affect their emotional expression when they are around others? Are people's emotions when they multitask publicly visible on their faces for others to see?

We decided to test this. With colleagues Ricardo Guttierez-Osana and Ioannis Pavlidis, and our graduate students, we conducted an experiment to investigate how people express their emotions when they multitask. We recruited sixty-three people for the experiment and brought them into a laboratory, where we simulated a multitasking office environment with interruptions. Since we know that email is a key source of interruptions, we decided to interrupt people with email.

We asked participants to complete a task, which was to write an essay. We chose the topic of technological singularity, which is what might happen when machines overtake human civilization. We expected that this topic would be provocative and engaging for the participants. Participants were then randomly assigned to one of two conditions. In the sequential task condition, they first received a set of emails, answered them, and then wrote the essay, and in the multitasking condition, they worked on the essay but were interrupted at random times with the same number of emails throughout the session and instructed to respond to them right away. The emails were pretested so that people had to give a thoughtful reply, and examples included asking for advice on domestic travel or opinions on white lies.

We videotaped the facial expressions of the participants in both conditions. We also measured their stress using a thermal imaging camera, which is quite accurate in detecting stress based on sweat in the perinasal region of the face, the triangular area between the nose and lips. We then used an automatic facial expression recognition program that has been tested to be quite accurate and recognizes seven distinct emotions: anger, disgust, fear, happiness, sadness, surprise and neutrality. We found that when people multitasked, their facial expressions displayed more negative emotions, particularly anger, which you can see in Figure 3. When they did not multitask, their emotional expressions were more neutral.[26] Interestingly, when people received the emails all at once, their expressions showed a rise in anger during the time they were working on the emails compared to when they worked on the essay task. We also gave participants the NASA-TLX scale, described earlier in Chapter 5, and those who were continually interrupted assessed themselves as having higher mental load and effort. Thus, the displayed emotions that were objectively measured appeared to match what people were experiencing. Remember also that cognitive load is believed to correspond to the underlying cognitive resources used[27]—so a higher mental load from those continually interrupted would mean more resources being expended.

Figure 3. *The image on the left is a person performing a task without interruptions, showing a neutral emotion. The three images on the right show the same person while multitasking and continually being interrupted, showing angry expressions.*[28]

While we can't know for sure if people's facial expressions show what they are actually feeling, we do know that the emotions that people feel and express are closely intertwined.[29] So it is likely that if your face shows you're looking sad, you may feel sad, but not always. Similarly, if your face shows that you are bubbling with excitement, then likely you are feeling positive, but again, not always. People's emotional expressions and behavior can have an impact on others, especially in a public setting. Emotions can have contagion effects, where one person's emotion can influence another person to express a similar emotion,[30] leading researcher Sigal Barsade to refer to people as "walking mood inductors."[31] Thus, what we do on our devices affects our emotions, and these can be on public display. In short, it's not just that people feel stressed when they multitask and are exhausted, but they may convey these negative emotions to others.

The rabbit hole of contentment

Given the amount of multitasking and interruptions that people experience, rote work can serve a function—to elicit positive emotions in a stressful environment. The positive emotional rewards that people get from doing rote activity can help explain why people are drawn to non-taxing activities such as social media and simple games, which are effortless and bring us pleasure. The writer Nicholson Baker sets aside time for what he calls "daylight kind of work": low-pressure, non-cognitively demanding work of typing up notes or transcribing an interview.[32] In the different rhythms of attention that we found in Chapter 3, we also found that people take time to ramp up to focused work, and Baker's activities might ready him for the hard task of writing. In our digital age, facing a screen for much of our day, we have many more opportunities for rote activity that happen to be peripheral to our work such as browsing Twitter or watching TikTok videos. Turning to digital rote activity may be a consequence of our stressful, time-pressured, multitasking days but it has an upside as it can help release tension.

You may not have thought that low effort mindless activities could help your work. With mindless activity, we can let problems incubate in our minds, and thinking about other things that do not tax our cognitive resources can help us generate solutions.[33] Because positive feelings are associated with more choices of how to act, if we glean positivity and can replenish from rote activity, then it can even potentially help us be more creative. It can reset our emotions back to a desirable state, and this can perhaps explain why we are so attracted to such mindless activity. It can help us achieve a psychological balance.

Remember that attention is goal-directed. When we lose sight of our goals, then attention can be pulled by our inner thoughts or by external stimuli towards less effortful and potentially more positively rewarding emotional activity. But on the other hand, if you keep your higher-level goals in mind and view rote activity as a means towards achieving an end in the same way that Maya Angelou's Little Mind worked in concert with her Big Mind, then you face less risk of falling into the rote attention trap.

Can rote activity help us achieve productivity? If you were an efficiency expert like Frederick Taylor (who, if you recall, used stopwatches to measure worker productivity), it would be hard to measure how rote activity helps productivity. B. F. Skinner, the noted psychologist who believed in behaviorism, described gardening and swimming as time not "profitably spent" because it cut into his work hours.[34] In Skinnerian fashion, he used a buzzer to record his work start and stop times and set his alarm to ring four times during the night, waking him so that he could work for an hour. There was no room for rote activity for Skinner. Today, productivity apps used to track your time when you're using your devices provide you with information about when you are on sites like Twitter and when you are using applications like Word. They are intended for you to maximize your work in a quantifiable way. However, for knowledge workers, such apps cannot capture how working on mindless tasks other than our main project can actually make us happy, de-stress us, and potentially help us solve problems by letting them incubate. Such productivity apps would not have classified Wittgenstein as being productive when he peeled potatoes (he noted that he thought his best when doing so) nor Einstein as being productive when he spent long hours lost in thought or playing the violin. Einstein even claimed that music helped him in his work and led to his intuition of relativity theory.[35] We will next take a broader view of our attention to look at it in relation to all the media that we use beyond our computers and phones.

CHAPTER ELEVEN:

How the Media Conditions Our Attention

As a parent, I take as a source of pride the fact that my children were raised in a household without television. When our family moved back to the US from Germany in the year 2000, my husband insisted that we not have a television set in our home. From his European perspective, American TV had too much violence. It was not easy though to raise kids in America without TV. There was intense peer pressure from their friends to follow shows, and they felt left out. I began to wonder if we were doing the right thing. But then an interesting thing happened. A few years later, we lived in Berlin for a year while on sabbatical. We rented a flat that had two TV sets. One day when I was trying to work, my children were hovering, and I couldn't concentrate. So I said what was unthinkable just a few months earlier: "Go watch TV." They then protested loudly with, "No, it's boring!" I knew I had done something right.

Most of us in our daily lives are exposed to an array of media beyond what is on our computers and phones. It turns out that our attention switches quickly not only when on our computers, but also when watching TV and films, music videos, and commercials—but in these cases, directors and editors determine the pace of your attention shifts. In this chapter, I will show how fast attention-switching is also found with a range of media we consume. I argue that through our broader media immersion, we have developed expectations for fast screen changes, and this can influence our attention-switching on our personal devices in ways in which we may not even be consciously aware.

Influences by the broader media landscape

Most children from a young age are exposed to television, averaging about two hours and fifteen minutes per day in front of a TV screen.[1] But also, it runs in the family. According to the 2021 Nielsen Total Audience Report,[2] American adults eighteen and over average four hours and twenty-four minutes a day on television, which is more than in other countries. For example, in the UK, the daily viewing time averages three hours, twelve minutes;[3] in France, three hours, forty-nine minutes;[4] in Japan, two hours, forty-one minutes;[5] and in China, two hours, thirty minutes.[6] This is not counting the amount of time spent on streaming sites. It also does not account for the amount of screen time spent on other computer and phone activity— Nielsen reports that Americans spend on average five hours and thirty minutes daily of screen time on their computers, tablets and phones.[7] This average is based on all Americans, all ages, and not just people who use computers in their jobs. But what is really astonishing is that when we add in the time watching other media like TV and films to this, then we see that our attention is fixated on some form of screen, in some type of mediated environment, *for nearly ten hours a day*.[8]

But what does all this time spent watching TV or film have to do with our attention spans when we're on our devices? When we watch a TV show, film or music video, our attention is directed from one camera shot to another—at a very fast rate. A shot is the shortest unbroken unit of film that the viewer perceives.[9] Each shot is composed of twenty-four or thirty frames per second; because of this fast speed, an individual frame is not discernable by the human eye. The length of the shot itself is carefully crafted in the editing room. The length, along with motion and lighting within each shot, is designed to steer a viewer's interest and emotions and create tension.

The type of motion within shots has been changing. According to film scholar James Cutting and his colleagues at Cornell, shots containing the onset of motion (like a standing person who then runs) have increased because filmmakers believe that it will better attract viewers' attention.[10] People are more accurate at detecting objects that change from stationary to moving compared to objects that are already moving.[11] When an object begins to move, we perceive and process the stimuli—like we do with notifications that flash on our computer screens. We can't help but notice it.

Another change that has affected viewers' attention is that shot lengths have become shorter over decades. The introduction of films with synchronized sound in the late 1920s initially led to shot lengths becoming longer, as this allowed for more focus on the dialogue. The average film shot length in 1930 was twelve seconds, but then began to shorten, reaching an average of less than four seconds after the year 2010, as measured by James Cutting and colleagues.[12] Interestingly, the shot length for film sequels also decreased. For example, the shot length of the first *Iron Man* film averaged about 3.7 seconds; for *Iron Man 2*, 3.0 seconds; and for *Iron Man 3*, about 2.4 seconds.[13]

Television followed a similar pattern to film with decreasing shot lengths over the years. Figure 1 shows the average shot lengths of films (starting in 1930 reported by James Cutting and colleagues) and television programs (starting in 1950 as measured by Jeremy Butler[14]) through the year 2010.

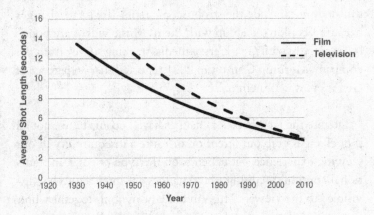

Figure 1. *Trends of average shot lengths of films and TV programs over the decades (data from Cutting et al.[12] and Jeremy Butler[14]).*

As the figure shows, the general trend has been for the average length of both film and television shots to decrease over decades. Television shots averaged around thirteen seconds in 1950 (similar to the average of twelve seconds in film in 1930) and both film and television shots shortened to average less than four seconds in 2010. Considering the extensive four and a half hours daily that people spend watching TV, I maintain that people have come to expect short, rapidly switching content with so much viewing.

Short shot length is also visible in music videos. The median shot length of 155 MTV award winners and nominees for Best Editing from 1984 to 2014 was found to be only 1.6 seconds.[15] As described on the Cinemetrics website, this average shot length has been used in MTV videos for thirty years. Of the top ten most watched YouTube clips, all are music videos, which have short, rapidly changing shots.[16] One of the most popular music videos of all time on YouTube, Psy's "Gangnam Style," with over four billion views, clocks in at 4 minutes, 12 seconds, with an average shot length of 2.9 seconds by my own count. But this does not include the stroboscopic rapid-fire scene changes because I couldn't keep up with them. Music videos are popular, especially with Gen Z'ers: a media-tracking survey from the company Morning Consult in 2021 reported that 36 percent of Gen Z'ers watch them daily.[17]

Despite the fact that shot changes have become faster, not all shot changes grab our attention or cause a discontinuity in our viewing experience—it depends on the type of edits. In traditional continuity editing, shot changes are intended to be "invisible" to the viewer. This kind of editing joins together shots that are similar enough in time and space to allow the viewer to cognitively knit together the film fragments and create the illusion of a continuous narrative.[18] There is a parallel between how our attention switches while viewing films and on our computers: a continuity edit would be like flipping to the next page of an ebook, while an abrupt edit would be like switching from an Excel spreadsheet to your email inbox.

However, even when rules of continuity editing are followed, people can still be aware of the shot changes. In a study examining whether people could detect cuts, participants were shown excerpts from various genres of film and told to press a button when they observed an edit. Overall, people could detect 84 percent of the cuts made in the films. As you might expect, people detected fewer edits when the shots cut to different perspectives within the same scene compared to switching between different scenes.[19] Other editing styles are intentionally abrupt, designed to jolt attention, and these are now becoming more popular, seen in music videos, advertisements, YouTube, and especially in blockbuster action films like *The Incredible Hulk* or *Transformers*, which we'll talk about shortly.

The evolution of film cuts and our attention

While fast shot changes on TV and film are common practice now, there is a long history of how we got here. Very early film originally had one-shot takes without any editing. But that soon changed. The innovation of shot changes within a film can be attributed to the Englishman Robert William Paul, born in 1869. Paul started his career as a scientific instrument maker, and his stature and renown in filmmaking came about by chance.[20] In 1894, Paul was asked by two entrepreneurs to build a reproduction of Thomas Edison's kinescope, a device through which a person could watch films. He was able to do so because Edison's kinescope was not patented in England. But there happened to be few films at the time to watch, and so Paul, a clever instrument maker, designed a film camera a year later. This launched a career in which he would go on to make nearly eight hundred films.

The first edit in the history of cinema occurred in Paul's 1898 film: *Come Along, Do!* In the first scene, lasting forty-four seconds, the camera has a full shot of a man and woman sitting outside an art gallery, eating their lunch. This scene establishes the tranquility of the couple's relationship.

The scene then abruptly changes to inside the art gallery for thirteen more seconds, changing background from light to dark, where the man is carefully inspecting a statue of a nude, and the woman, with an annoyed expression on her face, tries to tug him away. The cut jolts us and shows a clear shift in space and time.

Continuity editing, as mentioned to create a seamless transition among cuts to move the linear narrative along, was soon developed in the 1910s by the filmmaker D.W. Griffith. This editing became emblematic of classical Hollywood cinema (a period that spanned from the 1910s to the 1960s). An example of continuity editing is found in the 1954 Hitchcock film *Rear Window*. In one part of the film, the main character, a photographer, is viewing his neighbor through his telephoto camera lens. The shots switch back and forth from the photographer looking through his camera to the image of his neighbor, who he's watching. The switches do not disrupt the space-time continuum of the scene, and without much effort, the viewer can understand that it is the neighbor who the photographer is seeing.

In parallel to the rise of continuity editing in the US, in the mid-1920s in the Russian film school, the filmmaker Sergei Eisenstein developed a very different technique, called dialectical montage. Modeled after the Soviet ideology of dialectical materialism, the idea of pitting opposing forces against each other, Eisenstein believed that meaning in film is created through contrasting different but related ideas in sequential shots. For example, in his famous film *Battleship Potemkin*, a scene of a priest tapping a cross immediately cuts to a scene of a soldier tapping a sword. This required more effort by the viewer to find an association between the shots, but Eisenstein believed that this type of cut should lead to deeper thinking about the film.

Edits became more jarring during the French new wave in the 1950s. Jump cuts create a discontinuity in film, so that the narrative seems to instantaneously "jump" to a different point in time within the same scene. The first jump cut is credited to the director Georges Méliès in his 1896 horror film *The Haunted Castle*. French new wave directors like Jean-Luc Godard revolutionized and popularized jump cuts, which jolt your attention as they come as a surprise and feel a bit unnatural.

In a scene of Jean-Luc Godard's 1960 film *Breathless* (average shot length of 11.8 seconds), as the main character is driving a stolen car, he glances to the open glove compartment, and then a jump cut reveals that it contains a gun inside. He reaches for it. Then another jump cut and the gun is suddenly in his hand. The interruption to the flow of the action startles you a bit, but you can still follow the narrative. The experience is more like cutting out parts of the scene and relying on your attention to fill in the blanks. The viewer has to do some work to follow the story: carefully watching the shots, holding them in memory, and then piecing them together to construct the narrative. The British critic Penelope Houston claimed that Godard had developed a style of "visual cubism" to put the emphasis on the filmic medium rather than the story; on the other hand, Godard's rival, Claude Autant-Laura, claimed that he intentionally was trying to ruin *Breathless* with jump cuts.[21] Godard himself claimed that he utilized this technique to shorten a film that was an hour too long.

Whereas Jean-Luc Godard used jump cuts masterfully to enhance a scene (in the words of *New York Times* film critic Boswell Crowther,[22] to communicate the "raw and rootless young Parisians in the raw and restless flow of the French new wave"), jump cuts have become a characteristic YouTube aesthetic, mainly to hold your attention.

Jump cuts and YouTube

The goal of using jump cuts on YouTube is to maximize the amount of content within the shortest length of time. Jump cuts are also easier to do than more seamless editing techniques such as varying the shot sizes from, say, medium to close-up shots, especially for people inexperienced in editing. The rise of jump cuts on YouTube have created new expectations for viewers. In film, expert editors skillfully edit dialogue to condense speech while retaining its naturalistic sense. But on YouTube, the goal of eliminating "dead" airtime of pauses and short utterances like *ums* and *ohs* packs more action and content into a shorter time frame to hold one's attention. I watched an instructional video on how to make jump cuts on a YouTube video, and it was explained that once the dead air is eliminated, the video will appear smoother.[23] However, in real conversation, such filler words like *um* and *oh*—the words we use to buy time while we compose our speech—are essential for signaling transitions and making human conversation appear natural. YouTube has created a cinematic language where jump cuts during dialogue have now become normal. Visually, the video is jarring, choppy and energetic, speech is without pauses, and it serves the purpose to condense the video to hold our shorter attention spans.

Cinema originally created a spell that drew in the viewer so they could get lost in another world. Now, in newer forms of video, the goal is to make sure that the viewer doesn't get bored inside this world. As a result, the editing must continuously incorporate fast cuts and jump cuts to keep jolting the viewer's attention—it's like playing a fast-paced video game. Ironically, it turns out that if film editing is too dynamic, it works against people's natural tendency to perceive the coherence of a story and can actually lead to worse recall of the film.[24] Your visual attention might be held to a YouTube video with jump cuts, but you may have more trouble remembering what you saw.

Nonlinear and chaos editing

To understand the rise of fast edits and their impact on our attention from the perspective of someone who creates the shots, I spoke with Doug Pray—twice an Emmy-award-winning director, a pioneer in the field of nonlinear editing, and who learned to edit on analog film. Throughout his career, Pray has not only been an observer of shot developments, but also a participant in the changes, as he both directs films and edits them. During our Zoom call, Pray sat in his editing room. In the background, colorful index cards mapped out the story of his current project. At one point, Pray reached out of the frame and came back in to reveal an analog film reel. He explained that he learned to edit on 16 mm film and then unrolled the spool: "You know, film." He remembers back to the intensive process of analog editing before the 1990s: "You had a big bin by your editing system, and it had hundreds of little hooks, and there's hundreds of little pieces of film on each hook. So for every shot, you have to first find the film, then put it down, splice it, put a piece of tape on it. Imagine, if I wanted to have twenty shots for a minute of screen time, that's hours of work. And if you want to adjust a few frames in a shot, you would have to do the process all over again. If you wanted to do something that's abstract or artistically challenging in terms of shots per minute, it would take an insane amount of time. We're talking days and days of something that you can now do in one minute."

The first digital nonlinear editing system, the CMX-600, which enabled one to quickly access any frame in any order, came out in 1971. Its high price tag of $250,000, bad monitor quality and low storage space prohibited it from becoming popular among filmmakers. But in 1989, the company Avid released Avid Media Composer, software that revolutionized the emerging field of nonlinear editing. Pray remembers the first time he sat down at an Avid machine in 1992: "I was just thinking, 'Oh my God.' It was mind-boggling. It changed everything."

Suddenly, Pray said, he could try out a new shot on a whim. Or a dozen. And swap them out, or flip the order, in minutes, not hours or days. "And because you can, you will. And we started having fun with it. In terms of storytelling, you suddenly had an exponential number of options at your fingertips. We could advance the story rapidly, and a different kind of thinking opened up." Editing had become more efficient: it became quick to insert more cuts, and this resulted in shortening the overall shot length.

Pray also believes that the shortening of shot lengths has to do with a modern audience that has a good understanding of "filmic language" or conventions. An earlier audience would have been confused by a sequence showing a character on the street followed by a hard cut of them in a room. This audience would have needed to follow every step: "You had to do an establishing shot, show the person walking up to the house, get a close-up of their hand on the door and show how they open the door." Nowadays, audiences are far more sophisticated, and these intermediary shots can be taken out or reduced in length.

The shortening of film shots also has to do with the advent of MTV and the rise of music videos, believes Pray, who describes this as the "number one game changer" in terms of film style and aesthetics. The music had become "punchier" and faster. It took the form of punk rock, grunge, speed metal and new wave. And there was hip-hop, which Pray says is nonlinear: "It's a collision of two ideas that don't belong together. You put this scratch over this beat and put this person's voice over this other song." These new music styles led to the birth of new types of film edits such as the flash cut (a white flash between cuts) that draws attention to the cut, and which Pray describes as "visual percussion." These new music forms greatly influenced Pray's work, from his documentary *Hype!* (about the commodification of the grunge scene) to *Scratch* (about the emergence of hip-hop DJs).

It wasn't just his filmic aesthetics that were influenced, but also his shot length—more specifically, the idea that "faster is better." In the 1980s, Pray was working on music videos that were more "cutty," and he explains, "Everyone wanted them, because it seemed to be more exciting. I don't know why. It was just exciting, and every single producer would ask, 'Can you make it a little more cutty—more fun—more energetic?' In a way, it's this capitalistic: More! Faster! Bigger! Better! You're selling the band, you're selling the song. You're selling three minutes of time. It's real estate."

Last, Pray feels that the decrease in shot lengths also has to do with the proliferation of different media sources. With early TV, the US had three channels, and now there are nearly two thousand TV stations, not to mention other streaming media you can watch on sites like Netflix, YouTube and the web. So your choices have expanded, but not your time and attention capacity, and it is this limited real estate of your mind that media is targeting. As Pray describes, "Editing is omitting. If a shot doesn't further the story, then take it out. If a shot length is six seconds and can be three and it doesn't hurt the story, why not make it three?" The competition for your attention has become fiercer, and Pray believes that people will more likely pay attention to what is shorter.

To get a professional viewer perspective on how editing affects our attention spans, I spoke with longtime film critic Glenn Kenny, who writes for *The New York Times* and *RogerEbert.com*, teaches a language and film class at NYU, and is the author of *Made Men: The Story of Goodfellas*. Kenny loves film; not much has changed since he was a kid watching movies at a drive-in from the back seat of his parents' car, which is how he became interested in the first place. Kenny appreciates film that can provoke contemplation. But he feels that with the evolution of fast cuts, being able to ruminate is becoming rarer. Really fast cuts, like those averaging two seconds in action films, are now common practice, and Kenny explains that this is known as chaos editing.

The work of the filmmaker Michael Bay, who made the *Transformers* films, is emblematic of this technique. If you watch the 2007 film *Transformers* (average shot length 3.0 seconds), in one film clip you see a scene of robots destroying a pyramid, then the shot switches to explosions, then to people falling through the air, and then to robots hurtling through a long arcade with columns. All of this happens within fifteen seconds. If you happen to miss even a moment of the film, then you can still come right back and pick up the story. You haven't missed any plot development; you've just missed out on part of the havoc. You cannot help but notice the film cuts with chaos editing. You won't get a film that you can contemplate, Kenny notes, but "you'll get a head rush. It's asking for your attention, but if you don't pay full attention, you just miss more of the chaos." Chaos editing does have a function for action films, as it can be thrilling to watch such fast cuts. You will get bombarded with sensory information: the content within each scene races across the screen at dizzying speed like you're on a roller coaster. Kenny says that visually we can follow the action from cut to cut, but mentally we don't have time to apprehend what is going on in any type of meaningful way. He wonders whether the purpose of this type of fast cutting is just to create visual anarchy.

There is a parallel here in the evolution of shortening film cuts and the shortening of our attention spans on our computers. Decades ago, film shots lasted longer. But now your attention pivots from shot to shot of rapidly changing scenes. This is similar to the mental "cuts" that you make from screen to screen on your computer, between types of content often with little connection to each other. And when our attention rapidly switches on our devices in a kinetic fashion, it can be like we are creating our own chaos editing.

The shortening of advertisements

Like in TV and film, shot lengths in television commercials also shortened over time. The average shot length of commercials in 1978 was 3.8 seconds, dropping down to an average of 2.3 seconds in 1991.[25] I watched *Mind Reader*, the most viewed Super Bowl commercial of 2022 (according to *Variety* magazine), which portrays Amazon's Alexa as a psychic, and measured its average shot length as 2.4 seconds. Perhaps shot lengths in ads have reached their limit.

It's not just the shot lengths, though, that are short—the overall length of advertisements on TV has also decreased. The majority of ads started out as sixty seconds in length in the 1950s,[26] but that length comprised only 5 percent of ads shown in 2017. In the 1980s, advertisers started experimenting with showing fifteen-second ads instead of thirty-second ads. They discovered that fifteen seconds was even more persuasive than thirty seconds, especially when the ads used elements expressing cuteness and humor.[27] In 2014, 61 percent of ads were thirty seconds in length, but three years later, that percentage decreased to 49 percent.[28] Interestingly, in 2018, the Nielsen company filed a patent to compress video ads into shorter time frames. Video ads that were originally thirty seconds were found to perform as well when they were compressed into fifteen-second time frames, for example, by removing frames.[29] There is a financial motive behind the madness. A fifteen-second ad costs 60 to 80 percent of a thirty-second ad.[30] The more fifteen-second ads that can be fit into a commercial break, the more money the network will make. Thus, the bottom line pushed ads to have more information packed into a shorter time frame, further reinforcing our short attention spans.

On YouTube, people have the option to skip the ad, usually after the first five seconds. Hulu gives viewers a chance to choose shorter ads throughout a show instead of a longer one at the beginning. On its website, Facebook issues best practices for designing mobile video ads for its platform. At the top of the list, it states, "Keep Your Video Short," and recommends the length be fifteen seconds or less in order to hold people's attention.[31] Implicit in this recommendation is that people's attention spans have shrunk so much that fifteen seconds seems to be about the maximum at which attention can be held for an ad. In the same way that TV and film acclimate us to having shorter attention spans, the time duration of ads also fits to our short attention spans, explicitly driven by the profit motive. In fact, now six-second ads are commonly shown.[32]

Snacking culture and our attention

Let's return for a moment to consider our attention spans on social media. It's not just the ads that are short in length on social media; many of these platforms restrict the length of content that can be posted, enforcing us to read or view it in short snippets. In our digital world, we are seeing an evolving culture of snacking—a term that originated in South Korea, referring to the fact that young people consume content on their devices in ten-minute chunks on average at a time.[33] But social media platforms also help enforce such short sampling of content by setting boundaries for the length of posted content. This of course constrains how much time we can actually pay attention to any single post. In the case of TikTok, it had originally confined the time duration of videos that people create, share and watch to fifteen seconds, then expanded it to sixty seconds, and now it's three minutes. The company claims that they expanded it to allow for more creativity, but it also allows more ads to be inserted.[34] With over 130 million monthly active users worldwide at the time of this writing[35] and with about half of US adults age eighteen to twenty-nine using the platform, TikTok reaches a huge audience. While this expansion of the time duration might seem to be good news for our attention spans, unfortunately it is also the case that short videos of nine to fifteen seconds seem to perform the best to maximize viewing.[36]

It's not just TikTok but the structure of other popular social media platforms as well that constrain our ability to watch (and create) longer content. Both Instagram and Snapchat cap their video lengths at sixty seconds. The culture of texting is to write sparingly, and tweets are limited in characters. Just as advertisers discovered that shorter length ads can capture our attention better and more persuasively, these sites have also discovered that our attention can best be captured with short lengths of content. TikTok, Instagram and Snapchat cater to younger users who then grow up with expectations that content will be short. Small bites of content fit the mobile lifestyle well. We can easily fit online snacking into our daily routines while in meetings, taking short breaks from work, in the midst of watching other media, and even during in-person conversations.

Media effects on our attention

But while these trends occurred in parallel, what evidence exists for a relation between shorter media shots and our shorter attention spans when we use our computers and phones? Research supports the idea that there are crossover influences of TV and computer viewing that could in turn affect our attention spans. S. Adam Brasel and James Gips brought forty-two people into a lab at Boston College, where they were seated at a table with a laptop computer and five feet away from a thirty-six-inch television screen. Participants were told they could visit whatever website or use whatever computer application they liked and could use the TV remote to switch to any of the fifty-nine network and cable channels. The screen they looked at as well as their attention durations on each screen were tracked. The findings revealed very short attention durations on both: 75 percent of gazes on the TV screen and 49 percent of gazes on the computer screen lasted less than five seconds. What was especially interesting was that people's attention switched rapidly between the TV and computer (four times a minute). The fact that attention durations were so short on each medium, plus that attention switched so rapidly between them, supports the idea that there can be a crossover influence.[37] This study was done with people using media in a laboratory, but it's possible that these results could apply to real life: watching TV (and film) and using our computers and phones multiple hours a day over years can have crossover effects. Our habits of viewing swift scene changes in other media may be related to our kinetic attention behaviors observed on our devices. But viewing habits need not only be passive: think of flipping channels on the remote.

With films and TV that move at a fast pace and with short cuts, people have to reorient their visual attention fast, taking in the new content, angles, motion and perspectives, about every four seconds.[38] It can be taxing on your limited cognitive resources. Similar to how switching screens on our computers can drain our cognitive resources, watching fast-paced film and television also uses cognitive resources, based on evidence collected over years by Annie Lang at Indiana University.[39] Especially when shot changes are noticeable and abrupt, people have to use their limited attentional resources to continually reorient to the new shot. It is not surprising, then, that studies have shown that heart rate and arousal increase with faster pacing of film.[40]

But sometimes film cuts are so fast that we can process them visually but our minds can't keep up with them, like with chaos editing or music videos. Film and TV editors and directors are walking a fine line to control your attention: they determine the rate of switching shots so as to create tension and a dynamic viewing experience. The cuts made in the editing room are intended to support the pace of the story: they direct the images you see, their motion and how fast they change.

Research shows that fast edits may wear down the ability of our executive function. If you recall, executive function, the governor of the mind, is responsible for many things, among them inhibiting responses. So if your executive function is too taxed, then it may not be able to work effectively to stop you from impulsively clicking on the email icon. Conditioning starts when we're young, and the effect of swift film shot changes on executive function and control of attention is indeed found in children. In one experimental study, forty seven-year-old children were brought into a laboratory and shown videos that were either fast-paced or slow-paced. After the video, they were given a task called "go/no-go," where the child was told to press the button every time a digit appeared on the screen but not to press it when a letter appeared. The job of executive function is to control responses that we don't want to do, and in this case, it was to prevent the child from clicking on the letter. But after watching the fast-paced video, the children were less able to restrain themselves from clicking when the letter appeared, and they made more errors. Their executive function had been overloaded by having to continually follow and reorient to the fast scene changes in the videos. In fact, the responses showing poorer inhibition were even evident at the neural level in the brain's cortex based on an EEG recording.[41]

A similar finding came in a laboratory study of four-year-olds who were put in one of two conditions: they either watched fast-paced videos or made drawings.[42] They were better able to control their urges after drawing pictures than after watching the fast-paced videos. Taken together, we would expect these results to apply to children's lives outside the laboratory: after watching a fast-paced video, children should have less ability to restrain their impulses. We know that for adults, the same type of inability to inhibit responses can happen when we're low on cognitive resources.

These results are consistent with the idea that watching media with fast-paced shot changes can wear down our executive function, leading to more impulsivity, which could translate into less ability to keep our attention fixed for some length on other things, like a book, whiteboard or computer screen. Of course, these laboratory studies tested attention immediately after watching the videos, when people's executive function was taxed. So we might expect similar attention difficulties right after watching, say, a string of music videos or a blockbuster film like *Transformers*. But people can develop deep-seated habits after doing something for a long time, and after years of watching fast-paced videos for multiple hours a day, such habits can carry over to when we use our devices.

The idea that such habits can be formed is backed up by evidence that shows that the amount of television that children watch leads to attention problems later in adolescence. A long-term study in New Zealand followed 1,037 children over a period from the ages of three to fifteen years. The researchers found that the more television children watched, the greater were their attention problems later in adolescence, even after controlling for other things that could potentially affect the results: the child's gender, their socioeconomic status, early problems with attention, and the child's cognitive ability. The authors explain that exposure to fast-paced switching of screens, like on television, may make people less tolerant of longer-attention viewing.[43] This study lends further weight to the idea that watching television or films with short shot lengths can condition us to be less willing to pay longer attention on other devices, like our computers and phones.

A media culture of short attention spans

We live in such a fast-paced media environment that we are immersed in for ten hours a day, that I argue it's hard for our attention spans to not be affected. It is not only the content that affects us, but it is also the *structure* of the media, with fast shot lengths in high-action films, TV, YouTube, music videos and short advertisements. And of course we face restricted content length on social media platforms. How can our attention spans not be influenced when we're using so much media?

So what is driving the trend? To what extent are directors' fast scene cuts informed by their own shorter attention spans? Is the trend of shortening shot lengths unwittingly being reproduced in the editing process? Are people in the editing room just as subject to the same viewer expectations as the audience? Or, perhaps directors' fast scene cuts are rather informed by their belief that our attention spans are getting shorter and shorter? It is a chicken-and-egg question. What we are experiencing rather seems to be a cycle where our attention spans are getting shorter and the culture is at the same time adapting to and creating conditions for our attention spans to remain short.

We are seeing a cultural evolution where multiple avenues collude to shift our attention rapidly—every time we turn on the TV, watch films or use social media. A new generation is growing up amid this culture. In fact, shot lengths are starting to parallel the pattern of our mental fluctuations—how the mind naturally changes from thought to thought as measured in the laboratory.[44] Researchers James Cutting and colleagues from Cornell, who have tracked film shots over seventy-five years, claim that we have become used to and are even conditioned to expect such swift shot changes in film.

But also, we are creating the culture. Jonathan Gottschall writes in his book *The Storytelling Animal* how we are a storytelling species.[45] We are producers as well as consumers—everyone can be a maker, putting their stories into media. It's a key aspect of YouTube and social media. So it is not just film and TV directors or tech platforms who are responsible for changing the media structures—it is also all of us.

Film and TV use cuts to convey a story, or, in the case of high-action films, to pump up our adrenaline. But when we shift our attention among apps and screens on our computers and phones, the narrative we create for our own projects breaks down. We keep writing and rewriting our internal whiteboards. The media theorist Marshall McLuhan keenly observed, "We become what we behold."[46] Our attention spans have shaped the media, and the media in turn is shaping our attention.

Part Three:

Focus, Rhythm and Balance

CHAPTER TWELVE:

Free Will, Agency and Our Attention

Given the reach of sociotechnical forces on our attention that we have covered—the structure of the internet, targeted algorithms, social dynamics, our personalities, our emotions, and our widespread exposure to media in our society—how much of an influence do these forces have on our control of attention when we use our devices? When on one's computer and smartphone, to what extent is a person's attention completely due to their own volition, in the way William James thought about it? Do people really have free will in the digital world?

Let's talk more about free will. There has been a long-standing debate as to whether people have free will going back to Plato and Aristotle that continues today. This debate remains relevant in our digital age. We tend to believe that the choices we make in our lives, such as who to vote for or what career to pursue, are arrived at through free will. But we now live in a digital world where many complain that they can't stop themselves from going on social media or responding to clickbait. If free will is the command over our thoughts and actions, are we exercising free will when we respond to an impulse to check our smartphones or check social media? Is this action truly stemming from our own volition, or have we become conditioned by sociotechnical influences that cue us, or even coerce us, to perform these actions?

Let's consider two different experiences that illustrate contrasting positions on free will in the digital world. Ben, who works as a software developer in a tech company, told me that he has no trouble focusing his attention when he uses his devices. He stated adamantly that he freely chooses how much time to spend on social media, is in full control of when to use his email, and is not someone who gets sucked into playing a game for hours. He claims he can stop whenever he wants and is in complete command of his actions with his devices.

But on the other hand, Matt, one of our study participants, who works as a research analyst, felt he had little agency when he was on his computer. In describing his relationship with email, he said, "I let the sound of the bell and the pop-ups rule my life." He says his multitasking behavior is "foisted on me as opposed to being self-imposed," even though he does not want to work this way and did not envision it when he first started using computers and smartphones. The way he put it, he feels helpless. There is not a lot he can do "to change the way the world imposes itself upon me," he said, referring of course to the digital world.

There is clearly a stark difference here—Ben and Matt contrast in their worldviews on how much free choice they have in their behaviors in the digital world. Who is right? When someone goes to TikTok and can't seem to pull themselves away, despite knowing that they have other work to finish, why can't this person make a conscious choice to stop watching? Can people exercise free will in resisting distractions and choosing how to productively control and direct their attention? I have argued and shown that susceptibility to distraction varies based on our available cognitive resources, the different states of attention we experience throughout the day, our personality, technology design, emotional rewards, social dynamics, and exposure to a range of media in the environment. Is how we direct attention on our devices completely a matter of free will, or is that an illusion?

Let's briefly examine the case against free will, along the lines of what Matt expressed. One of the strongest skeptics of free will is probably not who you imagined. In 1905, the paper "On the Electrodynamics of Moving Bodies" shook the physics community and then soon the whole world and changed how we thought about space and time. Its author, Albert Einstein, became a world celebrity. He held a surprising belief about his abilities, far more extreme than just mere modesty. "I claim credit for nothing. Everything is determined," he said. "We can do what we wish but can only wish what we must. Practically, I am compelled to act as if freedom of the will existed."[1]

What does Einstein mean? We commonly believe that he was born with a genetic predisposition for a great intellect, and that he also worked hard to achieve the discovery of special relativity. But Einstein believed that everything has a prior cause. Just as the moon might believe it is charting its own course, he said, humans falsely believe they are freely choosing their own paths.[2] Einstein's view is that of a hard-core skeptic of free will, a belief that people ultimately do not have complete free choice in how they act.

Einstein was certainly not alone in his view. Strict behaviorist psychologists considered that human behavior is molded through exposure to stimuli in the environment, and this shaping of behavior is done automatically. B. F. Skinner believed that human behaviors, or for that matter the "minds and hearts of men and women," are changed by the contingencies in the social and physical environment.[3] To Skinner, human cognition is a fallacy. He argued that our environments condition us in how we behave in our daily lives. In fact, Skinner believed this so strongly that he designed an "Air Crib" for his daughter that carefully controlled the environment she would sleep and play in. It was an enclosed metal box with a glass pane and provided air flow, an optimal temperature and bedding, and he raised her in it for the first two years of her life. About three hundred American children used his Air Crib in the mid-1940s. Skinner's daughter and the other children apparently turned out normal, but it illustrates the extent to which he believed the environment shapes humans.

Evidence from brain scans seemingly adds to the case against the existence of free will. These studies have shown that some types of actions are precipitated by unconscious mechanisms. In a classic study by Benjamin Libet,[4] and replicated many times, subjects were told to make a motion with their hands such as flicking their wrists—they could choose when to do this. It turns out that *before they made any conscious actions*, a brain activity called the readiness potential preceded their wrist motion by four hundred milliseconds. Libet's experiment showed that a person's action first began at the unconscious level before they even became aware of moving their wrist. In other words, people first responded unconsciously, and then the conscious part of their brains kicked in. Yet people in these experiments believed that the origins of their wrist movements had been due to their conscious decisions. Libet's study would seem to apply broadly to actions such as picking up and checking our smartphones for messages. If asked, we would likely say that we made a conscious decision to do so. Yet we usually reach for them reflexively, which would appear to be more of an unconscious decision.

The idea of free will is strongly embedded in Western cultures. In fact, if I were to ask people in North America and Europe, chances are most would intuitively say they have free will. But should we take this at face value? The philosopher Daniel

Dennett, a professor at Tufts University who has tackled the question of free will for many years, believes that humans are endowed with the ability to act however they choose, and to also reflect on how they act. It is this free will that makes us morally responsible for our actions. Dennett believes that we can still have free will even in a world that is deterministic—that is, where effects are determined by prior causes.[5]

But here's the dilemma: If people truly have free will in the digital world, then why aren't they simply practicing it and choosing to be more focused? Why don't they exercise volition in their attention in the way that William James expressed? Free will means not only choosing how we want to behave, but also being able to self-regulate our actions. This means having control of attention and being able to resist checking Twitter or Instagram or responding to interruptions. People report that they want to self-regulate. If we really do have complete free will to choose to act how we want, why would our self-regulation decline just because of circumstances, say, when we lack sleep or when we try to resist choices for hours? When people check their email a lot, and yet complain about it, why don't they exercise free will and simply stop checking? Over the years of our studies, people have expressed a desire to be more focused, yet we find that their attention often shifts in a kinetic manner nevertheless.

Exercising free will can differ when it comes to desires rather than actions. Smokers do not have control over their yearning for that cigarette.[6] Similarly, people cannot stop wanting to visit Instagram or play Candy Crush. If free will exists, then people can override desires. For example, they can resist that urge to go on Instagram and instead work on that overdue report. Certain personality traits, such as Conscientiousness and low Impulsivity, play a role in resisting desires, as we discussed earlier. But must the rest of us use software blocking tools to restrain ourselves just as Odysseus had himself strapped to his ship's mast when he knew he could not resist the sirens' calls?

There is a third stance on free will, though, that might best explain our digital behaviors. This view, named by some as soft determinism, falls between belief and skepticism of complete free will. Soft determinism recognizes that other factors or conditions can shape how we behave. Our behavior may have antecedents, such as our genetic makeup, our cultural upbringing, or environment, yet these antecedents don't completely determine our actions. Within these constraints, in this view we do have some ability to shape our actions. It's hard to deny that circumstances play a role in our decisions. If we look back at where we chose to go to school or what career path we took, these decisions likely were shaped by circumstances and perhaps even luck. A person born into poverty is likely to have a lower socioeconomic status thirty years later than someone who is born into wealth. Further, being born into poverty also increases the probability that later in life, that person will have worse health outcomes and die younger. Girls who are discouraged from taking math classes generally don't go into science and engineering fields. These are examples that point to the role of circumstances that guide or constrain behaviors. Random chance can also play a role in our decisions: we may have gotten a job because of someone we met at a party. I met my husband after first declining an invitation to go out to eat with colleagues, but then decided to go at the last minute and sat across from him at the restaurant. We are also born with unique personalities that predispose us to act in certain ways. Likewise, social encounters early in life can affect behaviors: whether a person had been bullied, exposed to drugs, or met an inspiring role model—any of these experiences can shape how a person may relate to others later in life. Yet soft determinism provides us with optimism: despite the circumstances that might influence behavior, both earlier in life and in the present, it is still possible for people to freely choose how to act. This is good news as it suggests that despite so many different factors that might steer our behaviors and create distractions, we can take control of our attention in the digital world.

Conscious actions, automatic reactions and free will

Conscious and automatic decisions are distinct in their properties, and neuroscience research shows they originate from different locations in the brain. Free will involves conscious control,[7] and it's clear that we regularly make conscious decisions when we use our devices, where we use endogenous, or goal-driven, attention. The performance of conscious actions is driven by a series of processes that take place in different regions of the brain. When we open our laptops, we first generate possible plans. For example, we decide whether to check the news, browse Twitter or Facebook, or work on that overdue report. This decision occurs in the frontal cortex of the brain, the part of the brain responsible for planning, located right behind the forehead. Next, reward circuitry in the brain evaluates what will bring us a positive or negative experience. Then, in our brain's attentional areas, we choose the positive experience.

But if we refer back to Libet's studies, some actions that we consider conscious and intentional might actually be automatic. For example, we may not be acting with intention but rather behaving automatically when we respond to a targeted ad based on an algorithm that knows our personality or to a flashing notification designed to grab our attention. Free will skeptics might say that these actions are driven by neural mechanisms outside of our conscious awareness. As in the Stroop test discussed earlier, it is hard to resist our automatic responses.

From a neuroscience perspective, these types of digital notifications have what is called bottom–up salience. Salience operates through a part of the brain called the ventral attentional network (also called the exogenous attentional network), which informs us that we should attend to this moving, blinking object, in the same way that our ancestors would have been on high alert to respond to movement in the bush signaling a predator. Thus, when a targeted ad flashes across the screen or has enticing key words that capture your interest, people have an automatic response to look at it, as though they are operating on autopilot. Other common examples of such automatic responses are when we reach for our phone nearby, when we click on the Facebook notification at the top of the screen, or when we click on the email icon, which may be prompted by social forces such as wanting to maintain our social capital with others. And we act before we're even aware we're doing it.

Automatic responses do have their advantages as they do not tap into our pool of attentional resources, and as such, this behavior in theory saves mental energy. But this type of automaticity can be detrimental if it leads us to engage in behaviors that are contrary to our higher-level goals. Further, the more often we perform the same automatic responses, like checking our phone or email, the stronger they become. Once automatic responses become well established, it becomes difficult for executive function to assert control. This is why, after many instances of checking your phone over the years, it is hard to resist picking up and clicking your Home button when your phone is within sight.

Forces that shape human agency in our digital behavior

In our everyday use of computers and phones, we are constantly faced with the challenge of keeping our attention on our goals. But too often, our high-level goals get undermined by all the tempting things on the web that lure us away from them. We spend two hours on social media instead of finishing that report. We get lost in watching YouTube videos. This challenge to gain control of what we do, and not yield to undesirable behaviors, has not been ignored by psychologists. Albert Bandura turned the broader argument on free will into a more focused and actionable problem of human agency. To act with agency means that a person can act intentionally the way they want in this very complex world. With agency, people can make choices within the bounds of their strengths and weaknesses, are aware of the causes and effects of their actions, can self-regulate, and can understand the constraints in their environments.

Bandura realized that our environments circumscribe and limit our options for how we can act. For example, a person in prison cannot leave the four walls of their cell but can still exert agency in how they think. California occasionally imposes power cuts that limit what people can do during these outages (e.g., they can't use their microwave), but those cuts may give people more choices for action in the future if they prevent wildfires and safeguard the power supply. Bandura's position is optimistic as he believed that people can overcome environmental influences and choose their own futures. It may not be possible for most people to override circumstances of poverty to become a partner in a top law firm, but people can at least strive to influence their directions and, say, get a law degree.

Many psychologists' research interests were inspired by personal events that shaped their lives. Similarly, Bandura was drawn to study human agency by his early experience growing up in the rough terrain of northern Canada. He grew up in Mundare, Alberta, a small town of 400 people with only a single school. With only two teachers to cover all the high school courses, he largely took control of his own education. His homesteading experience and his schooling, as well as his exposure to the rough lifestyle in the Yukon—where he worked before college—planted a seed for his interest in the study of self-efficacy. He eventually received his PhD from the University of Iowa (Kurt Lewin had recently left the faculty there a few years earlier), and then joined the faculty at Stanford. Having started out in a pioneering lifestyle, he ended up becoming one of the most famous social psychologists of the twentieth century.

Bandura, who passed away while I was working on this book, spent his long career in understanding how people can develop beliefs in their ability to take control over their actions. He came to the idea that human agency has four properties: intentionality; forethought; self-regulation; and self-reflection and corrective behavior.[8] It is easy to imagine how these properties reflect agency when we act in the physical world. For example, a person might make an intentional choice to attend college. Using forethought, that person can imagine what the future might look like if she decides to go to an out-of-state school. That same person would demonstrate self-regulation by avoiding wild parties and instead studying for exams. The last property of agency, self-reflection and corrective behavior, would occur when a person realizes that she made a bad decision when accepting a job offer after graduation, and then takes the initiative to change jobs to correct the mistake.

It might be a bit harder, though, to think about how these properties of agency might operate in the digital world, especially if we want to apply them to exert control over our attention. With the first property, intentionality, we can make plans and consciously choose to work on that monthly report, deal with those accumulating emails in our inbox, or check the Twitter feed. The second property of agency, forethought, might not be obvious, say, in thinking about how going on social media will impact our future, especially if the action stems from an in-the-moment choice. If we think though about how going on Facebook might affect our work later in the day, then this is using forethought. Writing this book is also a good example. Whenever I set aside time to spend on my computer, I try to think ahead to how the book might turn out. Bandura's third property, self-regulation, as we have seen earlier in this book, is a challenge for many people in the digital world. People may have a hard time self-regulating their gaming behavior, the checking of their phone throughout the day or night, or their excessive use of social media—all of which can interfere with endogenous (internal) goals. Of course, those born with personality traits that give them a predisposition for low Impulsivity and high Conscientiousness have a much easier time because they were dealt a good set of cards to begin with. But your hand isn't necessarily fixed, as we'll talk about next.

This brings us to Bandura's fourth property of agency, self-reflection and corrective behavior. This aspect of agency is very important in controlling our attention, because it means being able to reflect on what we do on our devices and to use this awareness to change our behavior. For example, when you have agency, you not only realize you are spending excessive time on a game, but you also have the power to take action to stop doing it. But how can we do this? We know that change is not easy, but in order to reflect about our behavior, and then ultimately change it, we first need to be aware of the underlying factors that cause it. In other words, to develop the belief that we can change our behavior, which is a key part of practicing human agency, we first need to understand why we are carrying out such behaviors in the first place. This helps us develop our own internal tools to be able to change course. According to Bandura, the act of generating such understanding is an important foundation for developing agency because it can then lead to self-reflection and ultimately a course correction of behavior.

A strange and complicated partnership

So, given all the complexity that exists in the digital world, how can we act with agency? How can we behave in a way consistent with our higher-level goals? Let's step back first and remember that we don't use technology in a vacuum. Our attention is subject to so many influences beyond the self—it is bound up in a complex relationship with multiple factors both internal and external to us that guide, enable and constrain our attention in the digital world. Some of the factors on our attention are causal (an algorithmically designed ad that comes into our field of view on the screen and captures our attention). Other factors seem to affect our attention in a reciprocal way. For instance, we devote attention to building up our online social network, and then in turn we're distracted by the people in it. Our relationship with our devices is complicated and messy. Let's look now more closely at how the factors we discussed in Part II of the book might work in concert to affect our attention. This examination can help first of all with developing awareness of our behavior—Bandura's first property associated with agency. Achieving awareness of our actions is paramount for change. In the next chapter, we'll talk about how we can develop a meta-awareness of our actions, a deep "in-the-moment" awareness of what we are doing. We will also look later at other aspects of agency in relation to achieving control of our attention.

First, algorithms exert a direct effect on our attention by leveraging information about us, information that we unwittingly contribute based on our activity on the internet. Ads, recommendations, and news feeds are precisely tailored to lure us to click on them. Of course, we can try to resist them, but they are powerful and relentless.

A less direct influence is our personality, which does not determine our attention behavior, but it does set the stage for how we might respond. A person born with a personality trait of impulsiveness will likely have to work harder than others to resist distractions compared to those who score lower on that trait. As my research showed, a person who scores high in Neuroticism will on average shift their attention more among screens than someone who scores lower on this trait.

Social influences on our attention can also be forceful. People create social structures, and then their behaviors are shaped by the structures they create. In the physical world, people produce institutions like schools and workplaces and clubs with norms that they conform to. People also produce social structures such as groups and communities where the exchange of social capital and the exertion of social influence strongly urge them to remain socially connected. People form such social structures which in turn shape how people behave within them.

In the digital world, tech companies provide the platforms upon which people establish social structures such as a Facebook friend network or a Twitter following. We thus create our own digital social structures that shape our attention. We may have decided to limit our friend network only to close friends, or we may have accepted a lot of invitations and invited many others to the party so that we are part of a circle of one thousand people. Most likely a friend network of one thousand people will eat up our attention more than a network of fifty people, with more notifications and more posts to scroll through. Or, we may have constructed a large follower base on Instagram, and the likes we receive incentivize us to post even more, and thus the cycle of distraction continues.

Another type of reciprocal relationship involves the design of the internet and our attention. The vision for the design and structure of the internet was democratic with an open architecture. The fact that anyone—individuals or companies—can contribute content and develop the structure fosters the continual growth of new content, and this ties to our innate curiosity, which wants to discover new things. Many also experience FOMO (fear of missing out). We build on what others post, contributing more information and more links and thus offering more for everyone's attention. If a museum keeps growing in its offerings, we will keep returning again and again. Plus, the node and link structure provides a slick path for attention-wandering through our internal semantic memory network.

Software designers have cleverly designed interfaces that nudge us to perform certain actions, leading us to believe that we are doing these through willful intent. For example, we sit on the edge of our seats after a video episode, and Netflix automatically plays the next one, which we believe we have voluntarily decided to keep playing. In fact, we are lured, perhaps by the tension of the countdown of seconds, into continuing to watch. Another example is the Share button on Twitter, which nudges us to share tweets. When we are caught up in the momentum, we perform those actions. But the people who designed these types of nudges also refine their designs based on how users react—to maximize their effectiveness.

Similar reciprocal relations can be found in our broader media environment. Fast-changing shots and jump cuts on film, TV, YouTube and music videos may have been developed to move the plot along, and they steer our attention as we watch them. Or perhaps the choices of some directors and editors are made because they believe that swift shot changes are the way to keep people with short attention spans engaged. Or perhaps their choices are driven by a profit motive to pack in as much as possible in the shortest amount of time. Or perhaps their own short attention spans are influencing their aesthetic choices. Our attention is being targeted in a brutally competitive market for our mind's real estate.

Our attention behavior is also very much influenced by our situation and context. A person who feels that their personal tank of mental resources is near empty from an exhausting day of meetings will have little resistance against clicking on that algorithmic targeted ad or an inner urge to head to TikTok to get a reward of laughter. Or, as shown from my research, that person will likely prefer doing lightweight activities because they're easy (think Instagram or Candy Crush) and also make us content. If it's late in the evening and you are an adolescent, sleep-deprived and have homework looming, it will likely be very hard to not respond to your friend's Instagram notification.

A way forward using agency

So, have we created a digital world that makes it hard, or impossible for some, to exert free choice? Our digital world and how we behave in it are shaped by our culture, our current practices and our histories, and we could not have created a digital world free of these. Cultural influence is especially clear when we look at technology design: the signs and symbols of the digital world can be traced to those of the Western physical world such as the metaphors of files, folders and a trash can in personal computer interfaces, and the "friend" and "network" terms on Instagram and Facebook. These symbols are intended to signal to us how to act in the digital world, and we follow them willingly because they relate to our lives in the physical world. We can't just blame our short attention spans on algorithms and notifications; our attention behavior when we're on our devices is enveloped in a much broader culture beyond just the technology. We shouldn't forget that we are embedded also in a physical world that affects our digital behaviors.

If we reframe the goal of striving for free will in the digital world into a quest for agency, and if we believe that developing agency in the digital world is possible—and I believe it is—then we need to understand how these underlying factors can steer and constrain our attention in complex ways. Awareness and self-reflection on the reasons for our behaviors can lead us towards mastering our attention in the digital world.

Like Ben described earlier, some people may believe they are in control in the digital world and can easily stick to their higher-level goals when they use their devices. But for many participants in my studies, this is not the case. Most of us are susceptible to individual, environmental and technological forces that direct our attention behavior, and we may not even realize this. Bandura's view of agency, though, offers us a path forward. It does suggest that we can become aware of our conditioning and circumstances, and while we may not be able to control our desires, we can control our behaviors. This awareness can help us construct new ways of working. With such agency, we can achieve our higher-level attentional goals of finishing our tasks, we can strategically regulate attentional states and balance them better, and we can learn how to utilize our tendency for kinetic attention to our benefit. Next, we'll look specifically at what can be done to achieve that agency and control in our attention.

CHAPTER THIRTEEN:

Achieving Focus, Rhythm and Balance

As mentioned at the beginning of this book, it is time to rethink our relationship with our personal technologies. We need to reframe our goal from that of maximizing human productivity with our devices to instead using them and maintaining a healthy psychological balance while still achieving our aims. Outside of using our devices, there are of course so many things that can upset our psychological balance, such as having an argument with a partner, dealing with an unruly child, or being passed over for a long overdue promotion. But the fact is that we spend much of our waking hours on our computers, tablets and phones, and so in this chapter, I will focus on how we can feel positive and energetic and not stressed and exhausted—in other words, how we can achieve a psychological balance while using our devices.

What do we mean exactly by psychological balance? The autonomic nervous system controls certain body processes and is comprised of two parts: the parasympathetic and sympathetic systems. The parasympathetic system regulates the "rest and digest" functions when the body is relaxed, i.e., it lowers the heart rate and controls digestion. The sympathetic system, on the other hand, is associated with the fight-or-flight reaction, i.e., it increases heart rate and the flow of blood to the muscles in response to stressful situations. As my research showed, multitasking, with its rapid attention-shifting, interruptions, and too much sustained focus, results in stress, and when this happens for a long time, it creates too much dominance of the sympathetic nervous system. If the sympathetic system dominates over the parasympathetic system, then the body stays in a fight-or-flight state, and this can lead to all sorts of bad health outcomes such as hypertension.[1] If we are continually experiencing stress, then our psychological system is also thrown off balance. We can take action to achieve an internal psychological balance, which is called *psychological homeostasis*.[2]

When our autonomic nervous system is in balance, we can perform better. The mood associated with psychological homeostasis is positive: a combination of feeling content, happy and energetic.[3] When we feel positive, we can accomplish more. Positive emotion is shown to be an antecedent to creativity,[4] and as we discussed with the broaden-and-build theory in Chapter 10, positive emotion expands the breadth of thoughts and actions we can take so that we generate a greater range of solutions to problems.[5]

If you recall from Chapter 3, my research showed that attention is not just a binary of being focused and unfocused—our attention varies in types over the day, and each has a different purpose. Focused attention enables us to deeply process material, and rote attention enables us to pull back and refresh. Boredom, though too much of it can make us feel negative, can also help relieve cognitive load. We follow natural rhythms in our lives: our circadian rhythm signals to us when to sleep and wake, we adjust our routines to the rhythm of night and day, and we use rhythm in our speech.[6] Our attention also has a rhythm—sometimes we have the resources to be deeply focused, and sometimes not so much. Keep thinking of your internal gauge and recognize when your tank is full and ready for hard, creative work, but also when you need to stop and replenish that tank. Using your different types of attention purposefully while considering your resources can help you achieve your goals and still maintain an internal psychological balance.

Gaining agency to control your attention

In order to maintain an internal balance, you will need to develop agency to control your attention, and you also need to internalize this into your daily practice. In the last chapter, we discussed Bandura's notion that agency involves four properties: intentionality; forethought; self-regulation; and self-reflection and corrective behavior.[7] These properties can also be applied to gain control of attention in the digital world.

Being in control of your attention means first of all developing a conscious awareness of how you use it. For example, after years of using Facebook habitually, I began to question what I was really gaining from social media. I found face-to-face interactions or telephone calls to provide much more value, and they helped build trust in relationships. During the pandemic, I scheduled regular social Zoom chats with friends but also with colleagues who I ordinarily would see at work or conferences. What I had gained minimally in friend resources from using social media was now much stronger thanks to real-time conversations. But you can use social media strategically to gain benefits in your friendships, and I'll say more about that shortly.

Meta-awareness of your digital behaviors

To gain control of your attention, let's start with Bandura's first property for achieving agency: intentionality. You can learn how to practice *meta-awareness* of your actions, which is a powerful technique for bringing your attention and actions to a conscious level, enabling you then to be more intentional in your choices. Meta-awareness means knowing what you are experiencing as it is unfolding, like when you are conscious of your choice to switch screens from work to read *The New York Times*. If you have been on TikTok and fail to realize how much time has passed or you have fallen down a rabbit hole on the internet, then you lacked meta-awareness of your behavior.

Meta-awareness is an analytical mindset that helps you process your behavior and the reasons you are doing something more deeply. It is about observing your behavior like an outsider would, which then leads you to bring habitual actions to a conscious level. I came to this idea when the pandemic first began, and I took a course my university offered in mindfulness meditation. Mindfulness teaches you to focus on what you experience in the present, like your breathing, or external stimuli such as sounds, or on physical sensations in your body. As a result, you become more aware of the present.

I realized that a similar kind of process could be applied to make one more aware of their behavior on their devices. I am trained to observe people's behavior and have done so in the wild, and I realized that it's possible to apply a similar type of observation inwardly to my own behavior. So I tried it out and found that it helped me learn more about my online behavior and become more deliberate in my actions. Granted, I have a lot of experience in conducting observation, so it was fairly easy for me to learn how to observe my own behavior. But anyone can learn to observe oneself like another would—it's a skill you can develop. It's not necessary to take a course in mindfulness to develop meta-awareness when using your devices; rather, you can learn how to ask yourself the right questions to control your attention. You become better at practicing mindfulness the more you do it, and I found that practicing meta-awareness works the same way.

Remember the framing errors that can be made in choices from Chapter 2: people can misjudge how worthwhile a choice is and also the amount of time they might plan to spend doing something. You can try to avoid such framing errors by asking yourself questions to make you more conscious of your behavior. For example, before you go to, say, a social media site, ask yourself: What value will I gain by going there? If you're already there, you can ask: How much time have I spent here already? Am I gaining any value by staying here? When you use meta-awareness, you switch your frame of mind from being a passive to an active user of your attention. Asking such questions stopped me many times from clicking on a news or social media site. You can, of course, adopt an analytical mindset anytime, but I found that there are three main points when it works well: (1) to assess my level of cognitive resources; (2) when I am tempted to switch screens, to go to a site that's not central to my task at hand such as social media, news or a shopping page; and (3) when I'm already doing rote activity, to judge whether the activity is still worthwhile.

Practice meta-awareness to learn to recognize if your attentional resources are low and if you need a break. I used to work straight through the day without taking enough breaks, and then I realized too late that I was exhausted. Now I have learned to ask myself: How do I feel? Shall I continue working or do I feel fatigued? Do I need to take a break and replenish my energy? Such questions made me more conscious of the level of my personal resources, and I find that I can even be proactive in taking breaks before I get too exhausted. Of course, sometimes we go to social media or play simple games because our cognitive resources are low. That's perfectly fine. These mindless activities are great for short breaks, though a better choice is to get up and move around. But even if you go on social media or play simple repetitive games, you can learn to be aware of when you feel enough time has passed. Ask yourself: Do you feel replenished? Or rather, are you trying to avoid tough work? If so, what is making it tough? Is there some part of the task that you don't understand that someone can help you with? Are you on social media because you're bored with your work? The more you analyze your behavior, the easier it is to get out of that rabbit hole. By continuously asking yourself these questions, you can become a professional observer of yourself.

While I was writing this book, there was a news flash about a verdict in a high-profile trial. My impulse was to switch screens to read about it, but I paused first and asked myself: Will this really bring me value? Do I need a break now to read about it? I decided to wait until I would be at a break point in my work. (By then my excitement had cooled down.) While I read, say, a news story, I ask myself: Have I already learned the gist of the story? Am I still learning something new and interesting? If I keep at it, will I just experience diminishing marginal returns? If so, then I stop—it's that simple. This prevents one from getting too deep into the sunk cost attention trap where it's psychologically hard to pull out.

Developing the ability to use meta-awareness is like a muscle that you can develop. At first you might forget to pause and ask yourself such questions, but the more you practice, the more naturally it comes. You might start out by writing down simple questions to ask yourself, like on Post-it notes, and keeping them in view. The better able you are to gain a meta-awareness of your behavior, the more intentional you can be in your actions. With practice you will develop an analytical mindset when considering your behavior.

Developing forethought of your digital behavior

Bandura's second property, using forethought, is another tool to help you gain agency with your attention. Forethought means imagining how your current actions might affect your future. This also makes you more conscious and intentional in your behavior. Before you go on social media or play an online game, spend a moment to think ahead and imagine what your end of the morning or end of the day might look like if you indulge. You know your habits, and you probably know how long you usually spend on social media or a news site. If you know you are someone who goes down the social media rabbit hole, visualize how spending twenty minutes (or two hours) of your time will affect your work (and personal life) some hours from now. Let's imagine you need to finish multiple tasks: you have to do a PowerPoint presentation, you have to write a memo, you need to deal with your emails and keep up with Slack, and on top of this, you need to search for an apartment. You know that you like to visit social media, but you also know that once there, you tend to remain there easily for an hour. So pause before you go to social media and imagine then that you will spend an hour on social media. What will your end of the day look like?

Do you imagine that you will not be seeing that finished PowerPoint presentation, or do you see yourself staying up late making up for lost time? If you are a student, forethought is especially important—in our studies of college students, we found that social media takes up an inordinate amount of time for them. Visualize what your night will look like at 2 a.m. Will you be asleep or still be up finishing homework because you spent many hours earlier on social media? Do you visualize any regret? Expand your thinking beyond the current moment so that you consider the implications of your actions now on your life downstream in the day.

Goals are important, but without a visualization to go with them, they are abstract and hard to keep in mind. The more detailed your visualization is, even imagining what your emotions might be, the easier it is to take an action to course-correct if you need to. Envisioning the impact that spending time on these sites will have in the short term for you, and possibly even in the long term, will introduce speed bumps before you switch your attention. Visualizing this future can help you build awareness of how your present actions have consequences. A detailed picture of the future (finishing your work, having time to relax, watching the next episode of that Netflix series, and reading a book before bed) becomes a motivator for you to stick to your goals.

I admit that I'm a sucker for a certain anagram game called Pangram. The game has different levels, and it creates tension as I strive to achieve a higher level—this is intended by the game developers. When I start it, I stay in the game because I won't be able to relieve tension (following Kurt Lewin's notion of tension reduction) until I reach a higher level. I also know, given my own personality traits, that once I start, it's hard to stop until I finish. This game is not a good choice for taking a short break to reset—Zeigarnik's result on interrupted tasks is relevant for me as I won't be able to get the game out of my mind until I achieve that highest level. Sometimes even after succeeding, I continue playing to see if I can find even more words. It is something of an obsession for me. So before I even start that game, I practice forethought. I know that I can spend anywhere from thirty minutes to multiple hours before I reach the highest level, so I consider how it will interfere with what I plan to accomplish at the end of the day. If the circumstances allow (e.g., a long commute), then I give myself permission to indulge, knowing that I will have plenty of time to finish the game. Using forethought before I even begin has helped deter me from starting the game in the first place. But also, I know that doing the game at a later point when I have more time to finish it could provide me with even more rewards since I won't have the underlying tension that Lewin described of needing to finish my work. I do not even open the game unless I can visualize how playing this game will not impact my work.

When I used to play this anagram game a lot, even when I

did other tasks, the letters remained in the back of my mind, and I was crazily thinking of new words. That is the nature of being so obsessed. Even when you stop an activity, remnants of the task can stay in your mind and interfere with your subsequent tasks. Using meta-awareness has also helped me realize that the attention residue of the game has interfered with my other work. Visualizing the future consequences and also the future opportunity for when I can pick the game up again has helped me curtail my behavior.

Self-regulation of your digital behavior

Blocking software might seem like an easy way to promote self-regulation, Bandura's third property of agency. It may help in the short term, but it's not a permanent solution. While it did provide benefits in the short term for people in our study who had low self-control, if we take a step back, we realize that it is not actually teaching a long-lasting skill to self-regulate, but rather off-loading the work onto the software. People fail to learn the skills themselves, and that's what agency is all about. It's like keeping the training wheels on, and then you never learn to ride the bike on your own. When you use software to block sites, then you are no longer the agent responsible for your actions; the software has become a proxy agent, and you won't learn to develop an internal model to explain your own actions—the tool that you need to help you self-regulate. It is best to develop your own agency.

We're not all born with a personality trait for strong self-regulation, but it is a skill you can develop. If you would have grabbed that first marshmallow as a four-year-old like in Mischel's experiment, it does not mean that you're confined to a path of never being able to control your attention. You may just need to work more intently at it than others. Remember, we have a harder time self-regulating when our cognitive resources are low. So one of the first things you can do is not let yourself get expended. Become aware of your personal gauge of resources, and when you start feeling spent, then take a break.

Self-regulation through changing your structures

We create various kinds of structures for ourselves, such as schedules. But you probably don't realize that there are other types of structures that constrain and steer your attention in the digital world. The setup of your computer and phone interface is a structure that affects your attention by presenting visual cues of your files, apps and browser tabs. To gain control of your attention, the first thing you should do is restructure your interface environment to reduce stimuli that elicit automatic attention. You likely already know to remove visual cues in your interface that can distract you—you can turn off notifications, as they attract your attention through bottom-up salience and you respond automatically. You should also hinder access to things unrelated to your work, activities that you know you consciously choose. If you know that you like to play a certain game, hide the app in a folder so that you don't see it on your interface. Having to search for it will make you pause, and then you can ask yourself it it's worth doing now. If you don't get value from the time you spend on it, then delete it. But if it brings you pleasure and helps you de-stress, and you feel you can learn to moderate your behavior with it, then keep it. Do some housecleaning on your computer and phone.

You can also design a routine to help yourself self-regulate. If you know you are a person with a trait of high Impulsivity and you respond automatically to the sight of your phone, then design a personalized routine to create friction to make it harder to be distracted by your phone. When you sit down to work, leave your phone in another room or in a drawer and even lock it. The more friction you design into your routine to prevent distracting stimuli, the less likely you'll be interrupted—externally, but also internally, because your expectations of easily getting to that app will be revised. If I see a magazine next to me, I'm likely to pick it up to read it. If it's in another room, I may not even think about it, and if I do but have to walk to another room to get it, then probably I won't. So keep potentially distracting stimuli out of sight on your computer, phone and physical environment—and thus out of mind.

Self-regulation through creating hooks

Gaining control of your attention does not mean completely stopping social media use or surfing the web or reading news. That would be like throwing out the champagne with the cork. To retain social benefits, and also control of your attention, think of how to design what I call "hooks" into your digital world. Hooks can help prevent you from falling into an attention trap. Before you go on social media or read news, be proactive and plan a hook that can pull you out. For example, plan a social media break ten minutes before a scheduled phone call. The appointment becomes the hook, and you know you will have to stop browsing social media and take that call. (Of course, the danger is that you might miss that call, so be careful.) Another example is to save your game-playing obsession for your commute. The hook occurs when you reach your stop. Hopefully you won't miss your stop (like I did once on the New York subway when I was reading on my phone). You can also save your social media use for when you're in a waiting room, like a doctor's office, and then the hook to pull you out is when your name is called. You might think that you're not using agency if you rely on some external event to stop your behavior. But you are, because you're strategically planning ways to create an escape hatch in advance.

Self-regulation through not switching your screen

It's hard to resist eating that chocolate cake when it's already on your plate. Know that if you switch to another screen to follow your internal impulses, it will be doubly hard to return back to the original screen and original task. If you switch to YouTube, it's like you're putting that chocolate cake on your plate in full view. How can you not help but eat it? You won't get sucked into a rabbit hole of YouTube watching if you don't start looking at it in the first place. Remember, we may not have free will in our desires, but we can take agency in our actions. So when you have a desire to visit a social media site, you can help yourself self-regulate by just not switching your screen. It's easier to not switch the screen than to pull yourself out of social media once you're on the site. What you don't see becomes much less of a temptation in which to indulge. It's as simple as that. Take a deep breath, look out the window for a minute, or go for a short walk, and then pick up where you left off—on the same screen.

Self-reflection and correction

Now we'll turn to Bandura's fourth property of agency, self-reflection and course correction, and we'll look at different ways that behavior can be course-corrected to achieve control of attention and feel balanced. You can change your mindset about how you use social media, you can learn how to design your day considering your cognitive resources and your emotions, and you can keep your goals concrete and conscious in your mind.

Use your friend network meaningfully

Scrolling mindlessly through post after post on Facebook is like multitasking. You switch from person to person and topic to topic. Most posts barely register with you, some might be mildly interesting (or sad), and then every so often, just like with TikTok or Instagram, you'll get a hit with a charming story or a video that makes you happy or angry or sad. But it may take a long time to find that hit. You've then wasted your time, attention and energy.

As I mentioned, Facebook, or for that matter any social media, is not designed to develop deep relationships but simply to maintain relationships. However, because friend networks have grown to hundreds or even thousands of people, they have rendered even the idea of maintaining relationships somewhat meaningless. Think about the Dunbar number of one hundred fifty people with who you can have a stable relationship (and for deep relationships, it's only about five). Of course, if you really want to develop better relationships, then you'll have to do it outside of social media.

Remember, you get different kinds of rewards with your social network. Bridging social capital gives you input from a diverse group of people. It can help us solve problems, such as how to find an apartment, or can provide us with information that we may not have gotten otherwise, such as the latest news on climate change. The other type of social capital—bonding social capital—provides you with emotional and supportive rewards from those with who we have close relationships (and who we support in turn). Chances are, when you go on social media scrolling through posts, you probably don't think about these different types of rewards.

But you can leverage the rewards that your online network can offer you so you can make better use of your time and attention. My preference is to think about bonding social capital and how to interact meaningfully with one individual to gain something and give something in return. Perhaps it's an old friend you haven't contacted for a long time. When you take a break to do some rote activity, reach out and use social media to connect with that person and then arrange a follow-up with a phone call, video chat or meeting. I remember connecting once with an old friend from high school on Facebook, and it brought a flood of wonderful memories. Think of the first framing error: making a choice that is not worthwhile. Social media can be a time killer when you scroll through it mindlessly out of habit.

So rather than scrolling through hundreds or thousands of people in your network, who will likely become abstract to you, think about making your experience meaningful. Choose someone who makes you happy to be with and focus your time and attention on that individual. Visualize that interaction so it incentivizes you to pursue it. Write a positive message to tell that person that you value them. Of course, you can also pick up a phone and tell them this and arrange to meet them. But there is far less friction to kick off an interaction using an online network—this is a big advantage of our web connections. And by the way, once you've sent that nice message, then it's time to leave social media and get back to your work goals.

Designing your day to achieve a balance

The traditional practice of scheduling a day is to write down tasks to work on—it's what most of us have always done. Often what people do is write down meetings and deadlines in their calendars, make a to-do list, and sometimes even assign a start and stop time for each task. With this traditional practice, one thinks in terms of sticking to a schedule and finishing tasks. Maximizing productivity means squeezing as much work as possible into a limited amount of time, and of course the by-product is often higher stress. I have taught a project management course for years to students in my university department, a course that teaches people how to design and achieve their goals efficiently. We know from project management that there is usually slippage, and tasks almost always take longer than what one envisions. There is also no room for fitting human well-being into task schedules. We need to instead relearn what designing a day should be in the twenty-first century digital world. It should include strategies to not exhaust yourself and to improve your well-being, and it includes understanding your own rhythm of attentional states and the fact that you have limited and precious cognitive resources. Next we'll talk about strategies that you can use to design your day to better achieve a psychological balance.

Optimize your resources by knowing your rhythm

Throughout this book, we have used the theory of cognitive resources and applied it to your daily life, with the idea that some activities drain your resources while other activities replenish them. Design your day thinking that you have limited mental resources, knowing that taking time to replenish them will not only help you be less stressed and better able to resist distractions, but also more creative.[8] We know how different activities affect our physical energy in the world such as being with family or friends, coordinating a complex event, or taking a walk in nature. In the digital world, what taxes your mental energy? What things do you do that replenish your resources? What kind of rote activity relaxes you? At the end of the day, you want to feel energetic and positive. Don't end up with your tank of resources on reserve when it's only the early afternoon—there are carryover effects that bring stress to your personal life later in the day.

Plan your day thinking about how your tasks will impact your cognitive resources. Start by taking a big picture view of your work. Consider how your tasks fit together like a puzzle so that you're not doing one hard task right after another, overtaxing your attention. Remember, long stretches of sustained attention can be exhausting (unless you are in flow, which is rare in most knowledge work). What activity do you want to start your day with? Many people prefer to begin their day with rote work to ready themselves before diving into hard work. Consider your meetings. If you can, do not schedule one meeting right after the other—that's a sure way to feel exhausted. The problem with Zoom meetings is that we tend to schedule them back-to-back, and there's no chance to reset in between. Do something easy and positively rewarding before a long meeting that you know will be challenging, and then replenish your resources afterwards with social interaction, some rote activity, or best yet, a walk. Consider that you have precious mental energy that you'll need to distribute among your activities. Don't get exhausted by 11 a.m. when you still have the rest of the day to get through.

Design your day based on your own rhythm of attention, knowing that you have peak times for focus and taking advantage of these for tasks that need it. Your time for peak focus is affected by your chronotype—your natural circadian rhythm. Get to know your chronotype.[iii] We found in our studies reported in Chapter 3 that most people have peak focus times around 11 a.m. and midafternoon. Your own peak focus may differ depending on whether you are an early bird, in which case it is probably earlier than 11 a.m., or if you're a late type, then you may not hit your stride until later, perhaps even in the afternoon. Save your hardest tasks that require the most effort and creativity for your peak hours. Don't do email during your peak times—these will use up precious resources better spent on your other tasks. Remember, email creates stress, and can be done when you're not at your peak, perhaps first thing in the morning and at the end of your workday. Email ages fast, and if you wait to check your email at the end of the workday, you might discover that a lot of problems have been solved. Check your email in reverse chronological order and you will see how many issues have already been taken care of. Above all, don't do email before you go to bed—you don't want to bring that stress with you.

My own chronotype is moderate—I am neither an extreme early bird nor an extreme late-type. When I start my day, I first look at the news headlines and then usually do subordinate work of looking through my inbox. I know, though, that I can't open and then put aside important emails for later because they will become that unfinished task that Zeigarnik described, and I'll keep remembering that I need to answer them. My own peak focus time is around 11 a.m., and I save my most creative work for midmorning. Throughout the day, I envision my own personal

---

iii　You can take this survey to learn your chronotype: https://chronotype-self-test.info/

gauge of attentional capacity. I am aware that if I spend too much time, say, trying to understand tax law, then I'm using cognitive resources that may impinge on my attentional capacity when I need it for other creative work. Of course, it may be necessary for me to spend time on tax law, in which case I'll do it when I'm not spent. Thinking about my limited tank of resources also wakes me up from getting into a sunk cost trap if I start reading a long article. Better yet, I don't attempt to start it unless I know I'll have time reserved to finish it, and that's usually at the end of the day. Remember that as resources drain, we are also less resistant to distractions, and our kinetic attention impulses kick in.

Include negative space in your day

Design your day to include negative space. In art, negative space refers to the area around the image and is part of the art. In Japanese design, *yohaku no bi* refers to the beautiful and dynamic empty space around the objects in a painting or in garden design. It is like active silence in music, an integral part of the composition. Negative space is a good metaphor to use as you set aside respites in your day that surround hard work, so you can reset and boost your attention capacity. Use meta-awareness to assess if your cognitive resources are low. If they are, give yourself permission to do something that you know is non-taxing of your cognitive resources, that is rote and easy, that will make you feel positive and will bring a reward. Negative space is just as important as the work itself because it helps you achieve a balance where you are not overstressed.

However, you can't be in a zen state for too long during a workday because people do need some amount of arousal for good performance. The well-studied relationship between arousal and performance is called the Yerkes-Dodson law[9] and takes the form of an upside down U-shaped curve. The height of the curve represents your performance. The apex of the curve is where you need to be—that's where your performance is at its peak with the right amount of arousal. To the left of the apex, you don't have enough arousal, and your performance is also not great. If you need more arousal, take an energetic walk. Arousal is needed to be alert, but with too much arousal of the wrong kind (think of stress), performance starts to take a dive, and you end up to the right of the apex on the curve. Find your optimal point of arousal—think of it as your sweet spot of stress. Use the notion of combining negative space with hard tasks, and taking breaks to walk or do rote activity, to try and stay at that sweet spot. With practice you will get to know your rhythm and your attentional capacity.

Your tasks have an emotional valence

View your activities in the digital world not only in terms of how much attentional capacity they require, but also consider their emotional valence—the emotional quality associated with doing them that makes you feel positive or negative. Our research showed that people are happiest when they do easy, rote activity. We also found that handling email elicits negative emotions. Think about how you can design your day with the goal of ending it with net positive emotion. I know that jogging makes me happy, likely due to the endorphin release, so I fit it in when I want to feel more positive. Unfortunately, we can't do tasks all day that bring positive emotion. But you can limit the negative emotional effect of a meeting with a person you know to be ornery by timing it, say, right before lunch, when you can take a break (but not eating lunch in front of your screen). Or, you can manage unpleasant tasks like doing email by timing when you review your inbox and limiting your checking of it to once or twice a day. Perhaps you can collaborate with another person on a hard task, which might make it less onerous. For tasks that you can expect will have a negative valence for you—and if you can be flexible in scheduling them—change the time frame when you do them, such as before lunch. Intersperse them with tasks that bring positive emotions, or reset and replenish after you do them. So when you schedule your day, consider how the things you do will affect your emotions.

Choosing goals to achieve a balance

Your goals are your blueprints for the day outlining how you want to spend your precious cognitive resources and how to achieve an internal balance. Maintaining goals is not a static enterprise but is rather dynamic. Remember that attention is goal-directed, and to keep your attention on track, you have to keep a representation of your goals in your mind. When you design your day, ask yourself: What do you hope to accomplish? How do you want to feel? Visualize your goals to make them concrete and use forethought: What will your end of the day look like and how will you feel when you send out that finished report?

Also set emotional goals. A promising approach that shows the value of incorporating emotional goals with task goals is found in a study of work detachment and reattachment conducted at Microsoft Research by Alex Williams, which I was involved in. Each morning for fourteen days, thirty-four employees at a large organization answered simple questions posed by a computer software agent when they turned on their computer. The night before, people identified what they wanted to work on the next day and also how they wanted to feel. Say someone had identified that they wanted to work on a particular project, and they wanted to feel happy. This person would then be asked the next morning, "Do you still want to work on this project? What is the first step you can take towards completing this task? Do you still want to feel happy? What is the first step you can take towards feeling this way?" These questions primed people to think about their goals, and the experiment showed some success: people felt more productive and engaged in their first hour of work.[10] It brought people's plans and goals to a conscious level, and once they were recognized, people had agency to act on them. You can use this same technique to elevate your goals to a conscious level to keep them in mind. It was also found in this study that goals need to be reaffirmed throughout the day.

What kept me on track to finish this book was to use the practices described here to develop agency in my actions. I continually practice meta-awareness, to help me think more deeply about my actions, such as asking myself why I feel the need to stop writing and check news or email. It has become routine for me. I also used forethought. When I started work in the morning, I imagined what the end of my day would look like, and I envisioned what those several pages of a written chapter might also look like. Or, I imagined saving the document and moving it into the folder of finished chapters or sending it off. I also imagined how that would make me feel, which was happy, and that helped motivate me. It was a great incentive. Keeping my high-level goals in mind helped me from getting stuck in an attention trap. I know that my nature is to be obsessed once I start something, and therefore, I try not to start an activity unless I can imagine it fitting into my end of day vision. These practices helped me self-reflect on my digital activities and course-correct when I caught an issue.

Above all, I learned to recognize my own rhythm and to own it. I know when my peak writing time is, and I know when I tend to feel drained. For me, waking up too early doesn't work as I am not an early type. But I know that if I start at a reasonable time for my personal rhythm, with a bit of rote activity first, I will then hit full gear fast. I intentionally switch my activities depending on how I imagine my personal tank of cognitive resources. If I feel it is low, then I stop and refresh before I get exhausted. I schedule outdoor exercise into my day like I do a meeting (I admit, it helps to live in southern California), but you can also take a break and move around wherever you are, even inside your apartment or house. Sometimes I play short crossword puzzles (invoking Maya Angelou's Little Mind). This helps me clear my head, and when I return to writing, I can look at it with fresh eyes. Often by working on something else, when I returned to the book, I viewed it in a different light.

The important point is to use meta-awareness to take a break or switch to rote activity as soon as you detect yourself feeling low on resources, *before* they are exhausted, to use forethought to help keep you on track, and to develop your own hook before you do that lovely rote activity so that you don't end up trapped in a rabbit hole. I am very aware of the different forces that distract me, and I am also very aware of my own personality makeup, my strengths and weaknesses (I do tend to be neurotic), and use this knowledge, not as an excuse but rather to help me strategize how to be more intentional and purposeful in my attention when using my devices.

I wrote this book on sabbatical, which released me from teaching duties and service work. But I also ran research projects, held and attended meetings and workshops, wrote research papers, supervised two students writing their dissertations, sat on doctoral student defense committees, reviewed papers, wrote reference letters, and still managed to write this book in seven months. I also made sure to design my day carefully and schedule time for rote and other enjoyable activity. With my sabbatical in New York City, I made sure to enjoy the city's offerings in the evenings and on weekends. I also managed to do this while hovering close to that sweet spot of stress and not exceeding it. Yet I admit it was not always smooth sailing. Sometimes I did lose track of my goals, and sometimes I didn't pay attention to my personal gauge of resources, neglected to take breaks or pull back, and wore myself out. Each time, it made me more resolute to become more conscious of my actions and level of resources. In other words, when I encountered a challenge or a problem, I tried to recognize it as such. I then worked on developing agency to tackle the problem, and then could integrate this new learning into my repertoire of actions. My mother expressed this idea when she often said, "I take it, I take it over, I take it easy."

Breaking the myths and building a new foundation

In this book, I've aimed to use research findings to shift the public conversation in how we use our devices so that the main goal is to strive to achieve a healthy psychological balance, and to follow our natural attentional rhythm. But you might be thinking, wait a minute, what? Shouldn't striving for productivity be the number one concern? Just as we can't run a marathon all day, we cannot experience the high mental load of focused attention for long uninterrupted stretches without our performance degrading and stress increasing. So instead of forcing yourself into long periods of sustained focus with pressure to optimize productivity, instead find your rhythm of using different kinds of attention: there are times when you can be challenged, and other times when you need something easy and engaging. Design your day around using your cognitive resources wisely and aim to optimize your well-being.

The public narrative that we shouldn't allow for mindless rote activity is not based in science. Rote activity has a function in our lives: it makes people happy when they are engaged in activity that is not challenging and often relaxing and helps people step back and replenish their cognitive resources. Gardening and knitting are rote activities, for example. Similarly, in the digital world, there are things we can do to relax and reset and that can bring rewards such as connecting with other people. We need to consider rote activity as part of our work that supports our larger task and emotional goals. Of course, the best breaks are those where you can get up and move around (but not while checking your smartphone). Taking short breaks with easy tasks (and applying meta-awareness so you don't get too lost) helps replenish scarce cognitive resources, and the upshot is that with more resources, we can focus our attention better, self-regulate more effectively, be more productive, and importantly, feel more positive.

Give yourself permission to back off—you need not feel guilty. We can't all be like William James or the writer Stephen King, who are both known for writing two thousand words a day. We have created a culture intent on optimizing productivity, which also means more production of information, more communication, and more information to keep up with. In our current digital climate, we are fighting gale-force winds to keep the ship on course to maintain our well-being.

What you can do is develop agency to achieve better control of your attention, to get in sync with your attentional rhythm, and with it, strive for positive well-being. The great artists and writers knew the importance of finding their rhythms. They knew when they worked best and when to take breaks and when to fill their day with negative space. The writer Anne Beattie prefers to start writing at 9 p.m. and is at her best between midnight and 3 a.m.[11] She follows her own rhythm for her peak focus.

We need to change our conversation in our still relatively young digital age to prioritize our health and well-being. Computers were designed for us to extend our capabilities, but by doing so, we are losing control of our attention and stressing ourselves out. The idea that we get distracted, get interrupted and multitask because of our personal lack of willpower is incomplete. Nor is it useful to blame everything on powerful algorithms. The realm of influence is much bigger. Our attention behavior is influenced by a much larger sociotechnical world that we're part of, encompassing environmental, social, individual and other technological forces. It's not just about our own lack of discipline. However, we can use agency to *plan* and *take action*, like intentionally choosing how to use our attention, to harness our tendency for dynamic attention. Using our attention effectively in the digital world is really about understanding ourselves and the larger environment we live in.

CHAPTER FOURTEEN:

The Future of Attention

Personal computing, the internet and smartphones were intended to increase our human capabilities. But in my years of research, I have found that these technologies, though invaluable in improving our lives, are also often exhausting us. My research revealed results far worse that I had expected. In the long hours we spend on our computers and phones, we shift our attention rapidly and are interrupted by external sources and by ourselves. The result is that our work is fragmented, and we often feel overwhelmed and stressed. Stress, as I mentioned in the beginning of the book, is referred to as an epidemic of the twenty-first century,[1] and leads to a host of problems such as high blood pressure, sleep issues and fatigue. Of course, so many things in our lives cause stress, but we can change at least one potential source of it—our relationship with our personal devices. We can use our limited attentional capacity wisely and still achieve a psychological balance with positive well-being. We can also, yes, be productive.

Digital technologies have become an appendage to our minds and are embedded in our culture—no wonder it's so hard to pull away. We can't drive without our GPS, we no longer do calculations in our heads, and Google has become a partner in our conversations. Our computers and phones demand our constant attention. But let's not neglect the fact that we are part of a larger fast-changing digital world beyond our computers and smartphones: we ask voice assistants to do our shopping, set smart thermostats to heat our homes, and use robots to clean our houses. Change happens so fast in our digital world, and we don't always notice it.

Similarly, we have become inured to how our attention has decayed when using our personal devices—our attention spans have been declining over the years. Putting our own individual natures aside, a culture has developed that contributes to and reinforces our short attention spans. This culture has been created by tech companies, film, TV, and advertising, by social media platforms and organizational structures, but also by all of us. We contribute to a digital culture that reinforces our short attention spans by sharing content and stories through video and social media and developing new platforms to enable this.

My own story of how my attention was affected with the rise of computing is so similar to the stories of the people who I studied. As I continued with this research over the years, I became more aware of my own multitasking and stress. The more I looked outwardly to study others, the more I turned inwardly to examine my own behavior. I realized that I was neglecting my own psychological balance. In studying others, I soon realized it was not enough to document how much our attention is fragmented. I also wanted to understand why, and what we can do about it. My conclusion is that we do not have to remain locked into a path of more distractions and higher stress.

Developing a healthy relationship with technology requires change on three levels: individual, organizational and societal.

While as individuals we can't change our predispositions much nor our basic social drives, we can work with these and develop agency to control our attention in the digital world. Organizations can buttress our individual efforts through restructuring communication patterns and thus changing expectations, and society can enact policies and programs to help us develop new cultural practices.

Despite technology's current toll on our attention, I am continually excited by innovations and believe we can learn to master its use without it negatively impacting our happiness. We can change our popular narrative of needing to push ourselves to our limits to instead striving to achieve positive well-being with our technology use. Rather than getting engulfed by the ocean, we can learn how to swim with the current and ride the waves.

Looking towards the future

So can we simply cut ourselves off from email, Slack or social media, as is sometimes recommended as a way to limit distractions? We can take a digital detox, but it's not a permanent or viable long-term solution. If you're a knowledge worker of any type, a full- or part-time worker who needs to use computers and phones for work, a college or high school student or someone who needs to stay in touch with family and friends far away, it is not tenable to go off the grid for a lengthy period. Any individual who cuts themselves off will end up being penalized for missing out on critical information for work or important conversations with friends. This also shifts the burden of communication and work onto colleagues who then need to pick up the slack. Dropping out just doesn't work because we live in an interrelated web of people and information, and together are caught up in an ever-increasing circulation of information. It is the reality of the digital age we have created. Our devices are smart, but we must be smarter in how we use them.

While as individuals we can achieve agency over our personal actions, we also need to treat the issue of controlling our attention as a challenge for organizations. Pulling out of work tools like email and Slack can only be done collectively, as we found with our email cutoff study.[2] Batching email is widely proposed as a solution, but as I mentioned earlier, it is not the silver bullet that many imagine it to be, as we found in two studies: reading email in batches did not lower people's stress, nor did people report higher productivity. However, this doesn't mean that it can't provide some benefits. Limiting the arrival of email in the inbox can reset people's expectations. If everyone knows that email won't arrive until, say, 1 p.m., then it revises everyone's expectations collectively and relieves pressure (and guilt) to not respond right away. Perhaps this might cut down the volume of email sent. It can also change individual habits of checking email, so that people just go to their inbox once or twice a day and not seventy-seven times a day as I found. People may gain more time in the day. People learn pretty quickly that new email won't be there, so they'll stop checking it continuously, and habits can be broken. In the email cutoff study we did, even after a few days without email, people began to change their habits. Organizations can thus create new social conventions and new collective expectations around the use of work communications.

Designating a quiet time where no electronic communication can be sent can also set new expectations that there can be time without email. Perhaps even better, in the same way that phone service providers allot minutes of data use per month, organizations can allot a fixed amount of email minutes per week, or per day. Beyond that, well, people will just have to meet in person, which people in our email cutoff study enjoyed.

Organizations can do their part by not penalizing employees who do not respond to messages after work hours. Formal policy can help change employees' mindsets and rebuild the broken-down borders of work and personal life by supporting people's efforts to detach from work. Time spent dealing with emails after work hours adds to stress—simply put, after-work email use makes people feel angry.[3] Policies have already been introduced in some places to regulate intrusion so that people can turn off at an organizational level without penalizing any individual. German companies such as Volkswagen and the insurance company Allianz have adopted such a policy for their workers. Disconnection means not answering emails, Slack, or cell phones or doing video conferencing both before and after work hours.

On a broader, country level, Right to Disconnect laws are being enacted, which began in France with its El Khomri labor law, passed in 2017.[4] Other countries, such as Italy and the Philippines, are introducing similar legislation. In 2021, Ireland passed the Code of Practice, and the Canadian province of Ontario enacted the Working for Workers Act 2021, both of which grant employees the right to not answer work communications after normal work hours. Does this policy succeed? A survey of 107 French workers found the El Khomri law to be a mixed bag. They loved the idea, but in practice, some companies resisted implementing the policy because they felt it would interfere with their bottom line.[5] So the culture also has to change along with policy to put workers' well-being above the profit motive.

What is striking about these laws is that they treat detachment from digital devices as a basic human right. In other words, it is recognized as a basic human right for people to be able to disconnect from work after business hours without experiencing repercussions. The right to disconnect builds on Article 24 of the Universal Declaration of Human Rights, which states, "Everyone has the right to rest and leisure, including reasonable limitation of working hours and periodic holidays with pay."[6] There are still large problems to be addressed as more countries adopt Right to Disconnect laws, such as when people work with others across different time zones, but some countries are moving in a positive direction. Perhaps in due time, more countries will realize the necessity to reduce stress and give people a chance to replenish their attentional resources by enacting similar policies.

The pandemic experience, however, introduced a whole new way of thinking about work hours. People often interspersed personal life with work life during the day, such as caring for children, and so work hours stretched, the boundaries between work and personal life blurred, and it was no longer clear exactly what normal work hours meant. Many companies have already committed to continuing with hybrid or remote work, and many workers love the benefit of having flexibility in work hours, especially if they have to care for children or aging parents. For remote work, Right to Disconnect laws will become more important than ever before to prevent burnout from long evenings of doing email. Considering that people may have flexible hours, such laws could shrink the window for electronic communication for everyone in a company, say to a few hours per day. Change works best in organizations when it's incremental, and gradually shrinking the window of time can rewire expectations for all the employees about responding to communications.

Young people are especially vulnerable to the pull of technology, with their executive function and social identities still developing. Schools need to develop media literacy programs where young people are taught how to recognize and course-correct their digital behaviors—this can help them develop agency and positive habits of technology use. Already some school systems have enacted media literacy programs, such as California's Senate Bill number 830, approved in 2018.[7] This bill makes resources and instructional materials available to school districts for media literacy education. Learning how to have a healthy relationship with personal technology needs to start at a young age.

At a societal level, laws and policy can serve as a foundation to support us in becoming more balanced in our technology use. There is optimism for such societal change with individuals speaking out. As described in Chapter 7, in 2021, whistleblower Frances Haugen released internal Facebook files and testified before a US Senate committee about the harmful effects of the company. Her courage may inspire many others to step forward, and this can lead to new regulations to curb practices of social media companies. Other important efforts are underway to urge the US government to support more ethical use of social media through the Technology and Social Change Project at the Harvard Kennedy School[8] and the Center for Humane Technology,[9] as well as through further testimony before the US Congress. Though targeted personalization using algorithms is not slowing down, we are seeing an increase in awareness by the public of how our behaviors and attention are being manipulated. We saw the downfall of Cambridge Analytica after it improperly gained access to the sensitive Facebook data of 87 million users.[10] As legal fees escalated and clients turned away from them, it claimed insolvency. This serves as a strong public message to other companies that there are bounds of user privacy that cannot be breached. In Europe, data privacy is now enshrined in policy with the General Data Protection Regulation.

Optimism remains on hold as to whether the broader media environment of TV, film and advertising might change. The profit motive is strong, which drives more content to be packed into shorter and shorter time frames, and this is unlikely to change. However, if film shots become too short, then video will become incomprehensible (chaos editing seems to have reached its limit). Historically, the pendulum often swings back, so we will have to wait and see.

AI and our attention

Technological innovations can also give us reasons for optimism. A historical example of how innovations can change the course of societal trajectories is found with a study published in 1972, called *The Limits to Growth*,[11] commissioned by the Club of Rome, a network of one hundred top thought leaders whose goal was to address global problems. In this study, a group of MIT operations researchers used computer simulations to predict the decline of world resources, e.g., reporting that global food per capita will peak in 2020 and then plunge downward. We are past 2020, and so far the predictions did not hold. What the models did not account for was that interventions and innovations can happen along the way to thwart or slow the direction of such collapses—for example, new agricultural practices. Of course, significant changes still need to be made. There are still so many urgent societal problems such as climate change that are on a dangerous path and need innovations and changes in policy and practice.

Whereas we might feel that we are at the limit as to how much our attention can be fragmented, we cannot foresee what new technological and behavioral innovations might come along that might challenge or support our quest for agency. For example, in the future you may be the one to own the algorithm. You may have your own AI-based personal digital assistant that you control, and also, importantly, you would own your data associated with it. This means that what you do with your assistant will not and should not be owned or accessible by tech companies. These future personalized digital assistants will learn precise details of your attentional capabilities from your behavior, context, personality traits, sleep the night before, and mood, thus learning what builds up your personal attentional resources and what depletes them. It may also learn your ideal rhythms of different types of attention, what leads you to be distracted, and when you self-interrupt. It will give you feedback on a good time for a break and, because it knows you so well, might suggest an activity that will make you feel positive. An example of such a prototype digital assistant is Amber, deployed in a study at Microsoft Research with twenty-four people over fourteen days in 2019. Amber gave suggestions on when to take breaks;

participants liked these, and as a result they even made positive changes in their routines like taking fewer breaks in which they used social media.[12] Such agents will not do the work for you but will rather gather data to help you gain a deeper understanding of your behavior, far deeper than software that tells you how much time you have spent on different apps. The agent can nudge you to help you develop self-efficacy skills so that you can gain self-control in the digital world. Think of it as a personal coach, but one that puts you in control of your actions.

However, AI will affect our attention in other ways as it develops and becomes further integrated into our lives. It is good at handling routine tasks but is not good at handling ambiguity or complex decision-making. This can be a benefit as we assign it unpleasant, boring tasks that we may not want to do, but it also means that we will spend a greater proportion of our time and attention on handling complex tasks, so this will present new challenges for our attention.

Technology design to help us achieve a balance

Technology design plays a key role in steering our attention, as we saw with the design of the internet. Social media companies leverage the fact that humans are social beings and seek social rewards. For example, the Like button validates our social worth, and the endless feeds tap into our basic social curiosity, with no clear stopping point. Beyond individual efforts like restructuring your interface, friction can be designed into the interface that can lead to healthier technology habits—and longer attention spans. Infinite scroll runs counter to promoting goal-directed attention.[13] By cutting it out, people would have to do extra work to refresh the feed, and it can make nonconscious actions become more conscious. More brute force techniques would simply lock out a person from their social media account after ten minutes, requiring one to sign in again, or an allotment of minutes of use could be spread over a limited time period. This might also help people to focus their social media use on relationships that are most important to them. Or the platform could require one to renew their password every three days. You can see how at some point, people might just give up and go for a walk. Of course, these ideas are not likely to be built into the social media applications given the companies' profit motives, but they may be achieved in the form of a plugin in the browser.

On a broader level, design teams are urgently needed that include social and clinical psychologists as members—not to make social media systems more persuasive, but to strategically make the systems *less persuasive* to use, and to elevate our mental health and well-being as the priority in design. Currently design teams are generally comprised of people with technical backgrounds—computer scientists and engineers. I have worked on technology design teams, mostly as the lone psychologist on the project. I can attest to how important it is to bring a perspective to the team on how design decisions can impact human behavior. In fact, design teams should include perhaps the most important stakeholders of all—the users of the technologies. Remember the Google Glass story, where the designers did not foresee what would happen when the glasses were deployed in a social setting? Our priority should be to design social media to provide healthy social rewards that are merely supplementary to the rewards we get in real life. Design can and should work with our natural practices to promote a better psychological balance.

Attention to our physical lives

One of the consequences of our digital age is that spending so much of our time and attention on our devices can create an opportunity cost for interacting with people in person. Some results by Jean Twenge, Brian Spitzberg and W. Keith Campbell hint at this. Based on a large-scale nationally representative sample of middle school and high school students, the researchers found a decline of in-person interaction with these young people over the years 1976 to 2017.[14] However, while social media use has increased, this is a correlational study, so it cannot be claimed that the drop in interaction is due to the use of devices. Yet even when people are physically with one another, attention is often directed to their phones and not to those physically present. The phone often takes precedence over the person in front of us. The fact that messaging is asynchronous and that news is continually updated makes us always attentive to it even when we're face-to-face with someone. We keep checking our phone because we don't want to miss a beat.

As we create our future with technology, we have designed ways to be present in the digital world, such as when we work remotely with Zoom video calls. But we also have to think about how we can be more present in the physical world. Zoom conversation is better than no conversation at all, but don't let face-to-face conversation become a lost art. Online interaction restricts vital social cues that people use to communicate. Interacting online works when you can't meet in person, but it cannot fully substitute for the creativity and gratification that comes with in-person interaction. When people text, they lose the rich social cues found in face-to-face communication where intonation, gestures, body stance and facial expression communicate meaning. Even the enhanced media of audio or video conferencing also lack vital social cues that can help navigate and guide our interaction with others.

Conversation is an art, a dance among partners that is best enacted in the physical world, choreographed by the social information we use in a three-dimensional space. Context also matters in framing a conversation. Cues in the digital environment (such as a Zoom background) just don't create an expressive atmosphere for interaction in the same way as when you and your conversation partner share the same environment in an office, outdoors in a park, or in a candlelit dining room.

Perceiving two-dimensional stimuli as we do for much of our waking hours in front of screens cannot substitute for the three-dimensional stimuli that our minds have evolved to experience in the physical world. While virtual reality has become quite good at simulating physical environments, ultimately people's attention and behaviors are still restricted to using a screen interface and using avatars doesn't enable people to experience a kinesthetic sense of how they move. We need to think about how being immobile, situated in front of a screen for long hours, takes away the opportunity for us to use proprioception, our awareness of our body position and orientation in the physical world. Of course, when we move around the world with our gaze on our mobile phones, we're still missing out in perceiving the environment around us. While rote online activity has benefits, build in breaks from the screen where you can also experience the real-world environment: try taking a walk, especially outdoors in nature, which is shown to increase creativity. Stanford University researchers asked forty people to take a walk outdoors and found that walking (whether indoors or not) and being outside both contributed independently to higher creativity as measured by the subjects producing more novel ideas for uses of common objects (like using a tire for a flowerpot).[15] This study points to the importance of tearing away from the screen, getting out into the physical world and moving, and of course, leaving your cell phone behind.

The future of work environments and our attention

As we continue to try out different forms of work—working remotely from home in Vermont or going into the office three days a week for hybrid work—we need to understand how these different models might affect our attention spans. For example, in a work-from-home context, family or housemates or the home itself can be a major source of interruptions, both external and internal. Seeing that pile of dirty dishes can distract us—it is Zeigarnik's unfinished task. (However, I have a friend—an MIT professor—who finds pleasure in the rote activity of matching socks after the wash. Perhaps sock-matching or Kalman's ironing can be used as a break.) In physical workspaces, we can see if someone is in an absorbing phone conversation or else trying to get out of it—we use their body language and intonation cues for when to interrupt. But in a work-from-home context, the blurred borders of work and home life might lead us to get interrupted at 9 p.m., or we might interrupt someone else at 7 a.m. In remote work, we lack awareness of whether or not others are interruptible, and so we all become the interrupting fiends.

A completely different work configuration is the open office plan, which has also become popular in co-working spaces. The opportunities for informal interaction and collaboration are countered by it being a breeding ground for interruptions. In one of our observational studies of interruptions, we found not surprisingly that people who worked in an open office environment experienced far more interruptions—both external and internal—compared to people who worked in their own offices.[16] Also, not surprisingly, these interruptions were often peripheral to one's work, even when they came from others in the same workgroup. We observed how colleagues monitored the environment and gained an awareness of when to interrupt each other as soon as that opportunity presented itself (for example, when a person glances away from the computer). Thus, as we move towards a future of work where we can expect more remote and hybrid work, the benefits they provide will have challenges to address, like fostering new norms for interruptions, increased loneliness,[17] and especially more distractions.

We can create the digital world in our image

When it comes to predicting where we are heading, we need to remain aware that we are still inventing the digital world. In the history of computing, we are only still in its infancy. I'm reminded of the Emerson quote at the beginning of the book: "We think our civilization near its meridian, but we are yet only at the cock-crowing and the morning star."[18] Personal computers came into widespread use in the mid-1980s, the internet into widespread popularity in the mid-1990s, and smartphones, the supercomputer that you put in your pocket, took off only in 2007 with the invention of the iPhone. Technology is being developed at a rapid-fire pace, but an understanding of how it can be integrated into our daily lives without overtaxing our attention and overwhelming us with stress has lagged far behind. In the age of excess, where Western civilizations eat too much, purchase too many goods, and take too many substances, people also consume too much digital media, and often in the wrong way. We have not yet figured out how to direct our attention or curb our practices, or how to exert our agency in the digital world. We are in the Wild West era of the digital age.

We can be optimistic, though, in that the digital world has connected people together in ways that we could not have imagined, more than just with conversation and sharing content. A common digital culture has arisen, and not just for tech-savvy people, despite unique cultural practices across countries and global regions.[19] If you're a young person in Beijing or Rio, how you use Weibo or Twitter is not so different than someone living in Chicago or Paris. Essentially, we all have the same human natures and seek the same types of rewards when we use our devices. We are all battling for our attention, and we're all in this together, on a global level.

The digital world was invented by people and is shaped by people. We can collectively shape the culture; and we can each selectively create our own narratives of how technology can work for us. Corporations do lead the direction of the digital world, but ultimately, people, through their invention and sheer numbers, have the power to overrule them. Despite targeted notifications, social and environmental conditioning, and your own personality makeup, you still own your attention. No one can take that away from you. We can learn to effectively take control of our tendency for dynamic, kinetic attention to seek out what will benefit us, to use sustained focus when we need it, and to switch our attention to Little Mind when we need to step back. We are battling hurricane-force winds that try to divert our attention, but ultimately, humans can withstand the forces. We can create and live in the digital world in the image we want.

★ ★ ★ ★ ★

ACKNOWLEDGMENTS

Writing is a solitary pursuit, and I am inherently a social person. So in retrospect, it seems natural that I recruited others in this long journey. The book benefited from many people who were generous in their time and whose comments helped me expand my thinking. I am so fortunate to know so many wise and supportive people.

This book was written during the pandemic, and I would have loved nothing more than to sit down in person and discuss ideas. Instead, these conversations were relegated to Zoom calls and sometimes email threads. And so it was with Zoom as my window to the world that I got company along the way in writing this book.

There are so many people to whom I owe thanks for making this book possible. I wish to thank my dear friend Judy Olson, who I could always count on to give her honest opinion, her wisdom and her continuing support throughout this whole process. I thank Jim Guszcza, whose sharp philosophical mind kept me on my toes; Dan Russell, always clear-sighted and whose expertise about the internet broadened my perspective; Nick Belkin and Colleen Cool, who asked pointed and powerful questions and to whom I still owe a dinner; Barry Lazarowitz, for engrossing and fun conversations and who gave me new insight about rhythm; Doug Pray and Glenn Kenny, for helping me see different perspectives on film; Ellen Ensel, for her musical expertise and experience; Jonathan Grudin, a chronicler of history in human-computer interaction; and Dave Smith, who was there when it all began.

I also wish to thank Mary Czerwinski and Shamsi Iqbal, and other folks at Microsoft Research, for loads of fun and for opening my eyes to so many new possibilities in research. There are so many other colleagues to thank whom I've worked with on studies over the years, research that helped me develop my thinking about the relationship of our attention spans and our devices, especially Stephen Voida, Victor González, Erin Bradner and Yiran Wang. Without the generous support of the National Science Foundation, much of this research would not have been possible. Participants in my studies were always willing to talk about the pleasures and tribulations their devices brought them.

Many thanks also to Duncan Brumby and Max Wilson. I had wonderful conversations with Jofish Kaye, Javier Hernandez and Bart Knijnenburg. I also thank Judith Borghouts, Thomas Breideband, Alex Williams, Roya Farzaneh, Ted Grover, Fatema Akbar, Ioannis Pavlidis, Sidney D'Mello and Wendy Kellogg. I wish to acknowledge my dedicated students in my graduate seminar who were curious to learn about human-computer interaction and distraction.

I extend heartfelt thanks to Peter Joseph, my editor at Hanover Square, who was patient and tireless throughout this whole process; to Grace Towery at Hanover Square for her key comments; and to Jaidree Braddix, my agent, who I'm grateful to for planting the seed for this journey in the first place.

Of course, the whole premise for this book would not have been possible without the foundational research of Walter

Mischel, Kurt Lewin, Albert Bandura and so many other great psychologists, whom I thank for their inspiration.

Last, I thank my family. My daughters, Michaela and Natalie, gave me their unwavering support and feedback through thick and thin—they know that unconditional love means that you can be critical and not worry about the consequences. And Alfred, whom I could always count on for honest criticism, and for his unlimited patience with me.

ENDNOTES

Introduction

1 Fink, George. "Stress: the health epidemic of the 21st century." Elsevier SciTech Connect. http://scitechconnect.elsevier.com/stress-health-epidemic-21st-century/.

2 Mark, Gloria, Stephen Voida, and Armand Cardello. "A pace not dictated by electrons, an empirical study of work without email." *Proceedings of the SIGCHI Conference on Human Factors in Computing Systems*, New York: ACM Press, 2012: 555–64.

3 Simon, H. A. "Designing organizations for an information-rich world." In *Computers, Communication, and the Public Interest,* edited by Martin Greenberger, 40–1. Baltimore: The Johns Hopkins Press, 1971.

4 Song, Peige, Mingming Zha, Qingwen Yang, Yan Zhang, Xue Li, and Igor Rudan. "The prevalence of adult attention-deficit hyperactivity disorder: a global systematic review and meta-analysis." *Journal of Global Health* 11 (2021).

5 Danielson, Melissa L., Rebecca H. Bitsko, Reem M. Ghandour, Joseph R. Holbrook, Michael D. Kogan, and Stephen J. Blumberg. "Prevalence of parent-reported ADHD diagnosis and associated treatment among US children and adolescents, 2016." *Journal of Clinical Child & Adolescent Psychology* 47, no. 2 (2018): 199–212.

6 Seo, Mihye, Jung-Hyun Kim, and Prabu David. "Always connected or always distracted? ADHD symptoms and social assurance explain problematic use of mobile phone and multicommunicating." *Journal of Computer-Mediated Communication* 20, no. 6 (2015): 667–81.

7 Currey, Mason, ed. *Daily Rituals: How Artists Work*. New York: Knopf, 2013.

Chapter 1

1 James, William. *The Letters of William James*. Vol. 1. Little, Brown, 1920.

2 James, William. *The Principles of Psychology*. Vol. 1, New York: Holt, 1890, pg. 403.

3 James, William. *The Principles of Psychology*. Vol. 1, New York: Holt, 1890, pg. 402.

4 Raz, Amir, and Jason Buhle. "Typologies of attentional networks." *Nature Reviews Neuroscience* 7, no. 5 (2006): 367–79.

5 Kahneman, Daniel. *Attention and Effort*. Vol. 1063. Englewood Cliffs, NJ: Prentice-Hall, 1973.

6 Banich, M.T. "Executive function: the search for an integrated account." *Current Directions in Psychological Science* 18, no. 2 (2009): 89–94.

7 Kahneman, Daniel. *Attention and Effort*. Vol. 1063. Englewood Cliffs, NJ: Prentice-Hall, 1973.

8 Wickens, Christopher D. *Processing Resources and Attention*. CRC Press, 2020.

9 Valdez, Pablo, Candelaria Ramírez, Aída García, Javier Talamantes, and Juventino Cortez. "Circadian and homeostatic variation in sustained attention." *Chronobiology International* 27, no. 2 (2010): 393–416.

10 Wickens, Christopher D. "Multiple resources and mental workload." *Human Factors* 50, no. 3 (2008): 449–55.

11 Schneider, Walter, Sue T. Dumais, and Richard M. Shiffrin. *Automatic/Control Processing and Attention*. Illinois University Champaign Human Attention Research Lab, 1982.

12 Wickens, Christopher D. "Multiple resources and mental workload." *Human Factors* 50, no. 3 (2008): 449–55.

13 Sirois, Sylvain, and Julie Brisson. "Pupillometry." *Wiley Interdisciplinary Reviews: Cognitive Science* 5, no. 6 (2014): 679–92.

14 Warm, Joel S., Gerald Matthews, and Victor S. Finomore Jr. "Vigilance, workload, and stress." In *Performance Under Stress*, 131–58. CRC Press, 2018.

15 Warm, Joel S., and Raja Parasuraman. "Cerebral hemodynamics and vigilance." In *Neuroergonomics: The Brain at Work*, 146–58. 2007.

16 Hitchcock, Edward M., Joel S. Warm, Gerald Matthews, William N. Dember, Paula K. Shear, Lloyd D. Tripp, David W. Mayleben, and Raja Parasuraman. "Automation cueing modulates cerebral blood flow and vigilance in a simulated air traffic control task." *Theoretical Issues in Ergonomics Science* 4, no. 1–2 (2003): 89–112.

17 Midha, Serena, Horia A. Maior, Max L. Wilson, and Sarah Sharples. "Measuring mental workload variations in office work tasks using fNIRS." *International Journal of Human-Computer Studies* 147 (2021): 102580.

18 Norman, Donald A., and Tim Shallice. "Attention to action." In *Consciousness and Self-Regulation*, 1–18. Boston: Springer, 1986.

19 Wickens, Christopher D. "Multiple resources and mental workload." *Human Factors* 50, no. 3 (2008): 449–55.

20 Kalimo, Raija, and Theo Mejman. "Psychological and behavioural responses to stress at work." *Psychosocial Factors at Work and Their Relation to Health* (1987): 23–36.

21 Hunter, Mary Carol R., Brenda W. Gillespie, and Sophie Yu-Pu Chen. "Urban nature experiences reduce stress in the context of daily life based on salivary biomarkers." *Frontiers in Psychology* 10 (2019): 722.

22 Rosenberg, Monica, Sarah Noonan, Joseph DeGutis, and Michael Esterman. "Sustaining visual attention in the face of distraction: a novel gradual-onset continuous performance task." *Attention, Perception, & Psychophysics* 75, no. 3 (2013): 426–39.

23 Fortenbaugh, F. C., D. Rothlein, R. McGlinchey, J. DeGutis, and M. Esterman. 2018. "Tracking behavioral and neural fluctuations during sustained attention: a robust replication and extension." *Neuroimage* 171, (2018): 148–64.

24 Esterman, M., and D. Rothlein. "Models of sustained attention." *Current Opinion in Psychology* 29, (2019): 174–80.

25 Monsell, S. "Task switching." *Trends in Cognitive Sciences* 7, no. 3 (March 2003): 134–40.

26 Bartlett, Frederic Charles, and F.C. Bartlett. *Remembering: A Study in Experimental and Social Psychology*. Cambridge: Cambridge University Press, 1932.

Chapter 2

1 Chun, Marvin M., and Jeremy M. Wolfe. "Visual attention." *Blackwell Handbook of Perception*, (2001): 272310.

2 Birnbaum, I. M., and E. S. Parker. *Alcohol and Human Memory.* Lawrence Erlbaum Associates, 1977.

3 Stroop, J. Ridley. "Studies of interference in serial verbal reactions." *Journal of Experimental Psychology* 18, no. 6 (1935): 643.

4 Culler, Arthur Jerome. *Interference and Adaptability: An Experimental Study of Their Relation with Special Reference to Individual Differences.* No. 24. Science Press: 1912.

5 Blain, B., G. Hollard, and M. Pessiglione. "Neural mechanisms underlying the impact of daylong cognitive work on economic decisions." *Proceedings of the National Academy of Sciences* 113, no. 25 (2016): 6967–72.

6 James, William. 1890. *The Principles of Psychology.* Harvard ed. vol. 2. New York: Holt, 1890, pg. 404.

7 Chun, Marvin M., and Jeremy M. Wolfe. "Visual attention." *Blackwell Handbook of Perception*, (2001): 272310.

8 Monsell, S. (2003). "Task switching." *Trends in Cognitive Sciences* 7, no. 3 (March 2003): 134–40.

9 Nasar, J. L., and D. Troyer. "Pedestrian injuries due to mobile phone use in public places." *Accident Analysis & Prevention* 57 (2013): 91–5.

10 Shapiro, Emily. 2021. "How hiker overcame mental hurdles to survive 8 days missing in wilderness." ABC News, June 30, 2021, https://abcnews. go.com/US/hiker-overcame-mental-hurdles-survive-days-missing-wilderness/story?id=78533463.

11 Paxton, J. L., D. M. Barch, C. A. Racine, and T. S. Braver. "Cognitive control, goal maintenance, and prefrontal function in healthy aging." *Cerebral Cortex* 18, no. 5 (2008): 1010–28.

12 Braver, T. S., and J. D. Cohen. "On the control of control: the role of dopamine in regulating prefrontal function and working memory." *Control of Cognitive Processes: Attention and Performance XVIII*, (2000): 713–37.

13 Blain, B., G. Hollard, and M. Pessiglione. "Neural mechanisms under-lying the impact of daylong cognitive work on economic decisions." *Proceedings of the National Academy of Sciences* 113, no. 25 (2016): 6967–72.

14 Collopy, F. "Biases in retrospective self-reports of time use: an empirical study of computer users." *Management Science* 42, no. 5 (1996): 758–67.

15 Kane, Michael J., Leslie H. Brown, Jennifer C. McVay, Paul J. Silvia, Inez Myin-Germeys, and Thomas R. Kwapil. "For whom the mind wanders, and when: an experience-sampling study of working memory and executive control in daily life." *Psychological Science* 18, no. 7 (2007): 614–21.

16 Baird, Benjamin, Jonathan Smallwood, Michael D. Mrazek, Julia W. Y. Kam, Michael S. Franklin, and Jonathan W. Schooler. "Inspired by distraction: mind wandering facilitates creative incubation." *Psychological Science* 23, no. 10 (2012): 1117–22.

17 Kane, Michael J., and Jennifer C. McVay. "What mind wandering reveals about executive-control abilities and failures." *Current Directions in Psychological Science* 21, no. 5 (2012): 348–54.

18 Levy, David M., Jacob O. Wobbrock, Alfred W. Kasizniak, and Marilyn Ostergren. "The effects of mindfulness meditation training on multi-tasking in a high-stress information environment." *Proceedings of Graphics Interface*, (2012): 45-52.

19 Herrnstein, R.J. On the law of effect 1. *Journal of the Experimental Analysis of Behavior* 13, no. 2 (1970): 243-66.

20 Johnson, Samuel. *The Works of Samuel Johnson*. London: Jones & Co., 1825.

21 Baudrillard, J. *Simulacra and Simulation*. Ann Arbor, MI: University of Michigan Press, 1994.

22 "The state of online gaming." Limelight, 2020. Accessed July 2022. https://de.limelight.com/resources/white-paper/state-of-online-gaming-2020/.

23 Kahneman, D. *Attention and Effort*. Englewood Cliffs, NJ: Prentice Hall, 1973.

24 James, William. *The Principles of Psychology*. Vol. 1, New York: Holt, 1890.

Chapter 3

1 Charney, Noah. "Maya Angelou: how I write." *The Daily Beast*, April 10, 2013, https://www.thedailybeast.com/maya-angelou-how-i-write.

2 Locke, John. *An Essay Concerning Human Understanding.* Philadelphia: Kay & Troutman, 1847.

3 James, William. *The Principles of Psychology.* Vol. 1, New York: Holt, 1890.

4 Tellegen, Auke, and Gilbert Atkinson. "Openness to absorbing and self-altering experiences ('absorption'), a trait related to hypnotic susceptibility." *Journal of Abnormal Psychology* 83, no. 3 (1974): 268.

5 Lifshitz, Michael, Michiel van Elk, and Tanya M. Luhrmann. "Absorption and spiritual experience: a review of evidence and potential mechanisms." *Consciousness and Cognition* 73 (2019): 102760.

6 Angiulo, Michael J., and John F. Kihlstrom. "Dissociative experiences in a college population." Unpublished manuscript, University of Arizona, 1993.

7 Webster, Jane, and Hayes Ho. "Audience engagement in multimedia presentations." *ACM SIGMIS Database: The DATABASE for Advances in Information Systems* 28, no. 2 (1997): 63–77.

8 Csikszentmihalyi, Mihaly. *Flow: The Psychology of Optimal Experience.* New York: Harper & Row, 1990.

9 Friedman, William. *About Time: Inventing the Fourth Dimension.* The MIT Press, 1990.

10 Hektner, Joel M., Jennifer A. Schmidt, and Mihaly Csikszentmihalyi. *Experience Sampling Method: Measuring the Quality of Everyday Life.* Thousand Oaks, CA: Sage, 2007.

11 Plimpton, George. "Maya Angelou, the art of fiction." *The Paris Review* 119, no. 116 (1990). https://theparisreview.org/interviews/2279/the-art-of-fiction-no-119-maya-angelou.

12 Nakamura, Jeanne, and Mihaly Csikszentmihalyi. "The concept of flow." In *Flow and the Foundations of Positive Psychology*, 239–63. Dordrecht: Springer, 2014.

13 Mark, Gloria, Shamsi T. Iqbal, Mary Czerwinski, and Paul Johns. "Bored Mondays and focused afternoons: the rhythm of attention and online activity in the workplace." *Proceedings of the SIGCHI Conference on Human Factors in Computing Systems*, New York: ACM Press, 3025–34. 2014.

14 LeFevre, Judith. "Flow and the quality of experience during work and leisure." Cambridge: Cambridge University Press, 1988.

15 Curry, David. "Candy Crush revenue and usage statistics." *Business of Apps*, 2021. https://www.businessofapps.com/data/candy-crush-statistics/.

16 Sweney, Mark. "More than 9m play Candy Crush for three hours or more a day." *The Guardian*, June 26, 2019. https://www.theguardian.com/games/2019/jun/26/more-than-9m-play-candy-crush-for-three-hours-or-more-a-day-addiction.

17 Mikulas, William L., and Stephen J. Vodanovich. "The essence of boredom." *The Psychological Record* 43, no. 1 (1993): 3.

18 Fisher, Cynthia D. "Boredom at work: a neglected concept." *Human Relations* 46, no. 3 (1993): 395–417.

19 Valdez, Pablo, Candelaria Ramírez, Aída García, Javier Talamantes, Pablo Armijo, and Jorge Borrani. "Circadian rhythms in components of attention." *Biological Rhythm Research* 36, no. 1–2 (2005): 57–65.

20 Carrier, Julie, and Timothy H. Monk. "Circadian rhythms of performance: new trends." *Chronobiology International* 17, no. 6 (2000): 719–32.

21 Busch, Niko A., and Rufin VanRullen. "Spontaneous EEG oscillations reveal periodic sampling of visual attention." *Proceedings of the National Academy of Sciences* 107, no. 37 (2010): 16048–53.

22 Mark, Gloria, Shamsi T. Iqbal, Mary Czerwinski, and Paul Johns. "Bored Mondays and focused afternoons: the rhythm of attention and online activity in the workplace." *Proceedings of the SIGCHI Conference on Human Factors in Computing Systems*, New York: ACM Press, 3025–34. 2014.

23 Mark, Gloria, Shamsi T. Iqbal, Mary Czerwinski, and Paul Johns. "Bored Mondays and focused afternoons: the rhythm of attention and online activity in the workplace." *Proceedings of the SIGCHI*

Conference on Human Factors in Computing Systems, New York: ACM Press, 3025–34. 2014.

24 Mark, Gloria, Shamsi Iqbal, Mary Czerwinski, and Paul Johns. "Focused, aroused, but so distractible: temporal perspectives on multitasking and communications." *Proceedings of the 18th ACM Conference on Computer Supported Cooperative Work & Social Computing*, New York: ACM Press, 903–16. 2015.

25 Abdullah, Saeed, Elizabeth L. Murnane, Mark Matthews, Matthew Kay, Julie A. Kientz, Geri Gay, and Tanzeem Choudhury. "Cognitive rhythms: unobtrusive and continuous sensing of alertness using a mobile phone." *Proceedings of the 2016 ACM International Joint Conference on Pervasive and Ubiquitous Computing*, 78–189. 2016.

26 Valdez, Pablo, Candelaria Ramírez, Aída García, Javier Talamantes, and Juventino Cortez. "Circadian and homeostatic variation in sustained attention." *Chronobiology International* 27, no. 2 (2010): 393–416.

27 Behrens, John. *America's Music Makers: Big Bands and Ballrooms: 1911-2011.* Bloomington: AuthorHouse, 2011.

Chapter 4

1 Metcalfe, Bob. "Microsoft and Netscape open some new fronts in escalating Web Wars." *InfoWorld*, Aug. 21, 1995: 35.

2 Smith, Monica L. *A Prehistory of Ordinary People.* Tucson: University of Arizona Press, 2010.

3 Medeiros-Ward, Nathan, Jason M. Watson, and David L. Strayer. "On supertaskers and the neural basis of efficient multitasking." *Psychonomic Bulletin & Review* 22, no. 3 (2015): 876–83.

4 Poposki, Elizabeth M., and Frederick L. Oswald. "The multitasking preference inventory: toward an improved measure of individual differences in polychronicity." *Human Performance* 23, no. 3 (2010): 247–64.

5 Kaufman, Carol Felker, Paul M. Lane, and Jay D. Lindquist. "Exploring more than 24 hours a day: a preliminary investigation of polychronic time use." *Journal of Consumer Research* 18, no. 3 (1991): 392–401.

6 Cherry, E. Colin. "Some experiments on the recognition of speech, with

one and with two ears." *The Journal of the Acoustical Society of America* 25, no. 5 (1953): 975–9.

7   Taylor, Frederick Winslow. *The Principles of Scientific Management.* New York: Cosimo Classics, 2010.

8   González, Victor M., and Gloria Mark. "'Constant, constant, multi-tasking craziness': managing multiple working spheres." *Proceedings of the SIGCHI Conference on Human Factors in Computing Systems*, New York: ACM Press, 113–20. 2004.

9   Meyer, Andre N., Laura E. Barton, Gail C. Murphy, Thomas Zimmermann, and Thomas Fritz. "The work life of developers: activities, switches and perceived productivity." *IEEE Transactions on Software Engineering* 43, no. 12 (2017): 1178–93.

10 Akbar, Fatema. *Stress and Human-Computer Interaction at the Workplace: Unobtrusive Tracking with Wearable Sensors and Computer Logs.* Unpublished PhD dissertation, University of California, Irvine, 2021.

11 Mark, Gloria, Shamsi T. Iqbal, Mary Czerwinski, Paul Johns, and Akane Sano. "Neurotics can't focus: an in situ study of online multitasking in the workplace." *Proceedings of the 2016 CHI Conference on Human Factors in Computing Systems*, New York: ACM Press, 1739–44. 2016.

12 Akbar, Fatema. *Stress and Human-Computer Interaction at the Workplace: Unobtrusive Tracking with Wearable Sensors and Computer Logs.* Unpublished PhD dissertation, University of California, Irvine, 2021.

González, Victor M., and Gloria Mark. "'Constant, constant, multi-tasking craziness': managing multiple working spheres." *Proceedings of the SIGCHI Conference on Human Factors in Computing Systems*, New York: ACM Press, 113–20. 2004.

Mark, Gloria, Stephen Voida, and Armand Cardello. "A pace not dictated by electrons, an empirical study of work without email." *Proceedings of the SIGCHI Conference on Human Factors in Computing Systems*, New York: ACM Press, 555–64. 2012.

Mark, Gloria, Shamsi T. Iqbal, Mary Czerwinski, and Paul Johns. "Bored Mondays and focused afternoons: the rhythm of attention and online activity in the workplace." *Proceedings of the SIGCHI Conference on Human Factors in Computing Systems*, New York: ACM Press, 3025–34. 2014.

Mark, Gloria, Shamsi T. Iqbal, Mary Czerwinski, Paul Johns, and Akane Sano. "Neurotics can't focus: an in situ study of online multitasking in the workplace." *Proceedings of the 2016 CHI Conference on Human Factors in Computing Systems*, New York: ACM Press, 1739–44. 2016.

Meyer, Andre N., Laura E. Barton, Gail C. Murphy, Thomas Zimmermann, and Thomas Fritz. "The work life of developers: activities, switches and perceived productivity." *IEEE Transactions on Software Engineering* 43, no. 12 (2017): 1178–93.

Yeykelis, Leo, James J. Cummings, and Byron Reeves. "Multitasking on a single device: arousal and the frequency, anticipation, and prediction of switching between media content on a computer." *Journal of Communication* 64, no. 1 (2014): 167–92.

13 Leroy, Sophie. "Why is it so hard to do my work? The challenge of attention residue when switching between work tasks." *Organizational Behavior and Human Decision Processes* 109, no. 2 (2009): 168–81.

14 Horne, J. H., and T. Lupton. "The work activities of 'middle' managers—an exploratory study." *The Journal of Management Studies* 2 (1965): 14–33.

15 Mintzberg, H. "Structured observation as a method to study managerial work." *The Journal of Management Studies* 7 (1970): 87–104.

16 Sproull, L. S. "The nature of managerial attention." *Advances in Information Processing in Organizations* 1 (1984): 9–27.

17 González, Victor M., and Gloria Mark. "'Constant, constant, multitasking craziness': managing multiple working spheres." *Proceedings of the SIGCHI Conference on Human Factors in Computing Systems*, New York: ACM Press, 113–20. 2004.

18 Das Swain, Vedant, Koustuv Saha, Hemang Rajvanshy, Anusha Sirigiri, Julie M. Gregg, Suwen Lin, Gonzalo J. Martinez, et al. "A multisensor person-centered approach to understand the role of daily activities in job performance with organizational personas." *Proceedings of the ACM on Interactive, Mobile, Wearable and Ubiquitous Technologies* 3, no. 4 (2019): 1–27.

19 Das Swain, Vedant, Koustuv Saha, Hemang Rajvanshy, Anusha Sirigiri, Julie M. Gregg, Suwen Lin, Gonzalo J. Martinez, et al. "A multisensor person-centered approach to understand the role of daily activities in job performance with organizational personas." *Proceedings of the ACM on Interactive, Mobile, Wearable and Ubiquitous Technologies* 3, no. 4 (2019): 1–27.

González, Victor M., and Gloria Mark. "'Constant, constant, multi-tasking craziness': managing multiple working spheres." In *Proceedings of the SIGCHI Conference on Human Factors in Computing Systems*, New York: ACM Press, 113–20. 2004.

Horne, J. H., and T. Lupton. "The work activities of 'middle' managers-an exploratory study." *The Journal of Management Studies* 2 (1965): 14–33.

Hudson, J. M., J. Christensen, W. A. Kellogg, and T. Erickson. "'I'd be overwhelmed, but it's just one more thing to do': availability and interruption in research management." In *Proceedings of CHI 2002*, 97–104. New York: ACM Press, 2002.

Mintzberg, H. "Structured observation as a method to study managerial work." *The Journal of Management Studies* 7 (1970): 87–104.

Sproull, L. S. "The nature of managerial attention." *Advances in Information Processing in Organizations* 1 (1984): 9–27.

20 González, Victor M., and Gloria Mark. "'Constant, constant, multi-tasking craziness': managing multiple working spheres." *Proceedings of the SIGCHI Conference on Human Factors in Computing Systems*, New York: ACM Press, 113–20. 2004.

21 Mark, Gloria, Victor M. González, and Justin Harris. "No task left behind? Examining the nature of fragmented work." In *Proceedings of the SIGCHI Conference on Human Factors in Computing Systems*, New York: ACM Press, 321–30. 2005.

22 Van Merrienboer, Jeroen J. G., and John Sweller. "Cognitive load theory and complex learning: recent developments and future directions." *Educational Psychology Review* 17, no. 2 (2005): 147–77.

23 Mark, Gloria, Victor M. González, and Justin Harris. "No task left behind? Examining the nature of fragmented work." In *Proceedings of the SIGCHI Conference on Human Factors in Computing Systems*, New York: ACM Press, 321–30. 2005.

24 Jersild, Arthur T. "Mental set and shift." *Archives of Psychology*, (1927).

25 Wegner, Daniel M., and Ralph Erber. "The hyperaccessibility of suppressed thoughts." *Journal of Personality and Social Psychology* 63, no. 6 (1992): 903.

26 Adler, Rachel F., and Raquel Benbunan-Fich. "Self-interruptions in discretionary multitasking." *Computers in Human Behavior* 29, no. 4 (2013): 1441–9.

27 Bailey, Brian P., and Joseph A. Konstan. "On the need for attention-aware systems: measuring effects of interruption on task performance, error rate, and affective state." *Computers in Human Behavior* 22, no. 4 (2006): 685–708.

28 Westbrook, Johanna I., Magdalena Z. Raban, Scott R. Walter, and Heather Douglas. "Task errors by emergency physicians are associated with interruptions, multitasking, fatigue and working memory capacity: a prospective, direct observation study." *BMJ Quality & Safety* 27, no. 8 (2018): 655–63.

29 Loukopoulos, Loukia D., R. Key Dismukes, and Immanuel Barshi. "Cockpit interruptions and distractions: a line observation study." In *Proceedings of the 11th International Symposium on Aviation Psychology*, 1–6. Columbus: Ohio State University Press, 2001.

30 Leroy, Sophie. "Why is it so hard to do my work? The challenge of attention residue when switching between work tasks." *Organizational Behavior and Human Decision Processes* 109, no. 2 (2009): 168–81.

31 Mark, Gloria, Shamsi Iqbal, Mary Czerwinski, and Paul Johns. "Focused, aroused, but so distractible: temporal perspectives on multitasking and communications." In *Proceedings of the 18th ACM Conference on Computer Supported Cooperative Work & Social Computing*, New York: ACM Press, 903–16. 2015.

32 Wetherell, Mark A., and Martin C. Sidgreaves. "Secretory immunoglobulin-A reactivity following increases in workload intensity using the Defined Intensity Stressor Simulation (DISS)." *Stress and Health: Journal of the International Society for the Investigation of Stress* 21, no. 2 (2005): 99–106.

33 Mark, Gloria, Daniela Gudith, and Ulrich Klocke. "The cost of interrupted work: more speed and stress." In *Proceedings of the SIGCHI Conference on Human Factors in Computing Systems*, New York: ACM Press, 107–10. 2008.

34 Wetherell, Mark A., and Kirsty Carter. "The multitasking framework: the effects of increasing workload on acute psychobiological stress reactivity." *Stress and Health* 30, no. 2 (2014): 103–9.

35 Reinecke, Leonard, Stefan Aufenanger, Manfred E. Beutel, Michael Dreier, Oliver Quiring, Birgit Stark, Klaus Wölfling, and Kai W. Müller. "Digital stress over the life span: the effects of communication load and internet multitasking on perceived stress and psychological health impairments in a German probability sample." *Media Psychology* 20, no. 1 (2017): 90–115.

36 Mark, Gloria, Shamsi Iqbal, Mary Czerwinski, and Paul Johns. "Focused, aroused, but so distractible: temporal perspectives on multitasking and communications." In *Proceedings of the 18th ACM Conference on Computer Supported Cooperative Work & Social Computing*, New York: ACM Press, 903–16. 2015.

37 Mark, Gloria, Shamsi T. Iqbal, Mary Czerwinski, Paul Johns, and Akane Sano. "Neurotics can't focus: an in situ study of online multitasking in the workplace." In *Proceedings of the 2016 CHI Conference on Human Factors in Computing Systems*, New York: ACM Press, 1739–44. 2016.

38 Rideout, Victoria, and Michael B. Robb. "The Common Sense census: media use by kids age zero to eight." San Francisco: Common Sense Media, 2020. https://www.commonsensemedia.org/sites/default/files/uploads/research/2020_zero_to_eight_census_final_web.pdf.

39 Plude, Dana J., Jim T. Enns, and Darlene Brodeur. "The development of selective attention: a life-span overview." *Acta Psychologica* 86, no. 2–3 (1994): 227–72.

40 Welsh, Marilyn C., Bruce F. Pennington, and Dena B. Groisser. "A normative-developmental study of executive function: a window on prefrontal function in children." *Developmental Neuropsychology* 7, no. 2 (1991): 131–49.

41 Statement of Frances Haugen, Oct. 4, 2021. "United States Senate Committee on Commerce, Science and Transportation." https://www.commerce.senate.gov/services/files/FC8A558E-824E-4914-BEDB-3A7B1190BD49.

42 Anderson, Monica, and Jingjing Jiang. "Teens, social media & technology 2018." *Pew Research Center* 31, no. 2018 (2018): 1673–89.

43 Ceci, L. "TikTok—Statistics & Facts. 2022." Statista. https://www.statista.com/topics/6077/tiktok/#topicHeader__wrapper.

44 Auxier, Brooke, and Monica Anderson. "Social media use in

2021." *Pew Research Center.* 2021. https://www.pewresearch.org/internet/2021/04/07/social-media-use-in-2021/.

45 Wang, Yiran, Melissa Niiya, Gloria Mark, Stephanie M. Reich, and Mark Warschauer. "Coming of age (digitally): an ecological view of social media use among college students." In *Proceedings of the 18th ACM Conference on Computer Supported Cooperative Work & Social Computing*, New York: ACM Press, 571–82. 2015.

46 Mark, Gloria, Yiran Wang, and Melissa Niiya. "Stress and multitasking in everyday college life: an empirical study of online activity." In *Proceedings of the SIGCHI Conference on Human Factors in Computing Systems*, New York: ACM Press, 41–50. 2014.

47 Ophir, Eyal, Clifford Nass, and Anthony D. Wagner. "Cognitive control in media multitaskers." *Proceedings of the National Academy of Sciences* 106, no. 37 (2009): 15583–7.

48 Baumgartner, Susanne E., Winneke A. van der Schuur, Jeroen S. Lemmens, and Fam te Poel. "The relationship between media multitasking and attention problems in adolescents: results of two longitudinal studies." *Human Communication Research* 44, no. 1 (2018): 3–30.

49 Green, C. Shawn, and Daphne Bavelier. "Effect of action video games on the spatial distribution of visuospatial attention." *Journal of Experimental Psychology: Human Perception and Performance* 32, no. 6 (2006): 1465.

50 Boot, Walter R., Arthur F. Kramer, Daniel J. Simons, Monica Fabiani, and Gabriele Gratton. "The effects of video game playing on attention, memory, and executive control." *Acta Psychologica* 129, no. 3 (2008): 387–98.

Chapter 5

1 Carr, Nicholas. *The Shallows: What the Internet Is Doing to Our Brains.* New York: WW Norton & Company, 2020.

2 Goodreads. Martin Luther King Jr. Quotes. Available https://www.goodreads.com/quotes/211372-the-major-problem-of-life-is-learning-how-to-handle.

3 "Manuscript of S T Coleridge's 'Kubla Khan.'" The British Library. Available https://www.bl.uk/collection-items/manuscript-of-s-t-coleridges-kubla-khan.

4 Perlow, Leslie A. "The time famine: toward a sociology of work time." *Administrative Science Quarterly* 44, no. 1 (1999): 57–81.

5 Feldman, Elana, and David Greenway. "It's a matter of time: the role of temporal perceptions in emotional experiences of work interruptions." *Group & Organization Management*, (2020): 1059601120959288.

6 Zeigarnik, Andrey V. "Bluma Zeigarnik: a memoir." *Gestalt Theory*, no. 3 (2007): 256–68.

7 Zeigarnik, Bluma. "On finished and unfinished tasks." (1938). Originally published as *Das Behalten erledigter und unerledigter Handlungen (1927)*. https://scholar.google.com/scholar?hl=en&as_sdt=0%2C33&q=On+finished+and+unfinished+tasks+Zeigarnik&btn G=.

8 Lewin, Kurt. "Field theory and experiment in social psychology: concepts and methods." *American Journal of Sociology* 44, no. 6 (1939): 868–96.

9 Zeigarnik, Andrey V. "Bluma Zeigarnik: a memoir." *Gestalt Theory*, no. 3 (2007): 256–68.

10 González, Victor M., and Gloria Mark. "'Constant, constant, multi-tasking craziness': managing multiple working spheres." In *Proceedings of the SIGCHI Conference on Human Factors in Computing Systems*, New York: ACM Press, 113–20. 2004.

11 Jin, Jing, and Laura A. Dabbish. "Self-interruption on the computer: a typology of discretionary task interleaving." In *Proceedings of the SIGCHI conference on human factors in computing systems*, New York: ACM Press, 1799–808. 2009.

12 Lally, Phillippa, Cornelia H. M. Van Jaarsveld, Henry W. W. Potts, and Jane Wardle. "How are habits formed: Modelling habit formation in the real world." *European Journal of Social Psychology* 40, no. 6 (2010): 998–1009.

13 Dabbish, Laura, Gloria Mark, and Víctor M. González. "Why do I keep interrupting myself? Environment, habit and self-interruption." In *Proceedings of the SIGCHI Conference on Human Factors in Computing Systems*, New York: ACM Press, 3127–30. 2011.

14 Altmann, E. M., and J. G. Trafton. "Memory for goals: an activation-based model." *Cognitive Science* 26, no. 1 (2002): 39–83.

15 Altmann, Erik M., and J. Gregory Trafton. "Timecourse of recovery from task interruption: data and a model." *Psychonomic Bulletin & Review* 14, no. 6 (2007): 1079–84.

16 Mark, Gloria, Daniela Gudith, and Ulrich Klocke. "The cost of interrupted work: more speed and stress." In *Proceedings of the SIGCHI Conference on Human Factors in Computing Systems*, New York: ACM Press, 107–10. 2008.

17 Monk, Christopher A. "The effect of frequent versus infrequent interruptions on primary task resumption." In *Proceedings of the Human Factors and Ergonomics Society Annual Meeting* 48, no. 3, 295–9. Los Angeles, CA: SAGE Publications, 2004.

18 Hart, Sandra G., and Lowell E. Staveland. "Development of NASA-TLX (Task Load Index): results of empirical and theoretical research." In *Advances in Psychology* 52 (1988): 139–83. Amsterdam: North-Holland Publishing.

19 Mark, Gloria, Shamsi Iqbal, Mary Czerwinski, and Paul Johns. "Focused, aroused, but so distractible: temporal perspectives on multitasking and communications." In *Proceedings of the 18th ACM Conference on Computer Supported Cooperative Work & Social Computing*, New York: ACM Press, 903–16. 2015.

20 Mark, Gloria, Shamsi T. Iqbal, Mary Czerwinski, Paul Johns, Akane Sano, and Yuliya Lutchyn. "Email duration, batching and self-interruption: patterns of email use on productivity and stress." In *Proceedings of the 2016 CHI Conference on Human Factors in Computing Systems*, New York: ACM Press, 1717–28. 2016.

21 Pew Research. "Social media fact sheet." 2021. https://www.pew-research.org/internet/fact-sheet/social-media/.

22 Klosterman, C. "My zombie, myself: why modern life feels rather undead." *The New York Times*, Dec. 3, 2010.

23 Mark, Gloria, Stephen Voida, and Armand Cardello. "A pace not dictated by electrons, an empirical study of work without email." In *Proceedings of the SIGCHI Conference on Human Factors in Computing Systems*, New York: ACM Press, 555–64. 2012.

24 Mark, Gloria, Shamsi T. Iqbal, Mary Czerwinski, Paul Johns, Akane Sano, and Yuliya Lutchyn. "Email duration, batching and self-

interruption: Patterns of email use on productivity and stress." In *Proceedings of the 2016 CHI Conference on Human Factors in Computing Systems*, New York: ACM Press, 1717–28. 2016.

25 Akbar, Fatema, Ayse Elvan Bayraktaroglu, Pradeep Buddharaju, Dennis Rodrigo Da Cunha Silva, Ge Gao, Ted Grover, Ricardo Gutierrez-Osuna, et al. "Email makes you sweat: examining email interruptions and stress using thermal imaging." In *Proceedings of the 2019 CHI Conference on Human Factors in Computing Systems*, New York, ACM Press, 1–14. 2019.

26 Miyata, Yoshiro, and Donald A. Norman. "Psychological issues in support of multiple activities." *User Centered System Design: New Perspectives on Human-Computer Interaction*, (1986): 265–84.

27 McFarlane, Daniel C. "Comparison of four primary methods for coordinating the interruption of people in human–computer interaction." *Human-Computer Interaction* 17, no. 1 (2002): 63–139.

28 Bailey, Brian P., and Shamsi T. Iqbal. "Understanding changes in mental workload during execution of goal-directed tasks and its application for interruption management." *ACM Transactions on Computer-Human Interaction (TOCHI)* 14, no. 4 (2008): 1–28.

29 Adamczyk, Piotr D., and Brian P. Bailey. "If not now, when? The effects of interruption at different moments within task execution." In *Proceedings of the SIGCHI Conference on Human Factors in Computing Systems*, New York: ACM Press, 271–8. 2004.

30 Westman, Mina. "Stress and strain crossover." *Human Relations* 54, no. 6 (2001): 717–51.

31 Scullin, Michael K., Madison L. Krueger, Hannah K. Ballard, Natalya Pruett, and Donald L. Bliwise. "The effects of bedtime writing on difficulty falling asleep: a polysomnographic study comparing to-do lists and completed activity lists." *Journal of Experimental Psychology: General*, 147, no. 1 (2018): 139.

Chapter 6

1 Bush, Vannevar. "As we may think." *The Atlantic Monthly* 176, no. 1 (1945): 101–8.

2 Chan, Lois Mai, and Athena Salaba. *Cataloging and Classification: An Introduction*. Rowman & Littlefield, 2015.

3 Berkeley, Edmund·Callis. *Giant Brains or Machines that Think*. New York: John Wiley & Sons, 1949.

4 Berkeley, Edmund Callis. *Giant Brains or Machines that Think*. New York: John Wiley & Sons, 1949, 181–2.

5 Nelson, T.H. "Complex information processing: a file structure for the complex, the changing and the indeterminate." In *Proceedings of the 1965 ACM 20th National Conference*, (August 1965): 84–100.

6 Nelson, T.H. "Complex information processing: a file structure for the complex, the changing and the indeterminate." In *Proceedings of the 1965 ACM 20th National Conference*, (August 1965): 84–100. Quote on pg. 96.

7 Bardini, Thierry. *Bootstrapping: Douglas Engelbart, Coevolution, and the Origins of Personal Computing*. Stanford: Stanford University Press, 2000.

8 Russell, Bertrand. *Analysis of Mind*. Oxfordshire: Routledge, 2005.

9 Kumar, Abhilasha A. "Semantic memory: a review of methods, models, and current challenges." *Psychonomic Bulletin & Review* 28, no. 1 (2021): 40–80.

10 Mark, Gloria, Jörg M. Haake, and Norbert A. Streitz. "The use of hypermedia in group problem solving: an evaluation of the DOLPHIN electronic meeting room environment." In *Proceedings of the Fourth European Conference on Computer-Supported Cooperative Work ECSCW '95*. Dordrecht: Springer, 1995. 197–213.

11 Killingsworth, Matthew A., and Daniel T. Gilbert. "A wandering mind is an unhappy mind." *Science* 330, no. 6006 (2010): 932.

12 Smallwood, Jonathan, and Jonathan W. Schooler. "The restless mind." *Psychological Bulletin* 132, no. 6 (2006): 946.

13 Becker, Suzanna, Morris Moscovitch, Marlene Behrmann, and Steve Joordens. "Long-term semantic priming: a computational account and empirical evidence." *Journal of Experimental Psychology: Learning, Memory, and Cognition* 23, no. 5 (1997): 1059.

14 Bargh, John A., Peter M. Gollwitzer, Annette Lee-Chai, Kimberly Barndollar, and Roman Trötschel. "The automated will: nonconscious activation and pursuit of behavioral goals." *Journal of Personality and Social Psychology* 81, no. 6 (2001): 1014.

15 Nedungadi, Prakash. "Recall and consumer consideration sets: Influencing choice without altering brand evaluations." *Journal of Consumer Research* 17, no. 3 (1990): 263–76.

16 Anderson, John R. "A spreading activation theory of memory." *Journal of Verbal Learning and Verbal Behavior* 22, no. 3 (1983): 261–95.

17 Bargh, John A., and Ezequiel Morsella. "The unconscious mind." *Perspectives on Psychological Science* 3, no. 1 (2008): 73–9.

18 Loewenstein, George. "The psychology of curiosity: a review and reinterpretation." *Psychological Bulletin* 116, no. 1 (1994): 75.

19 Kang, Min Jeong, Ming Hsu, Ian M. Krajbich, George Loewenstein, Samuel M. McClure, Joseph Tao-yi Wang, and Colin F. Camerer. "The wick in the candle of learning: epistemic curiosity activates reward circuitry and enhances memory." *Psychological Science* 20, no. 8 (2009): 963–73.

20 Clark, Andy. *Natural-Born Cyborgs: Minds, Technologies, and the Future of Human Intelligence.* Oxford: Oxford University Press, 2003.

21 Fisher, Matthew, Mariel K. Goddu, and Frank C. Keil. "Searching for explanations: how the Internet inflates estimates of internal knowledge." *Journal of Experimental Psychology: General* 144, no. 3 (2015): 674.

22 Liu, Xiaoyue, Xiao Lin, Ming Zheng, Yanbo Hu, Yifan Wang, Lingxiao Wang, Xiaoxia Du, and Guangheng Dong. "Internet search alters intra- and inter-regional synchronization in the temporal Gyrus." *Frontiers in Psychology* 9 (2018): 260.

23 McLuhan, Marshall. *Understanding Media: The Extensions of Man.* MIT Press, 1994.

24 Wan, Catherine Y., and Gottfried Schlaug. "Music making as a tool for promoting brain plasticity across the life span." *The Neuroscientist*, 16, no. 5 (2010): 566–77.

25 Small, Gary W., Teena D. Moody, Prabha Siddarth, and Susan Y. Bookheimer. "Your brain on Google: patterns of cerebral activation during internet searching." *The American Journal of Geriatric Psychiatry* 17, no. 2 (2009): 116–26.

Chapter 7

1 Masood, Rahat, Shlomo Berkovsky, and Mohamed Ali Kaafar. "Tracking and personalization." In *Modern Socio-Technical Perspectives on Privacy*, Cham, Switzerland: Springer, 2022, 171–202.

2 Bornstein, Robert F. "Exposure and affect: overview and meta-analysis of research, 1968–1987." *Psychological Bulletin* 106, no. 2 (1989): 265.

3 Pereira, Carlos Silva, João Teixeira, Patrícia Figueiredo, João Xavier, São Luís Castro, and Elvira Brattico. "Music and emotions in the brain: familiarity matters." *PloS One* 6, no. 11 (2011): e27241.

4 Baker, William, J. Hutchinson, Danny Moore, and Prakash Nedungadi. "Brand Familiarity and Advertising: Effects on the Evoked Set and Brand Preference." In *NA—Advances in Consumer Research* Volume 13, eds. Richard J. Lutz. Provo, UT: Association for Consumer Research, 1986, 637–642.

5 Presbrey, F. "The history and development of advertising." *Advertising & Society Review* 1, no. 1 (2000).

6 The Eno Story. Accessed July 2022. https://www.eno.co.za/history-fruit-salts/.

7 Barnard, E. *Emporium: Selling the Dream in Colonial Australia*. National Library of Australia, 2015.

8 Plotnick, M., C. Eldering, and D. Ryder. Expanse Networks Inc., 2002. *Behavioral Targeted Advertising*. U.S. Patent Application 10/116,692.

9 Deshpande, N., S. Ahmed, and A. Khode. "Web based targeted advertising: a study based on patent information." *Procedia Economics and Finance* 11, (2014): 522–35.

10 Watson, David, Lee Anna Clark, and Auke Tellegen. "Development and validation of brief measures of positive and negative affect: the PANAS scales." *Journal of Personality and Social Psychology* 54, no. 6 (1988): 1063.

11 Ryff, Carol D., and Corey Lee M. Keyes. "The structure of psychological well-being revisited." *Journal of Personality and Social Psychology* 69, no. 4 (1995): 719.

12 Hao, Bibo, Lin Li, Rui Gao, Ang Li, and Tingshao Zhu. "Sensing subjective well-being from social media." In *International Conference on Active Media Technology*. Cham, Switzerland: Springer, 2014, 324–35

13 De Choudhury, Munmun, Michael Gamon, Scott Counts, and Eric Horvitz. "Predicting depression via social media." In *Seventh International AAAI Conference on Weblogs and Social Media*. 2013.

14 Reece, Andrew G., and Christopher M. Danforth. "Instagram photos reveal predictive markers of depression." *EPJ Data Science* 6 (2017): 1–12.

15 Kosinski, M., D. Stillwell, and T. Graepel. "Private traits and attributes are predictable from digital records of human behavior." *Proceedings of the National Academy of Sciences* 110, no. 15 (2013): 5802–5.

16 Kosinski, M., D. Stillwell, and T. Graepel. "Private traits and attributes are predictable from digital records of human behavior." *Proceedings of the National Academy of Sciences* 110, no. 15 (2013): 5802–5.

17 Youyou, W., M. Kosinski, and D. Stillwell. "Computer-based personality judgments are more accurate than those made by humans." *Proceedings of the National Academy of Sciences* 112, no. 4 (2015): 1036–40.

18 Reynaud, Emmanuelle, Myriam El Khoury-Malhame, Jérôme Rossier, Olivier Blin, and Stéphanie Khalfa. "Neuroticism modifies psychophysiological responses to fearful films." *PloS One* 7, no. 3 (2012): e32413.

19 Matz, Sandra C., Michal Kosinski, Gideon Nave, and David J. Stillwell. "Psychological targeting as an effective approach to digital mass persuasion." *Proceedings of the National Academy of Sciences* 114, no. 48 (2017): 12714–9.

20 Wang, Weichen, Gabriella M. Harari, Rui Wang, Sandrine R. Müller, Shayan Mirjafari, Kizito Masaba, and Andrew T. Campbell. "Sensing behavioral change over time: using within-person variability features from mobile sensing to predict personality traits." *Proceedings of the ACM on Interactive, Mobile, Wearable and Ubiquitous Technologies* 2, no. 3 (2018): 1–21.

21 Nowak, Michael, and Dean Eckles. 2014. "Determining user personality characteristics from social networking system communications

and characteristics." Patent US8825764B2. https://patents.google.com/patent/US8825764B2/en.

22 LeDoux, J. *The Emotional Brain: The Mysterious Underpinnings of Emotional Life*. New York: Simon and Schuster, 1998.

23 Merrill, Jeremy B., and Will Oremus. "Five points for anger, one for a 'like': How Facebook's formula fostered rage and misinformation." *The Washington Post* (2021). https://www.washingtonpost.com/technology/2021/10/26/facebook-angry-emoji-algorithm/.

24 Manninen, Sandra, Lauri Tuominen, Robin I. Dunbar, Tomi Karjalainen, Jussi Hirvonen, Eveliina Arponen, Riitta Hari, Iiro P. Jääskeläinen, Mikko Sams, and Lauri Nummenmaa. "Social laughter triggers endogenous opioid release in humans." *Journal of Neuroscience* 37, no. 25 (2017): 6125–31.

25 Bennett, Mary P., Zeller, Janice M., Rosenberg, Lisa, and McCann, Judith. "The Effect of Mirthful Laughter on Stress and Natural Killer Cell Activity." *Alternative Therapies in Health and Medicine* 9 (2), (2003): 38–45. Available http://digitalcommons.wku.edu/nurs_fac_pub/9.

26 Ananny, Mike. "The curious connection between apps for gay men and sex offenders." *The Atlantic*. April 14, 2011. https://www.theatlantic.com/technology/archive/2011/04/the-curious-connection-between-apps-for-gay-men-and-sex-offenders/237340/.

Chapter 8

1 Becker, Barbara, and Gloria Mark. "Constructing social systems through computer-mediated communication." *Virtual Reality* 4, no. 1 (1999): 60–73.

2 Chung, Alicia, Dorice Vieira, Tiffany Donley, Nicholas Tan, Girardin Jean-Louis, Kathleen Kiely Gouley, and Azizi Seixas. "Adolescent peer influence on eating behaviors via social media: scoping review." *Journal of Medical Internet Research* 23, no. 6 (2021): e19697.

3 Puri, Neha, Eric A. Coomes, Hourmazd Haghbayan, and Keith Gunaratne. "Social media and vaccine hesitancy: new updates for the era of COVID-19 and globalized infectious diseases." *Human Vaccines & Immunotherapeutics* 16, no. 11 (2020): 2586–93.

4   Krafft, Peter M., Nicolás Della Penna, and Alex Sandy Pentland. "An experimental study of cryptocurrency market dynamics." In *Proceedings of the 2018 CHI Conference on Human Factors in Computing Systems*, New York: ACM Press, 1–13. 2018.

5   Siddiqui, Yusra, 2020. "Emma Chamberlain just resurrected the pants we used to wear instead of leggings." *Who What Wear*. 2020. https://www.whowhatwear.com/emma-chamberlain-flared-leggings/slide2.

6   Humphrey, K. "Hashtags seep into everyday speech." *Star Tribune*. 2012. https://www.startribune.com/hashtags-seep-into-everyday-speech/173909961/.

7   Asch, S. E. "Studies of independence and conformity: I. A minority of one against a unanimous majority." *Psychological Monographs: General and Applied* 70, no. 9 (1956): 1.

8   Brandstetter, Jürgen, Péter Rácz, Clay Beckner, Eduardo B. Sandoval, Jennifer Hay, and Christoph Bartneck. "A peer pressure experiment: recreation of the Asch conformity experiment with robots." In *2014 IEEE/RSJ International Conference on Intelligent Robots and Systems*, 1335–40. IEEE, 2014.

9   Vilhauer, Ruvanee P. "Characteristics of inner reading voices." *Scandinavian Journal of Psychology* 58, no. 4 (2017): 269–74.

10 Nesi, Jacqueline, Sophia Choukas-Bradley, and Mitchell J. Prinstein. "Transformation of adolescent peer relations in the social media context: part 2—application to peer group processes and future directions for research." *Clinical Child and Family Psychology Review* 21, no. 3 (2018): 295–319.

11 Ohannessian, Christine McCauley, Anna Vannucci, Kaitlin M. Flannery, and Sarosh Khan. "Social media use and substance use during emerging adulthood." *Emerging Adulthood* 5, no. 5 (2017): 364–70.

12 CareerBuilder survey. "Number of employers using social media to screen candidates at all-time high, finds latest CareerBuilder study." 2017. https://www.prnewswire.com/news-releases/number-of-employers-using-social-media-to-screen-candidates-at-all-time-high-finds-latest-careerbuilder-study-300474228.html.

13 Sherman, Lauren E., Patricia M. Greenfield, Leanna M. Hernandez, and Mirella Dapretto. "Peer influence via Instagram: effects on brain and behavior in adolescence and young adulthood." *Child Development* 89, no. 1 (2018): 37–47.

14 Braams, Barbara R., Anna C. K. van Duijvenvoorde, Jiska S. Peper, and Eveline A. Crone. "Longitudinal changes in adolescent risk-taking: a comprehensive study of neural responses to rewards, pubertal development, and risk-taking behavior." *Journal of Neuroscience* 35, no. 18 (2015): 7226–38.

15 Mark, Gloria, Yiran Wang, and Melissa Niiya. "Stress and multitasking in everyday college life: an empirical study of online activity." In *Proceedings of the SIGCHI Conference on Human Factors in Computing Systems*, New York: ACM Press, 41–50. 2014.

16 Bradner, Erin, and Gloria Mark. "Why distance matters: effects on cooperation, persuasion and deception." In *Proceedings of the 2002 ACM Conference on Computer Supported Cooperative Work*, New York: ACM Press, 226–35. 2002.

17 Tajfel, Henri, ed. *Social Identity and Intergroup Relations*. Vol. 7. Cambridge University Press, 2010.

18 Buzzfeed, 2020. "A college student behind a massively popular paint-mixing TikTok page was fired from Sherwin-Williams." https://www.buzzfeednews.com/article/tanyachen/college-student-behind-a-massively-popular-paint-mixing.

19 Goffman, Erving. *The Presentation of Self in Everyday Life*. Vol. 21. London: Harmondsworth, 1978.

20 Barash, Vladimir, Nicolas Ducheneaut, Ellen Isaacs, and Victoria Bellotti. "Faceplant: impression (mis)management in Facebook status updates." In *Fourth International AAAI Conference on Weblogs and Social Media*. 2010.

21 Putnam, Robert D. *Bowling Alone: The Collapse and Revival of American Community*. New York: Simon and Schuster, 2000.

22 Ellison, N. B., C. Steinfield, and C. Lampe. "The benefits of Facebook 'friends': social capital and college students' use of online social

network sites." *Journal of Computer-Mediated Communication* 12, no. 4 (2007): 1143–68.

23 Granovetter, Mark S. "The strength of weak ties." *American Journal of Sociology* 78, no. 6 (1973): 1360–80.

24 Burke, M., C. Marlow, and T. Lento. "Social network activity and social well-being." In *Proceedings of the SIGCHI Conference on Human Factors in Computing Systems*, 1909–12. 2010.

25 Russell, Bertrand. *Power: A New Social Analysis*, 10. Oxfordshire: Routledge, 2004.

26 Magee, Joe C., and Adam D. Galinsky. "Social hierarchy: the self-reinforcing nature of power and status." *Academy of Management Annals* 2, no. 1 (2008): 351–98.

27 Panteli, Niki. "Richness, power cues and email text." *Information & Management* 40, no. 2 (2002): 75–86.

28 Gilbert, Eric. "Phrases that signal workplace hierarchy." In *Proceedings of the ACM 2012 Conference on Computer Supported Cooperative Work*, New York: ACM Press, 1037–46. 2012.

29 Tchokni, Simo Editha, Diarmuid O. Séaghdha, and Daniele Quercia. "Emoticons and phrases: status symbols in social media." In *Eighth International AAAI Conference on Weblogs and Social Media*. 2014.

30 Anderson, Cameron, Oliver P. John, Dacher Keltner, and Ann M. Kring. "Who attains social status? Effects of personality and physical attractiveness in social groups." *Journal of Personality and Social Psychology* 81, no. 1 (2001): 116.

31 Fiske, Susan T. "Controlling other people: the impact of power on stereotyping." *American Psychologist* 48, no. 6 (1993): 621.

32 Dunbar, Robin I. M. "Coevolution of neocortical size, group size and language in humans." *Behavioral and Brain Sciences* 16, no. 4 (1993): 681–94.

33 Gonçalves, Bruno, Nicola Perra, and Alessandro Vespignani. "Modeling users' activity on Twitter networks: validation of Dunbar's number." *PloS One* 6, no. 8 (2011): e22656.

34 Buettner, Ricardo. "Getting a job via career-oriented social networking markets." *Electronic Markets* 27, no. 4 (2017): 371–85.

35 Wang, Yiran, Melissa Niiya, Gloria Mark, Stephanie M. Reich, and Mark Warschauer. "Coming of age (digitally): an ecological view of social media use among college students." In *Proceedings of the 18th ACM Conference on Computer Supported Cooperative Work & Social Computing*, New York: ACM Press, 571–82. 2015.

Chapter 9

1 Brown, Chip. "The epic ups and downs of Peter Gelb." *The New York Times*, March 21, 2013. https://www.nytimes.com/2013/03/24/magazine/the-epic-ups-and-downs-of-peter-gelb.html.

2 Mischel, W., Y. Shoda, and P. K. Peake. "The nature of adolescent competencies predicted by preschool delay of gratification." *Journal of Personality and Social Psychology* 54, no. 4 (1988): 687.

3 Moffitt, T. E., L. Arseneault, D. Belsky, N. Dickson, R. J. Hancox, H. Harrington, R. Houts, R. Poulton, B. W. Roberts, S. Ross, and M. R. Sears. "A gradient of childhood self-control predicts health, wealth, and public safety." *Proceedings of the National Academy of Sciences* 108, no. 7 (2011): 2693–8.

4 Ayduk, Ozlem, Rodolfo Mendoza-Denton, Walter Mischel, Geraldine Downey, Philip K. Peake, and Monica Rodriguez. "Regulating the interpersonal self: strategic self-regulation for coping with rejection sensitivity." *Journal of Personality and Social Psychology* 79, no. 5 (2000): 776.

5 Mischel, Walter. *Personality and Assessment*. Psychology Press, 2013.

6 McCrae, Robert R., and Paul T. Costa. "Self-concept and the stability of personality: cross-sectional comparisons of self-reports and ratings." *Journal of Personality and Social Psychology* 43 (1982): 1282–92.

7 Mischel, W., and Y. Shoda. "Toward a unified theory of personality." *Handbook of Personality: Theory and Research* 3 (2008): 208–41.

8 McCrae, Robert R., and Paul T. Costa Jr. "The five-factor theory of

personality." In *Handbook of Personality: Theory and Research*, edited by L. A. Pervin and O. P. John, 2nd ed. New York: Guilford, 1999.

9   Mischel, Walter, and Yuichi Shoda. "Personality psychology has two goals: must it be two fields?" *Psychological Inquiry* 5, no. 2 (1994): 156–8.

10 John, O. P., E. M. Donahue, and R. L. Kentle. 1991. *Big Five Inventory (BFI)* [Database record]. APA PsycTests. https://doi.org/10.1037/t07550-000.

11 Mischel, Walter, and Yuichi Shoda. "Personality psychology has two goals: must it be two fields?" *Psychological Inquiry* 5, no. 2 (1994): 156–8.

12 McCrae, Robert R. "Cross-cultural research on the five-factor model of personality." *Online Readings in Psychology and Culture* 4, no. 4 (2002): 1–12.

13 Terracciano, A., A. M. Abdel-Khalak, N. Adam, L. Adamovova, C.-k. Ahn, H.-n. Ahn, et al. "National character does not reflect mean personality trait levels in 49 cultures." *Science* 310 (2005): 96–100.

14 Costa, P. T., Jr., A. Terracciano, and R. R. McCrae. "Gender differences in personality traits across cultures: robust and surprising findings." *Journal of Personality and Social Psychology* 81 (2001): 322–31.

15 Kraaykamp, Gerbert, and Koen Van Eijck. "Personality, media preferences, and cultural participation." *Personality and Individual Differences* 38, no. 7 (2005): 1675–88.

16 Braun, Beate, Juliane M. Stopfer, Kai W. Müller, Manfred E. Beutel, and Boris Egloff. "Personality and video gaming: comparing regular gamers, non-gamers, and gaming addicts and differentiating between game genres." *Computers in Human Behavior* 55 (2016): 406–12.

17 Karim, Nor Shahriza Abdul, Nurul Hidayah Ahmad Zamzuri, and Yakinah Muhamad Nor. "Exploring the relationship between internet ethics in university students and the big five model of personality." *Computers & Education* 53, no. 1 (2009): 86–93.

18 Moore, Kelly, and James C. McElroy. "The influence of personality on Facebook usage, wall postings, and regret." *Computers in Human Behavior* 28, no. 1 (2012): 267–74.

19 Mark, Gloria, and Yoav Ganzach. "Personality and internet usage: a large-scale representative study of young adults." *Computers in Human Behavior* 36 (2014): 274–81.

20 Błażej Szymura, and Edward Nęcka. "Three superfactors of personality and three aspects of attention." *Advances in Personality Psychology.* (2005): 75–90.

21 Whiteside, Stephen P., and Donald R. Lynam. "The five factor model and impulsivity: using a structural model of personality to understand impulsivity." *Personality and Individual Differences* 30, no. 4 (2001): 669–89.

22 Cohen, Sheldon, Tom Kamarck, and Robin Mermelstein. "A global measure of perceived stress." *Journal of Health and Social Behavior,* (1983): 385–96.

23 Mark, Gloria, Shamsi T. Iqbal, Mary Czerwinski, Paul Johns, and Akane Sano. "Neurotics can't focus: an in situ study of online multitasking in the workplace." In *Proceedings of the 2016 CHI Conference on Human Factors in Computing Systems*, New York: ACM Press, 1739–44. 2016.

24 Forster, Sophie, and Nilli Lavie. "Establishing the attention-distractibility trait." *Psychological Science,* (Dec. 14, 2015): 203–12.

25 Mark, Gloria, Shamsi T. Iqbal, Mary Czerwinski, Paul Johns, Akane Sano, and Yuliya Lutchyn. "Email duration, batching and self-interruption: patterns of email use on productivity and stress." In *Proceedings of the 2016 CHI Conference on Human Factors in Computing Systems*, New York: ACM Press, 1717–28. 2016.

26 Mark, Gloria, Daniela Gudith, and Ulrich Klocke. "The cost of interrupted work: more speed and stress." In *Proceedings of the SIGCHI Conference on Human Factors in Computing Systems*, New York: ACM Press, 107–10. 2008.

27 Mark, Gloria, Mary Czerwinski, and Shamsi T. Iqbal. "Effects of individual differences in blocking workplace distractions." In *Proceedings of the 2018 CHI Conference on Human Factors in Computing Systems*, New York: ACM Press, 1–12. 2018.

28 Agarwal, Ritu, and Elena Karahanna. "Time flies when you're having fun: cognitive absorption and beliefs about information technology usage." *MIS Quarterly,* (2000): 665–94.

29 Moffitt, T. E., L. Arseneault, D. Belsky, N. Dickson, R. J. Hancox, H. Harrington, R. Houts, R. Poulton, B. W. Roberts, S. Ross, and M. R. Sears. "A gradient of childhood self-control predicts health, wealth, and public safety." *Proceedings of the National Academy of Sciences* 108, no. 7 (2011): 2693–8.

30 Mark, Gloria, Mary Czerwinski, and Shamsi T. Iqbal. "Effects of individual differences in blocking workplace distractions." In *Proceedings of the 2018 CHI Conference on Human Factors in Computing Systems*, New York: ACM Press, 1–12. 2018.

31 Chattu, Vijay Kumar, M. D. Manzar, Soosanna Kumary, Deepa Burman, David Warren Spence, and Seithikurippu R. Pandi-Perumal. "The global problem of insufficient sleep and its serious public health implications." In *Healthcare*, Vol. 7, No. 1, 1. Multidisciplinary Digital Publishing Institute, 2019.

32 Mark, Gloria, Yiran Wang, Melissa Niiya, and Stephanie Reich. "Sleep debt in student life: online attention focus, Facebook, and mood." In *Proceedings of the 2016 CHI Conference on Human Factors in Computing Systems*, New York: ACM Press, 5517–5528. May 2016.

33 Muraven, M., D. M. Tice, and R. F. Baumeister. "Self-control as a limited resource: regulatory depletion patterns." *Journal of Personality and Social Psychology* 74, no. 3 (1998): 774.

34 Mischel, W., Y. Shoda, and P. K. Peake. "The nature of adolescent competencies predicted by preschool delay of gratification." *Journal of Personality and Social Psychology* 54, no. 4 (1988): 687.

35 Watts, T.W., G. J. Duncan, and H. Quan. "Revisiting the marshmallow test: a conceptual replication investigating links between early delay of gratification and later outcomes." *Psychological Science* 29, no. 7 (2018): 1159–77.

36 Gottfredson, M. R., and T. Hirschi. *A General Theory of Crime*. Stanford University Press, 1990.

Chapter 10

1 Danner, Deborah D., David A. Snowdon, and Wallace V. Friesen. "Positive emotions in early life and longevity: findings from the nun study." *Journal of Personality and Social Psychology* 80, no. 5 (2001): 804.

2 Kalman, Maira. "How to iron a sheet, according to Maira Kalman." *New York Magazine*, April 15, 2020.

3 Currey, Mason, ed. *Daily Rituals: How Artists Work*. New York: Knopf, 2013.

4 Flanner, Janet, James Thurber, and Harold Ross. "Tender Buttons: a day with Gertrude Stein." (October 13, 1934). https://www.newyorker.com/magazine/1934/10/13/tender-buttons.

5 Diener, E. "Introduction to the special section on the structure of emotion." *Journal of Personality and Social Psychology* 76 (1999): 803–4.

6 Watson, D., D. Wiese, J. Vaidya, and A. Tellegen. "The two general activation systems of affect: structural findings, evolutionary considerations, and psychobiological evidence." *Journal of Personality and Social Psychology* 76, no. 5 (1999): 820.

7 Gibran, Kahlil, and Suheil Badi Bushrui. *The Prophet: A New Annotated Edition*. Simon and Schuster, 2012.

8 Zohar, Dov, O. Tzischinski, and R. Epstein. "Effects of energy availability on immediate and delayed emotional reactions to work events." *Journal of Applied Psychology* 88, no. 6 (2003): 1082.

9 Gross, Sven, Norbert K. Semmer, Laurenz L. Meier, Wolfgang Kälin, Nicola Jacobshagen, and Franziska Tschan. "The effect of positive events at work on after-work fatigue: they matter most in face of adversity." *Journal of Applied Psychology* 96, no. 3 (2011): 654.

10 Fredrickson, B. L., and C. Branigan. "Positive emotions broaden the scope of attention and thought-action repertoires." *Cognition & Emotion* 19, no. 3 (2005): 313–32.

11 Fredrickson, Barbara L., and Robert W. Levenson. "Positive emotions speed recovery from the cardiovascular sequelae of negative emotions." *Cognition & Emotion* 12, no. 2 (1998): 191–220.

12 Folkman, Susan, and Judith Tedlie Moskowitz. "Positive affect and the other side of coping." *American Psychologist* 55, no. 6 (2000): 647.

13 Agarwal, Ritu, and Elena Karahanna. "Time flies when you're having fun: cognitive absorption and beliefs about information technology usage." *MIS Quarterly*, (2000): 665–94.

14 Csikszentmihalyi, Mihaly. *Flow: The Psychology of Optimal Experience.* Vol. 1990. New York: Harper & Row, 1990.

15 Kabat-Zinn, Jon. *Wherever You Go, There You Are: Mindfulness Meditation in Everyday Life.* New York: Hachette Books, 2009.

16 Mark, Gloria, Shamsi T. Iqbal, Mary Czerwinski, and Paul Johns. "Bored Mondays and focused afternoons: the rhythm of attention and online activity in the workplace." In *Proceedings of the SIGCHI Conference on Human Factors in Computing Systems*, New York: ACM Press, 3025–34. 2014.

17 Posner, Jonathan, James A. Russell, and Bradley S. Peterson. "The circumplex model of affect: an integrative approach to affective neuroscience, cognitive development, and psychopathology." *Development and Psychopathology* 17, no. 3 (2005): 715–34.

18 Posner, Jonathan, James A. Russell, and Bradley S. Peterson. "The circumplex model of affect: an integrative approach to affective neuroscience, cognitive development, and psychopathology." *Development and Psychopathology* 17, no. 3 (2005): 715–34.

19 Lang, Peter J., Mark K. Greenwald, Margaret M. Bradley, and Alfons O. Hamm. "Looking at pictures: affective, facial, visceral, and behavioral reactions." *Psychophysiology* 30, no. 3 (1993): 261–73.

20 Keil, Andreas, Matthias M. Müller, Thomas Gruber, Christian Wienbruch, Margarita Stolarova, and Thomas Elbert. "Effects of emotional arousal in the cerebral hemispheres: a study of oscillatory brain activity and event-related potentials." *Clinical Neurophysiology* 112, no. 11 (2001): 2057–68.

21 Posner, Jonathan, James A. Russell, and Bradley S. Peterson. "The circumplex model of affect: an integrative approach to affective neuroscience, cognitive development, and psychopathology." *Development and Psychopathology* 17, no. 3 (2005): 715–34.

22 Carver, Charles S., and Michael F. Scheier. "Situational coping and coping dispositions in a stressful transaction." *Journal of Personality and Social Psychology* 66, no. 1 (1994): 184.

23 Smit, A. S., P. A. Eling, and A. M. Coenen. "Mental effort causes vigilance decrease due to resource depletion." *Acta Psychologica* 115, no. 1 (2004): 35–42.

24 Mark, Gloria, Shamsi Iqbal, Mary Czerwinski, and Paul Johns. "Capturing the mood: Facebook and face-to-face encounters in the workplace." In *Proceedings of the 17th ACM Conference on Computer Supported Cooperative Work & Social Computing*, New York: ACM Press, 1082–94. 2014.

25 Watson, David, Lee Anna Clark, and Auke Tellegen. "Development and validation of brief measures of positive and negative affect: the PANAS scales." *Journal of Personality and Social Psychology* 54, no. 6 (1988): 1063.

26 Blank, C., S. Zaman, A. Wesley, P. Tsiamyrtzis, D. R. Da Cunha Silva, R. Gutierrez-Osuna, G. Mark, and I. Pavlidis. "Emotional footprints of email interruptions." In *Proceedings of the 2020 CHI Conference on Human Factors in Computing Systems*, New York: ACM Press, 1–12. 2020.

27 Wickens, Christopher D. "Multiple resources and mental workload." *Human Factors* 50, no. 3 (2008): 449–55.

28 Blank, C., S. Zaman, A. Wesley, P. Tsiamyrtzis, D. R. Da Cunha Silva, R. Gutierrez-Osuna, G. Mark, and I. Pavlidis. "Emotional footprints of email interruptions." In *Proceedings of the 2020 CHI Conference on Human Factors in Computing Systems*, New York: ACM Press, 1–12. April 2020.

29 Zajonc, Robert B., Sheila T. Murphy, and Marita Inglehart. "Feeling and facial efference: implications of the vascular theory of emotion." *Psychological Review* 96, no. 3 (1989): 395.

30 Bartel, Caroline A., and Richard Saavedra. "The collective construction of work group moods." *Administrative Science Quarterly* 45, no. 2 (2000): 197–231.

31 Barsade, Sigal G. "The ripple effect: emotional contagion and its influence on group behavior." *Administrative Science Quarterly* 47, no. 4 (2002): 644–75.

32 Currey, Mason, ed. *Daily Rituals: How Artists Work*. New York: Knopf, 2013.

33 Wickelgren, Wayne A. *How to Solve Problems: Elements of a Theory of Problems and Problem Solving*. San Francisco: WH Freeman, 1974.

34 Currey, Mason, ed. *Daily Rituals: How Artists Work*. New York: Knopf, 2013.

35 Root-Bernstein, Robert S. "Music, creativity and scientific thinking." *Leonardo* 34, no. 1 (2001): 63–8.

Chapter 11

1 Rideout, Victoria, and Michael B. Robb. *The Common Sense Census: Media Use by Kids Age Zero to Eight*. San Francisco: Common Sense Media, 2020. https://www.commonsensemedia.org/sites/default/files/uploads/research/2020_zero_to_eight_census_final_web.pdf.

2 "The Nielsen total audience report March 2021." https://www.nielsen.com/us/en/insights/report/2021/total-audience-advertising-across-todays-media/.

3 Statista 2020. "Average daily time spent watching TV per individual in the United Kingdom (UK) from 2005 to 2020." https://www.statista.com/statistics/269870/daily-tv-viewing-time-in-the-uk/.

4 Statista 2020. "Audience distribution among the leading television channels in France in 2020." https://www.statista.com/statistics/381685/audience-share-of-tv-channels-in-france/.

5 Statista 2019. "Average time people spent on watching real-time television per weekday in Japan from fiscal year 2012 to 2019." https://www.statista.com/statistics/1201929/japan-average-time-spent-real-time-television-per-weekday/.

6 Statista 2019. "Average daily time spent watching television in China from 2011 to 2019 with estimates until 2022." https://www.statista.com/statistics/467531/china-average-daily-time-spent-watching-tv/.

7 "The Nielsen total audience report March 2021." https://www.nielsen.com/us/en/insights/report/2021/total-audience-advertising-across-todays-media/.

8 "The Nielsen total audience report March 2021." https://www.nielsen.com/us/en/insights/report/2021/total-audience-advertising-across-todays-media/.

9 Cutting, James E., Jordan E. DeLong, and Christine E. Nothelfer. "Attention and the evolution of Hollywood film." *Psychological Science* 21, no. 3 (2010): 432–9.

10 Cutting, J. E., K. L. Brunick, J. E. DeLong, C. Iricinschi, and A. Candan. "Quicker, faster, darker: changes in Hollywood film over 75 years." *i-Perception* 2, no. 6 (2011): 569–76.

11 Abrams, Richard A., and Shawn E. Christ. "Motion onset captures attention." *Psychological Science* 14, no. 5 (2003): 427–32.

12 Cutting, J. E., K. L. Brunick, J. E. DeLong, C. Iricinschi, and A. Candan. "Quicker, faster, darker: changes in Hollywood film over 75 years." *i-Perception* 2, no. 6 (2011): 569–76.

13 Follows, S. (2017). "How many shots are in the average movie?" Stephen Follows Film Data and Education. Available https://stephenfollows.com/many-shots-average-movie/.

14 Butler, Jeremy G. "Statistical analysis of television style: what can numbers tell us about TV editing?" *Cinema Journal* 54, no. 1 (Fall 2014): 25–45.

15 Tsivian, Yuri. Lab: MTV Video. Cinemetrics. Accessed December 3, 2021. http://www.cinemetrics.lv/lab.php?ID=165.

16 Statista. "Most popular YouTube videos based on total global views as of August 2021." 2021. https://www.statista.com/statistics/249396/top-youtube-videos-views/.

17 Shevenock, Sarah. Exclusive: Vevo Data Reveals How Often Gen Z Watches Music Videos and Which Ones Overperform With Them. Morning Consult. 2021. Available https://morningconsult.com/2021/08/02/vevo-exclusive-data-gen-z-music-videos/.

18 Smith, Tim J. "The attentional theory of cinematic continuity." *Projections* 6, no. 1 (2012): 1–27.

19 Smith, Tim J., and John M. Henderson. "Edit blindness: the relationship between attention and global change blindness in dynamic scenes." *Journal of Eye Movement Research* 2, no. 2 (2008).

20 Barnes, John. *The Beginnings of the Cinema in England 1894-1901. Vol. 2.* Exeter: University of Exeter Press, 1996.

21 Raskin, Richard. "Five explanations for the jump cuts in Godard's Breathless," *P.O.V.: A Danish Journal of Film Studies*, no. 6. (1998), 141–53.

22 Crowther, Bosley. "French film 'Breathless' has shocking power." *The New York Times*, February 12, 1961. https://timesmachine.nytimes.com/timesmachine/1961/02/12/118022212.html?pageNumber=355.

23 BMAC. "How to jump cut like a pro." 2017. https://www.youtube.com/watch?v=p2BqEvoiX04.

24 Schwan, Stephan, Bärbel Garsoffky, and Friedrich W. Hesse. "Do film cuts facilitate the perceptual and cognitive organization of activity sequences?" *Memory & Cognition* 28, no. 2 (2000): 214–23.

25 MacLachlan, James, and Michael Logan. "Camera shot length in TV commercials and their memorability and persuasiveness." *Journal of Advertising Research* 33, no. 2 (1993): 57–62.

26 Elliott, Stuart. "TV Commercials Adjust to a Shorter Attention Span." *The New York Times*, April 8, 2005. https://www.nytimes.com/2005/04/08/business/media/tv-commercials-adjust-to-a-shorter-attention-span.html?searchResultPosition=1.

27 Stanton, John L., and Jeffrey Burke. "Comparative effectiveness of executional elements in TV advertising: 15- versus 30-second commercials." *Journal of Advertising Research* 38, no. 6 (1998): 7–8.

28 Friedman, Wayne. "Shorter-duration TV commercials on the rise." *Television News Daily*, Oct. 4, 2017. https://www.mediapost.com/publications/article/308248/shorter-duration-tv-commercials-on-the-rise.html.

29 Mandese, J. "Nielsen patents method for compressing TV ads, finds they can work better than longer ones." *MediaDailyNews*, June 11, 2018. https://www.mediapost.com/publications/article/320538/nielsen-patents-method-for-compressing-tv-ads-fin.html.

30 Newstead, Kate, and Jenni Romaniuk. "Cost per second: the relative effectiveness of 15- and 30-second television advertisements." *Journal of Advertising Research* 50, no. 1 (2010): 68–76.

31 "Facebook for business. Best practices for mobile video ads." Accessed August 31, 2021. https://www.facebook.com/business/help/144240239372256?id=603833089963720.

32 Fulgoni, Gian M. "Why marketers need new measures of consumer engagement: how expanding platforms, the 6-second ad, and fewer ads alter engagement and outcomes." *Journal of Advertising Research* 58, no. 3 (2018): 259–62.

33 Ah-young, Chung. "Snack Culture." *The Korea Times*, Feb. 2, 2014. http://www.koreatimes.co.kr/www/news/culture/2014/02/386_150813.html.

34 Hutchinson, Andrew. "TikTok tests even longer video uploads as it looks to expand its presence." *Social Media Today*, 2021. https://www.socialmediatoday.com/news/tiktoks-testing-even-longer-video-uploads-as-it-looks-to-expand-its-presen/605603/.

35 Ceci, L. "TikTok—Statistics & Facts. 2022." Statista. https://www.statista.com/topics/6077/tiktok/#topicHeader__wrapper.

36 Aldredge, J. "Your guide to social media video lengths." 2021. https://vimeo.com/blog/post/social-media-video-lengths/.

37 Brasel, S. Adam, and James Gips. "Media multitasking behavior: concurrent television and computer usage." *Cyberpsychology, Behavior, and Social Networking* 14, no. 9 (2011): 527–34.

38 Cutting, J. E., K. L. Brunick, J. E. DeLong, C. Iricinschi, and A. Candan, A. "Quicker, faster, darker: changes in Hollywood film over 75 years." *i-Perception* 2, no. 6 (2011): 569–76.

39 Lang, Annie. "The limited capacity model of mediated message processing." *Journal of Communication* 50, no. 1 (2000): 46–70.

40 Lang, Annie, Paul Bolls, Robert F. Potter, and Karlynn Kawahara. "The effects of production pacing and arousing content on the information processing of television messages." *Journal of Broadcasting & Electronic Media* 43, no. 4 (1999): 451–75.

41 Kostyrka-Allchorne, Katarzyna, Nicholas R. Cooper, Steffan Kennett, Steffen Nestler, and Andrew Simpson. "The short-term effect of video editing pace on children's inhibition and N2 and P3 ERP components during visual go/no-go task." *Developmental Neuropsychology* 44, no. 4 (2019): 385–96.

42 Lillard, Angeline S., and Jennifer Peterson. "The immediate impact of

different types of television on young children's executive function."
Pediatrics 128, no. 4 (2011): 644–9.

43 Landhuis, Carl Erik, Richie Poulton, David Welch, and Robert John
Hancox. "Does childhood television viewing lead to attention problems
in adolescence? Results from a prospective longitudinal study." *Pediat-rics* 120, no. 3 (2007): 532–7.

44 Cutting, J. E., K. L. Brunick, J. E. DeLong, C. Iricinschi, and A. Can-dan, A. "Quicker, faster, darker: changes in Hollywood film over 75
years." *i-Perception* 2, no. 6 (2011): 569–76.

45 Gottschall, Jonathan. *The Storytelling Animal: How Stories Make Us Human.*
Houghton Mifflin Harcourt, 2012.

46 McLuhan, Marshall, and Quentin Fiore. *The Medium is the Message.*
New York: Random House, 1967: 115.

Chapter 12

1 Viereck, George Sylvester. "What life means to Einstein." *The Saturday
Evening Post*, 1929. http://www.saturdayeveningpost.com/wp-content/
uploads/satevepost/einstein.pdf.

2 Strawson, Galen. "Nietzsche's Metaphysics?" in: *Nietzsche on Mind and
Nature* (editors: Manuel Dries, Peter J. E. Kail), Oxford University Press,
2015, quote, pg. 33.

3 Skinner, Burrhus Frederic. "Why I am not a cognitive psychologist."
Behaviorism 5, no. 2 (1977): 1–10.

4 Libet, Benjamin. "Unconscious cerebral initiative and the role of con-scious will in voluntary action." *Behavioral and Brain Sciences* 8, no. 4
(1985): 529–39.

5 Dennett, Daniel C. *Elbow Room: The Varieties of Free Will Worth Want-ing.* MIT Press, 2015.

6 Baumeister, Roy F. "Addiction, cigarette smoking, and voluntary con-trol of action: do cigarette smokers lose their free will?" *Addictive Behav-iors Reports* 5 (2017): 67–84.

7 Shepherd, Joshua. "Free will and consciousness: experimental studies."
Consciousness and Cognition 21, no. 2 (2012): 915–27.

8 Bandura, Albert. "The reconstrual of 'free will' from the agentic perspective of social cognitive theory." In eds., John Baer, James C. Kaufman,
   and Roy F. Baumeister, *Are We Free? Psychology and Free Will*. Oxford
   University Press, 2008: 86–127.

Chapter 13

1 Esler, Murray, Elisabeth Lambert, and Markus Schlaich. "Point: chronic
   activation of the sympathetic nervous system is the dominant contrib-
   utor to systemic hypertension." *Journal of Applied Physiology* 109, no. 6
   (2010): 1996–8.

2 Cummins, Robert A. "Subjective well-being, homeostatically pro-
   tected mood and depression: a synthesis." In *The Exploration of Happiness*,
   Dordrecht: Springer, 2013, 77–95.

3 Cummins, Robert A., Eleonora Gullone, and Anna L. D. Lau. "A model
   of subjective well-being homeostasis: the role of personality." In *The Uni-
   versality of Subjective Wellbeing Indicators*, Dordrecht: Springer, 2002, 7–46.

4 Amabile, Teresa M., Sigal G. Barsade, Jennifer S. Mueller, and Barry
   M. Staw. "Affect and creativity at work." *Administrative Science Quarterly*
   50, no. 3 (2005): 367–403.

5 Fredrickson, B. L., and C. Branigan. "Positive emotions broaden the
   scope of attention and thought-action repertoires." *Cognition & Emotion*
   19, no. 3 (2005): 313–32.

6 Ramus, Franck, Marina Nespor, and Jacques Mehler. "Correlates of linguistic rhythm in the speech signal." *Cognition* 73, no. 3 (1999): 265–92.

7 Baer, John, James C. Kaufman, and Roy F. Baumeister, *Are We Free?
   Psychology and Free Will*. Oxford University Press, (2008): 86–127.

8 Rowe, Gillian, Jacob B. Hirsh, and Adam K. Anderson. "Positive affect
   increases the breadth of attentional selection." *Proceedings of the National
   Academy of Sciences* 104, no. 1 (2007): 383–8.

9 Yerkes, Robert M., and John D. Dodson. "The relation of strength of
   stimulus to rapidity of habit-formation." *Punishment: Issues and Experiments*, (1908): 27–41.

10   Williams, Alex C., Harmanpreet Kaur, Gloria Mark, Anne Loomis Thompson, Shamsi T. Iqbal, and Jaime Teevan. "Supporting workplace detachment and reattachment with conversational intelligence." In *Proceedings of the 2018 CHI Conference on Human Factors in Computing Systems*, New York: ACM Press, 2018, 1–13.

11   Currey, Mason, ed. *Daily Rituals: How Artists Work*. New York: Knopf, 2013.

Chapter 14

1   Fink, George. "Stress: the health epidemic of the 21st century." Elsevier SciTech Connect. 2016. http://scitechconnect.elsevier.com/stress-health-epidemic-21st-century/.

2   Mark, Gloria, Stephen Voida, and Armand Cardello. "A pace not dictated by electrons, an empirical study of work without email." *Proceedings of the SIGCHI Conference on Human Factors in Computing Systems*, New York: ACM Press, 2012: 555–64.

3   Butts, Marcus M., William J. Becker, and Wendy R. Boswell. "Hot buttons and time sinks: the effects of electronic communication during nonwork time on emotions and work-nonwork conflict." *Academy of Management Journal* 58, no. 3 (2015): 763–88.

4   Maligorne, Clementine. "Travail: vous avez désormais le droit de vous déconnecter." 2016. https://www.lefigaro.fr/social/2016/12/31/20011-20161231ARTFIG00013-le-droit-a-la-deconnexion-qu-est-ce-que-c-est.php.

5   Pansu, Luc. "Evaluation of 'Right to Disconnect' legislation and its impact on employee's productivity." *International Journal of Management and Applied Research* 5, no. 3 (2018): 99–119.

6   United Nations. Universal Declaration of Human Rights. 1948. Available https://www.un.org/en/about-us/universal-declaration-of-human-rights.

7   Senate Bill no. 830. An act to add Section 51206.4 to the Education Code, relating to pupil instruction. https://leginfo.legislature.ca.gov/faces/billTextClient.xhtml?bill_id=201720180SB830.

8   Technology and Social Change Project. Shorenstein Center on Media,

Politics and Public Policy, Harvard Kennedy School. Accessed July 2022. https://shorensteincenter.org/programs/technology-social-change/.

9 Center for Humane Technology. 2021. https://www.humanetech.com/.

10 Lapowsky, Issie. "Facebook Exposed 87 Million Users to Cambridge Analytica." *Wired*, April 4, 2018. https://www.wired.com/story/facebook-exposed-87-million-users-to-cambridge-analytica/.

11 Meadows, D. H., D. L. Meadows, J. Randers, and W. W. Behrens. *The Limits to Growth*. New York: Universe Books, 1972.

12 Kimani, Everlyne, Kael Rowan, Daniel McDuff, Mary Czerwinski, and Gloria Mark. "A conversational agent in support of productivity and wellbeing at work." In *2019 8th International Conference on Affective Computing and Intelligent Interaction (ACII)*, IEEE, 2019 1–7.

13 Loranger, Hoa. "Infinite Scrolling Is Not for Every Website." Nielsen Norman Group. 2014. https://www.nngroup.com/articles/infinite-scrolling/.

14 Twenge, Jean M., Brian H. Spitzberg, and W. Keith Campbell. "Less in-person social interaction with peers among US adolescents in the 21st century and links to loneliness." *Journal of Social and Personal Relationships* 36, no. 6 (2019): 1892–913.

15 Oppezzo, Marily, and Daniel L. Schwartz. "Give your ideas some legs: the positive effect of walking on creative thinking." *Journal of Experimental Psychology: Learning, Memory, and Cognition* 40, no. 4 (2014): 1142–52.

16 Mark, Gloria, Victor M. González, and Justin Harris. "No task left behind? Examining the nature of fragmented work." In *Proceedings of the SIGCHI Conference on Human Factors in Computing Systems*, New York, ACM Press, 321-30. 2005.

17 Killgore, William D. S., Sara A. Cloonan, Emily C. Taylor, and Natalie S. Dailey. "Loneliness: a signature mental health concern in the era of COVID-19." *Psychiatry Research* 290 (2020): 113117.

18 Emerson, Ralph Waldo. *Essays: Second Series*. Boston: James Munroe and Company, 1844.

19 Su, Norman Makoto, Yang Wang, Gloria Mark, Tosin Aiyelokun, and Tadashi Nakano. "A bosom buddy afar brings a distant land near: Are bloggers a global community?" In *Communities and Technologies*, Dordrecht: Springer, 2005, 171–90.

INDEX